Meditations from the Tantras

With kind regards, ॐ and prem

Swami Niranjan

Meditations from the Tantras

Swami Satyananda Saraswati

Yoga Publications Trust, Munger, Bihar, India

Published by Bihar School of Yoga
First published 1974
Reprinted 1975, 1977, 1981
Second edition 1983
Reprinted 1992
Reprinted with corrections 2000

Published by Yoga Publications Trust
Reprinted 2001, 2004

ISBN: 81-85787-11-5
Price: Indian rupees one hundred and fifty only

Publisher and distributor: Yoga Publications Trust, Ganga Darshan, Munger, Bihar, India.

Printed at Thomson Press (India) Limited, New Delhi, 110001

DEDICATION

To all those who descended and then left, both known and unknown, who have created, developed and mastered the tantric and yogic sciences, thereby giving to mankind the gift of light, the tools which can aid in the task of human evolution.

It is with our deepest yet still most humble appreciation that we are naming a few of the greats who are known to us, and whose teachings have made the practices in this book available to all of us today.

Lords Brahma, Vishnu and Shiva in their various forms, the gurus of the ages such as Vashishtha, Vyasa and Shankaracharya, the nine nathas, eighty-four siddhas and sixty-four yoginis, to Abraham, Moses and the compilers of the Kabbala, to Jesus, the Essenes and the Christian saints, Mohammed and the Sufis, the mystical Mayans, Zoroaster, Mahavira, Lord Buddha, Padmasambhava, Guru Nanak, Babaji, Kabir, Tulsidas, Chaitanya Mahaprabhu, Patanjali, the bhairavas and bhairavis, kaulas, aghoris and avadhootas, the great white brotherhood, siddha tantrics like Ramprasad, Sarvananda, Vamakshepa, Paramahamsa Ramakrishna, Tailang Swami, Sai Baba (Shirdi), Lahiri Mahasaya, Sri Yukteswara, Swami Yogananda, John Woodroffe, Swami Vivekananda, Sri Aurobindo, Swami Nityananda, Meher Baba, Ramana Maharishi and Paramguru Swami Sivananda of Rishikesh.

SWAMI SIVANANDA SARASWATI

Swami Sivananda was born at Pattamadai, Tamil Nadu, in 1887. After serving as a medical doctor in Malaya, he renounced his practice, went to Rishikesh and was initiated into Dashnami sannyasa in 1924 by Swami Vishwananda Saraswati. He toured extensively throughout India, inspiring people to practise yoga and lead a divine life. He founded the Divine Life Society at Rishikesh in 1936, the Sivananda Ayurvedic Pharmacy in 1945, the Yoga Vedanta Forest Academy in 1948 and the Sivananda Eye Hospital in 1957. During his lifetime Swami Sivananda guided thousands of disciples and aspirants all over the world and authored over 200 books.

SWAMI SATYANANDA SARASWATI

Swami Satyananda was born at Almora, Uttar Pradesh, in 1923. In 1943 he met Swami Sivananda in Rishikesh and adopted the Dashnami sannyasa way of life. In 1955 he left his guru's ashram to live as a wandering mendicant and later founded the International Yoga Fellowship in 1963 and the Bihar School of Yoga in 1964. Over the next 20 years Swami Satyananda toured internationally and authored over 80 books. In 1987 he founded Sivananda Math, a charitable institution for aiding rural development, and the Yoga Research Foundation. In 1988 he renounced his mission, adopting kshetra sannyasa, and now lives as a paramahamsa sannyasin.

SWAMI NIRANJANANANDA SARASWATI

Swami Niranjanananda was born at Rajnandgaon, Madhya Pradesh, in 1960. At the age of four he joined the Bihar School of Yoga and was initiated into Dashnami sannyasa at the age of ten. From 1971 he travelled overseas and toured many countries for the next 11 years. In 1983 he was recalled to India and appointed President of Bihar School of Yoga. During the following 11 years he guided the development of Ganga Darshan, Sivananda Math and the Yoga Research Foundation. In 1990 he was initiated as a paramahamsa and in 1993 anointed preceptor in succession to Swami Satyananda. Bihar Yoga Bharati was founded under his direction in 1994. He has authored over 20 books and guides national and international yoga programs.

SWAMI SATYASANGANANDA SARASWATI

Swami Satyasangananda (Satsangi) was born on 24th March 1953, in Chandorenagore, West Bengal. From the age of 22 she experienced a series of inner awakenings which led her to her guru, Swami Satyananda. From 1981 she travelled ceaselessly with her guru in India and overseas and developed into a scholar with deep insight into the yogic and tantric traditions as well as modern sciences and philosophies. She is an efficient channel for the transmission of her guru's teachings. The establishment of Sivananda Math in Rikhia is her creation and mission, and she guides all its activities there, working tirelessly to uplift the weaker and underprivileged areas. She embodies compassion with clear reason and is the foundation of her guru's vision.

Foreword

Tantra is an ancient science dealing with many different systems for increasing the speed of human evolution. It predates all of the world's existing religions, and provides the esoteric basis on which many of these religions were later based. Tantra provides practical techniques applicable by men and women of every temperament and spiritual level, and aims at turning every action of life into an act of sadhana, or spiritual practice. A few thousand years after its creation, tantra was wedded with the philosophy of Vedanta by the Aryans to form the system of yoga which is quite popular today. It is the aim of this book to provide a practical glimpse into the most important meditation techniques which have their original basis in tantra, so that they may be practised in their original and correct form.

The practices included in this book are based in tantra, though many of them have been forgotten for thousands of years. The task of rediscovering them and putting them in a form which can be understood and practised by people of this age has been done solely by Swami Satyananda Saraswati, as his personal contribution to a civilization searching for a deeper understanding of the basis of life. We hope the world may gain a little and that humanity may advance, even if only a small step, through the publication of these techniques, many of which have never been written down or published in their practicable forms.

Contents

Foreword *ix*
Preface *xiii*
Introduction 1

The Theory of Meditation
1. What is Meditation? 9
2. Science, Spirit and Meditation 17
3. Meditation and Health 32
4. Yoga's Psychic Physiology 39
5. Reprogram Your Mind 48
6. Yoga Philosophy 62
7. The System of Raja Yoga 67
8. Other Forms of Yoga 84

Preparation for Meditation
9. General Instructions and Suggestions 101
10. Meditation Poses 108
11. Mudras and Bandhas 120
12. Pranayama 138

Practices for Meditation
13. Japa Yoga 153
14. Mantra Siddhi Yoga 160
15. Ajapa Japa 165
16. Yoga Nidra 181
17. Antar Mouna 211
18. Inner Visualization 225
19. Chidakasha Dharana 242
20. Trataka and Antar Trataka 254

21. Nada Yoga 269
22. Abstract Meditations 277
23. Miscellaneous Meditations 282
24. Prana Vidya 297
25. Kundalini Kriyas 308

Appendices
A. Phonetic Pronunciation Guide 329
B. Mantras from Different Religions 330
Glossary 349
Further Reading 359
Index of Practices 361
General Index 365

Preface

This book was written because the writer feels that the majority of mankind is searching for happiness, yet very few seem to find anything that approaches contentment in their lives. People look to television, cinema, sports and so on for happiness, but though it might come for a short time, any lasting happiness seems to elude them. People seek power, status and material possessions. In return most people suffer from fear, hatred, insecurity, ulcers, heart attacks, mental disturbances, etc.

Yet the way, the path towards contentment in life and a positive, exuberant attitude towards life is simple, so simple, in fact, that people never try or even think of trying it. The answer is to raise your awareness, to dive deep into the infinite depths of the mind. It is here that you will find a peace that will transcend all other types of peace that you have experienced. When you know your deeper mind, all the pettiness and conflict will cease to be important. You will still live in the world and do your work, interact with other people, but you will feel a continual state of contentment. You will be in contact with that which has meaning, and which is not concerned with the superficialities that most people tangle themselves with.

It is the way one's mind works that is important, the way one's mind interprets outside phenomena as well as the information that is already stored in the mind. One sees people living in squalid conditions, yet they seem to be very happy, though not always. The answer lies in their mind, in the way their mind responds to outside events as well as to itself. So we say to you: change your mind, increase your awareness of the deeper workings of your mind, and happiness will come of itself. The method to attain happiness and contentment is to meditate.

Introduction

Man has evolved much during the last few thousand years. He has evolved from a nomadic being, concerned only with obtaining the necessities of basic existence and controlled completely by the vicissitudes of nature, to his present condition where nature is beginning to be the servant of man. Man is now able to devote a large proportion of his life to things outside earning a living. The process of evolution is a continuous movement of the disordered to the ordered, the unrefined to the refined and the gross to the subtle. With the majority of mankind this has occurred on the physical and mental planes and can of course continue in its present direction through the rapidly changing sophistication of science and technology. But this is not the only alternative and is not the only path on which man can tread. People today are finding that their values are lopsided, that something is missing from their lives.

All of us know subconsciously, though perhaps not consciously, that the spiritual path exists and that it leads somewhere. It is not merely wishful thinking on the part of a few people with their heads in the clouds. The great saints throughout the ages have been living examples of where the spiritual path leads. They have even explained the means, the way, though in general their teachings have been misinterpreted, either by accident or on purpose, by politically motivated groups. All these highly evolved souls have said the same thing using different words. All of them have said: Look within and know thyself.

For example, Christ said: "The kingdom of God is within you." Greek philosophers said: "Man, know thyself, and thou shalt know the universe." All the Eastern religions put forth the same idea. Paramahamsa Ramakrishna said: "The fabled musk deer searches the whole world over for the source of the scent which comes from within." In the *Bhagavad Gita* Lord Krishna says: "Meditation is better than intellectual knowledge."

Therefore, learn from other people's experiences. The path of evolution, of the evolution of the spirit to self-realization, towards the truth, does not lie in the outside world. It lies within your own being, only waiting to be discovered. You must dive deep inside yourself to find that which has been always there and was even there before your birth. So the choice is yours: either you continue to devote all your attention to fumbling around in the outside world, the way that most people now lead their lives with its unhappiness, or you start to develop a new direction, inwards, and follow the advice of wise men throughout the history of mankind who have made the same journey. You do not have to give up your present lifestyle. All you have to do is to supplement it with spiritual aspiration and practices of yoga which will gradually lead you along the path to meditation.

You might say, "Yes, I want to tread the spiritual path, but how do I start?" One of the ways is to do yoga, proceeding from the preliminary lower and simpler stages such as asanas to the more advanced stages such as concentration and meditation. It is in the practices of meditation that the key finally unlocks the door to the higher realms of being, higher consciousness, or whatever you want to call the infinite scope of experience that exists within and without.

Let us change our way of looking at our inner self or being. Many eminent scientists have emphatically stated that much of our mental faculties and potential remains unused. Some have said that 95 percent, others that 99 percent of our latent capacity remains dormant. Actually the given figures are only illustrative. What is meant is that almost all of our inner potential is untapped. It is only waiting to be utilized. It has also been predicted that the greatest adventures of the future will lie in the exploration of the largely unknown realms of the mind. Instead of confining our travels to the outside world, we will also start to make deeper and deeper journeys into the depths of inner space. Our slogan for the future should be 'Wake up the mind'.

Most people have the naive idea, even though yoga and psychology have told them otherwise, that the mind only thinks what they are conscious of at any particular time. This of course couldn't be further from the truth. At any time, scientists have estimated that the mind is sorting out, receiving, rejecting, analyzing millions of visual, acoustical and bodily sensations. We are aware only of that which comes to our consciousness. The rest remains at a level below our consciousness.

In western psychology, the unknown part of the mind is known as the subconscious or the unconscious. The known part is called the conscious mind. It is commonly compared to the upper tip of an iceberg, lying above the water, and the unconscious mind to the far larger submerged portion of the iceberg. In yoga the mind is regarded as one entity, with progressively more subtle layers. The less subtle or grosser layers of mind correspond to the parts of the mind which contain our basic urges and instincts, together with the rational part of the mind. The awareness of most people stays predominantly in these layers of the mind, completely neglecting the intuitive, inspirational, creative, and spiritual aspects of being. By treading the spiritual path, one is able to bring consciousness to these normally unknown realms. Modern psychology and yoga are saying virtually the same thing about the mind.

The opening up or exploration of these progressively more subtle layers of the mind leads to what is commonly called expansion of consciousness. Knowledge of all the realms of the mind as well as the very centre of your being, the self, that which illuminates your whole existence, is known as self-realization, *nirvana, satori*, unitive life or oneness with God.

The external world can be likened to an infinite horizontal circle. Our development of mind, or perhaps the awakening of the mind, can be likened to various lines at right angles to the horizontal circle all aiming at the centre. The circle represents the realm of time-space and the centre represents the realm of eternity, of timelessness. The centre is the very essence of our inner being. By giving our attention only to the outside world we remain on the circumference of the circle, totally unable to reach the centre. But by awakening our mind, while simultaneously living in the external world, we start to follow one of the perpendicular lines that leads towards the centre. The more we awaken the mind, the nearer we approach the central core of our being, the potential oneness of existence. So start your journey to the centre *now*. Don't delay.

Yes, but how? If one wants to explore the external world, the method is known. One merely uses a material vehicle, either one's own body to go to the nearby park or countryside, or one goes by train or bus to the nearby town, or one travels by ship or aeroplane, even by spaceship if one wants to go to another planet. But how does one go inwards? The answer we have already mentioned – it is through meditation. Meditation is the vehicle which takes one on the inner trip. You don't have to buy a ticket, The ticket is one's mind. So start meditation *now*.

In this book, we have tried not to get too carried away by the theoretical and non-practical aspects of meditation. Our general aim has been to show the possibilities open to the practitioner of meditation, the preparation that is necessary, how meditation relates to the different types of yoga, as well as practical methods, so that the reader can attain meditational experiences himself (after all, this is what meditation is all about). We feel that personal experience, even the slightest, is worth far more than any number of words. Words in themselves cannot begin to adequately describe what the meditator feels during meditation. The whole point of meditation is to transcend words and the rational mind, and not to become enmeshed in a web of empty platitudes. Words or any attempt at describing the transcendental experiences of meditation will not leave any deep impression on the individual, while a practical experience, even at a low level, can change his or her whole life. So we have given various practical methods and we ask you to try a few, not necessarily all, and find out what meditation is all about for yourself. Don't live vicariously in other people's experiences. If you want to read long descriptions of other people's experiences, preferring these to your own, then we suggest sincerely you read another book.

We have emphasized the importance of individual effort to change the mind. Most of our thinking and reactions in life operate on an instinctive level. We are programmed to respond in fixed ways to different life situations according to our likes, dislikes, ego-motivated needs and so on. If the outside world and other people don't fit in with our thought patterns, we become unhappy, depressed etc. These are serious impediments to meditation. Therefore, to attain success in meditation, it is essential that we change our mind.

Meditational practices are an excellent method of confronting the complexes, phobias and conflicts which are hidden in the usually inaccessible recesses of the unconscious part of the mind. Each person can become his own psychoanalyst. Once the problems are recognized they can be removed by autosuggestion (given in chapter 4) and by the system of psychic desensitization. As these problems are progressively removed, one's life will simultaneously undergo a transformation towards integration and happiness.

Yoga and meditation do not offer any opposition to religious or philosophical beliefs or non-beliefs. On the contrary, the practice of yoga and meditation makes an individual a much more active and better practitioner of his or her own particular way of life. What will surely happen is that the practitioner will gain more understanding of other people's beliefs and hence a more harmonious interaction with them in everyday life.

A word of warning. Don't expect to be able to attain a high state of meditation on your first attempt, for meditation, true meditation, is a high stage in spiritual life. Practice is required, but all effort is well worth it because of the illumination that it can bring. Speaking personally, I must admit that I was very sceptical about meditation when I was first introduced to it. I couldn't quite understand how merely closing my eyes could possibly have any influence on me. Many times I had previously closed my eyes, apart from sleep, and nothing had ever happened, but with some practice my doubts and naiveté were slowly but surely removed. And again it must be said that no amount of reading books on the subject could have removed my doubts and made me realize what an indispensable part of life meditation really is. My gradual conversion to the regular practice of meditation was through personal practice and experience and nothing else.

Remember, the practice of meditation though only performed for a short time every day (forgetting the great saints, etc., who are and were in an almost continual state of meditation) has vast repercussions on one's daily life. The insight and bliss one will experience during meditation will affect one's mental and physical state throughout the whole day. With constant practice of meditation, one's whole personality and behaviour will undergo an almost miraculous change in a positive direction. One's whole existence will turn over a new leaf.

Swami Nischalananda Saraśwati
Editor

The Theory of Meditation

1

What is Meditation?

Meditation is something that most people have heard about, few have any true conception about and even fewer have actually experienced. Like all other subjective experiences it cannot really be described in words. The reader must try to find it for himself to know what it is really about. The experience is real whereas a description is really non-experience, especially in the case of meditation. However, we will do our best to throw some light on the subject.

Let us first define the way that modern psychology has categorized different factors of the mind. The subconscious or unconscious mind can be roughly divided into three groups as follows: the lower mind, the middle mind and the higher mind. The lower mind is concerned with the activation and coordination of the various activities of the body, such as respiration, circulation, the abdominal organs, and so on. It is also the area of mind which gives rise to instinctive urges, and it is from this part of the mind that complexes, phobias, fears and obsessions manifest.

The middle mind is the part of the mind that concerns itself with data that we use during the waking state. It is this part of the mind that analyzes, compares and reaches conclusions in relation to incoming data. The results of its work manifest to our conscious attention as required. It is this part of the mind that gives us answers. For example, most of us have been faced with a problem which we cannot solve at the time, only to find that the answer surfaces to consciousness at some later time. It is the middle subconscious that has done the problem solving without our awareness. This is the realm of rational or intellectual thinking.

The higher mind is the area of so-called superconscious activity. It is the source of intuition, inspiration, bliss and transcendental experiences. It is from this region that geniuses derive their flashes of creativity. It is the source of deeper knowledge.

Throughout our waking hours we have consciousness of certain phenomena. We are conscious only of a small part of the activities of the mind, usually in the realms of the middle mind. It is this consciousness that is allowing you to read these words and to be aware of their meaning.

Another part of the mind is the collective unconscious that Carl Jung did much to bring to scientific acceptance. It is in this part of the mind that we have records of our evolutionary past. It contains records of the activities of our ancestors and the archetypes. It is the part of the mind that links us to all other human beings because it is the blueprint of our common past.

Behind all these different parts of the mind is the self or the very core of existence. It is the self that illuminates everything that we do, though we are not aware of it. Most of us assume that the centre of our being is the ego, yet the ego is really no more than another part of the mind. It is the self that illuminates even the ego.

So what happens when we meditate? When we meditate we are able to take our consciousness to the different parts of our mind. Normally, as we have already explained, our consciousness is confined to surface activity in small areas of the middle or rational parts of the unconscious. We are able to move away from intellectualization during meditation.

It is the usual experience of most people who start to meditate that they see grotesque apparitions, or they become aware of deep rooted complexes that they perhaps didn't know existed within them. They realize they have fears that they were not aware of before. The reason is that the consciousness is now functioning in the domain of the lower mind. The consciousness is now highlighting complexes, fears, etc., of which it was not previously aware. Before it was only aware of the manifestations of these fears in the form of anger, hatred, depression, etc. Once these deep-rooted complexes are confronted they can be removed (refer to chapter 5) and greater happiness attained in life. Also many people become very aware of the internal processes of their body during meditation. This is because the consciousness becomes aware of the activities that control these bodily functions.

Higher stages of meditation are difficult to attain if we don't remove most of the compulsive fear that we have in the lower mind. It is not possible to go into deeper states of meditation because these complexes are so compulsive that they seem to almost automatically draw the consciousness to their attention. Though there are many other places where the consciousness can go, it seems to be drawn like iron to a magnet to the lower mind's activities. It seems to take perverse delight in dwelling on our fears, phobias and anxieties.

In higher states of meditation the consciousness moves to the higher mind, or the region of superconsciousness. The consciousness rises above rational thought and we see the activities that seem to be closer to reality. The meditator enters the dimensions of inspiration and illumination. One starts to explore the deeper truths and aspects of existence. One enters new spheres, new lands of existence, which until this time seemed impossible and mere figments of the imagination.

The culmination of meditation is self-realization. This occurs when even the higher mind is transcended. The consciousness leaves the exploration of the mind and identifies with the central core of one's existence, the self. At this point it becomes pure consciousness. When a person achieves self-realization it means that he has contacted his central being and now identifies his existence, his life, from the viewpoint of the self and not from the standpoint of the ego. When he acts from the centre of his being, the body and mind operate almost as separate entities. The mind and body cease to be the real him; they are merely manifestations of the self, his true identity. So it can be seen that the aim of meditation is to explore the different regions of the mind and eventually to transcend the mind completely.

Passive and active meditation

There are two types of meditation: *passive* and *active*. Active meditation is that which occurs when one performs one's daily duties, when one walks, talks, eats and so on. This in fact is the aim of yoga, to allow one to meditate while being involved in worldly activities. It does not mean that the activities will not be done, or not done with enthusiasm. In fact the work or external activities will be performed with more efficiency and energy. Active meditation can be developed by performing the passive meditational practices given in this book and by developing one's self-identity, as well as perfecting the techniques of karma and bhakti yoga (refer to chapter 8).

Passive meditation is the aim of sitting in one pose and performing a meditational practice such as the ones given in this book. Its aim is to still the ever restless and wandering mind and make it one-pointed, so that meditational experience will automatically follow. It can be roughly divided into four various stages of proficiency:

1. Fixing the mind on a meditational practice, an object, sound, the breath, a picture and so on. This calms the mind and makes it introverted.
2. Success in stage 1 automatically leads to the free flow of thoughts, complexes, visions, memories, etc., from unconscious realms of the mind. It is possible now to probe the personality and lower mind and to remove undesirable contents.
3. When the lower mind has been fully explored one then starts to explore the superconscious realms. Now real

meditation begins. The limitless storehouse of knowledge and energy within each of us starts to show itself spontaneously. Eventually one's being starts to tune in with the cosmos and everything around us.

4. Eventually even the mind is transcended and the meditator attains oneness with the supreme consciousness. The goal of self-realization is reached.

Successful passive meditation will automatically lead to active meditation, for the deeper one dives into the mind in passive meditation the more one is likely to be able to live a perpetual meditational state even while performing worldly duties. In fact, the deeper one dives into the mind during passive meditation, the more powerful the surface expression in the form of external activities will become. As one explores the mind it becomes more powerful. As such, one's life, work, play, etc., becomes more powerful and one is able to accomplish things that were impossible before.

Eventually passive meditation becomes superfluous; this is when one attains self-realization. At this stage the individual lives completely according to the deepest inner and spiritual values, yet at the some time is able to express himself in the outside world. In this situation, the self-realized person is able to live both a spiritual and material life without conflict. In this state there is a continuous and spontaneous experience of active meditation.

People have a tendency to identify completely with objects of perception. For example, we see a beautiful sunset. Our whole awareness is wrapped up in it so that we completely forget our own identity. We forget the fact that we are experiencing the spectacle. As such, how can we really experience the joy of the sunset? The individual, the subject, the experiencer forgets his nature, for it is overshadowed by the object of perception. The consciousness has identified with the object to the exclusion of the subject. The reader should think about this now while reading these words. Are you aware of the fact that you are experiencing these words, or are you identifying completely with these words?

The ideal situation is where the sunset or any other object is experienced, yet at the same time the awareness of oneself is not lost. One should feel the objective experience of the perceiver. In this way the spiritual feeling of experiencing will be heightened; the self or soul now consciously knows the experience of the object. The bliss of the self can now show itself in response to the outer objective experience. Before, the nature of the self was overshadowed by the experience of the object, now the self can shine in its full pristine glory.

This should apply to our whole material existence. We should experience external phenomena for this is part of life. Yet we should supplement our outer life with the inner life. In this way we will be able to enjoy the material life more fully. At the moment most of us live an almost totally extroverted life through ignorance. We don't realize the ocean of bliss that exists in the inner depths of our being. One of the aims of meditation is to take our consciousness away from the external entanglements even for a short time and direct it inwards. The aim is to give a glimpse of the inner life and eventually to connect it with the outer life. This connection always exists yet we are never conscious of the fact. Meditation make us conscious of the connection and leads to spiritual happiness and peace. It makes us aware of the vital importance of the subjective experience, the inner, essential nature that is our heritage.

Meditation is the legacy of all. It is something that we all should and are able to experience spontaneously, yet we cannot because of the way we live. We are continually in a state of tension because we don't know ourselves, our inner nature. We are continually trying to do things because we feel we ought to, even though it might be contrary to our nature. There is a continual conflict between that which is and that which we want. We are always motivated to become something instead of just being. If we could only bring about a unity between what we are and what we want, then meditation would occur spontaneously.

The knowledge that most of us experience is in the form of intellectual knowledge. It is derived from the rational part of our mind. This is really a form of relative knowledge; it is not real knowledge. It consists of a limited field of facts and figures from which we deduce theories, concepts and our relationships with our environment. This is the form of scientific, technological, philosophical and other ways of reasoning which come from the rational mind. The fallacy is that the original assumptions are fundamentally adequate in themselves. Yet we find that knowledge of this type is continually being proved wrong as new light is thrown on the subject. Let's take an example from science. Newton expounded the theory of gravitation which was eventually accepted as being absolutely true. However, a few centuries later Einstein showed in his theory that gravity does not exist as such. Of course this does not only apply to science; it applies to every intellectual act that we perform. Any conclusion that we come to through the rational mind can be superseded in the light of new information.

We can also experience knowledge in the form of feeling or emotion. One can mentally feel the truth of an idea; at the same time one can also emotionally sense that something is true. Many people mistake this type of knowledge for intuitive knowledge.

Beyond emotional and intellectual knowledge there is another type of knowledge. This type of knowledge is achieved in states of meditation and is a more real form of knowledge. It is intuitive knowledge that comprehends the totality of a situation. Unlike rational knowledge which tries to build up a complete picture of the whole from the parts, intuition directly apprehends the whole, the totality. It comes from the superconscious part of the mind, of which we are usually unaware. This type of knowledge depends neither on the intellect nor on the emotions, which tend to colour or warp the real form of knowledge. Meditation does not depend on personal projection; if it did then it would not be meditation.

During meditation a link is made between the higher regions of mind associated with the so-called expansion of consciousness, the superconscious part of the mind, and the field of consciousness or awareness, the so-called waking consciousness. This link allows higher mental vibrations to be perceived by the consciousness of the meditator. These subtle higher vibrations exist all the time, yet they are not normally perceptible. Sometimes they are seen on rare occasions in the form of intuitive flashes, inspirations, creative illumination, etc. We are normally unaware of these vibrations, truths and higher knowledge because of the impure, complex ridden state of our minds. These higher forms of knowledge, higher vibrations, show more of the underlying cause and truth behind the manifestations that we see in our everyday lives. The deeper aspects of life show themselves during meditation.

2

Science, Spirit and Meditation

It is gratifying to find that science and yoga, which until recently seemed to be diametrically opposite to each other, are drawing closer together. Science is starting to study and utilize yogic techniques and yoga is starting to speak increasingly in scientific terms and to use scientific knowledge. No longer is science concerned totally with the material aspects of existence. More and more it is beginning to concern itself with, and to investigate, the spiritual or non-material facets of existence. Science, by showing modern intellectual people the physical by-products associated with spiritual phenomena, will surely open more minds to the truth and possibilities of religion, yoga and other spiritual paths or methods of mind exploration.

At the end of the last century many eminent scientists came to the conclusion that they knew so much that there was nothing important left to discover and investigate. Then Einstein, Freud and other open-minded scientists came and through their investigations showed that there was indeed much more to know and discover in the universe. Because of this, modern scientists are very aware of the possibilities open to them in the field of investigation and are very careful not to become complacent. It is for this reason that various research projects are currently investigating the phenomena of spiritual experiences. Actually, it is strange that science has not investigated this field before, considering that it was over fifty years ago that Freud published his findings on the lower unconscious mind, and that geniuses and saints throughout the ages have shown the possibilities of higher stages of mind awareness.

One of the most interesting fields of investigation of modern science is research into the physical manifestations of meditation. These are still in their infancy, but are already throwing much light on the utility of meditation for physiological, psychological and spiritual benefits. It seems more than a possibility that science will eventually greatly help people to tread the spiritual path. Devices such as biofeedback instruments (discussed later in this chapter) are being utilized by some to gain higher states of meditation. Modern forms of psychology, in particular, are very concerned with spiritual growth in an individual, as well as psychological health. A notable example is psychosynthesis, which actually has the same aims as yoga: integration of the whole being, of an individual and eventual self-realization.

Let us discuss various fields where science and yoga are approaching or have gained common ground. Modern ideas in the field of psychology are surprisingly like yogic ideas propounded thousands of years ago in the form of Samkhya philosophy. In yoga it is the whole nature of a person that is important. This means the physical, mental, emotional, psychic and spiritual aspects of man. All these aspects are developed, or rather we should say that the dormant faculties in each individual are revealed, through the practice of yoga. This is the true spiritual path, where all these aspects are integrated to make man a whole being.

Psychology in general (there are exceptions such as psychosynthesis, which was formulated by Roberto Assagioli in 1910) until comparatively recently has only been concerned with certain restricted facets of man's being, almost ignoring other influences on an individual's life. For example, Freud, the father of western psychology, postulated that man's prime motive in life was sexual satisfaction and self-preservation. This is, to say the least, a rather limited view of man's psychological being and his aspirations. Yet even today there are many psychologists who believe in this idea. Of course Jung was very progressive in his ideas, which accepted that there were deeper influences and aspects of man which most people are not aware of.

All psychological considerations of man have tended to treat him in isolation from his environment and other things that influence his being, such as the spiritual aspects of man's existence. As such, psychology could never really give anything that even slightly approaches a reasonable explanation of man. Consequently all psychological therapies that followed from the psychological theories were not very successful. They helped man in some ways, but not in any way that led to happiness or evolution of being.

Jung was probably the psychologist who most helped psychology to adopt a holistic or complete attitude to man's existence. His ideas, however, have only recently been considered seriously by other psychologists on a large scale. Partly from his teachings, various modern schools of thought have been indirectly or directly developed, for instance, growth psychology, gestalt psychology, organismic psychology, height psychology and various others. They all see man as a multi-dimensional being and all are very much in accordance with yogic thought. They all realize that any understanding of man must consider all aspects of existence, both objective and subjective. If any part of existence is omitted, such as the spiritual aspect, only a partial picture of man can be formulated.

All of the modern forms of psychology are very much concerned with the flowering of potential in each individual. This is referred to as self-actualization. It is the progressive unfoldment of each person's innate capacities. This is exactly what yoga is all about, but instead of self-actualization, yoga refers to self-realization in all spheres of being, or awareness of one's inner nature and its expression. The final aim of yoga is self-realization, where an individual has manifested all his potential to the peak, to the ultimate, where he is in tune, in perfect harmony with his inner being and his external environment.

In modern psychology a self-actualized person is exactly the same type of person, a person who has expressed all his latent potential, innate abilities and no longer reacts adversely to his personality and surroundings, harmonizing with everything external and internal. Both modern psychology and yoga stress the importance of evolution, of continual growth of each individual from 'less wholeness' to 'more wholeness'. The final aim according to yoga is oneness with existence, with God, with supreme consciousness. Psychologists as yet have not actually stated this as the final goal, but who knows, they may postulate this some time in the near future. Some schools, however, such as psychosynthesis, have said that self-realization is the ultimate aim of life.

In the past, psychology has tended to assume that a man is psychologically bound by fixed drives and motivations. It therefore assumed that a man should fulfil these so-called drives in endless repetition. However, this continual satisfaction of basic needs, though necessary, only removes tensions and frustrations for a short time. It in no way allows the individual to remove completely the basic tensions in his life. Modern psychology and yoga emphasize the importance of transcendence, the overall growth of an individual so that he does not stay in the same life mould. He should continually seek higher forms of fulfilment, the reason for higher aspiration being that the new aspiration is more joyous, more blissful than the previous. In this way the evolving individual leaves lower forms of drives behind because they are less satisfying. Yoga has always said this, and modern psychology is agreeing with yoga more and more in this context.

Modern psychologists have become greatly interested in meditation and have started to do research in this direction. They have not only performed scientific experiments but have even started referring to ancient texts on meditation to gain some insight into its implications and utility. They are even trying meditation for themselves and experiencing things that take them way beyond their normal intellectualization. Such has been the insight, obtained partly through meditation, that psychologists have started to redefine their definition of a normal human being. They have postulated that most people, from the day they were born, are subjected to constant classifications. In other words, people are indoctrinated that things are good/bad, persons are black/white, persons are Christian/Muslim/Hindu, persons are clever/dull and so on. We love or we hate. We become totally involved in a word categorization that prevents us seeing the world as it really is. People become automated. Many psychologists have declared that one of the main aims of psychology should be to de-automate people.

Modern thinkers, especially psychologists, are very concerned with the damaging effect that fast, competitive living can have on the mind. It is indeed a truth that mental problems and diseases are becoming epidemic. Psychologists realize that each person must have a mind that can face a bombardment of intense external activity. Many have realized that each person must become his own psychological adviser. The method that is being widely recommended and adopted is meditation. It is the universal way of removing or preventing excessive worry, conflict and stress. It is also the sure way to a positive and contented life.

At least it is becoming widely accepted that meditation is neither a sleep nor a hypnotic state. In this context, psychologists are only considering persons who sit down at a regular time to meditate for a short duration. The fact that certain highly evolved people are continually in a state of meditation, sleeping and waking, should indicate that meditation is beyond sleep and hypnotism. More and more psychologists are advising people to practise meditation so that they can observe their inner functioning. In this way they can become aware of overactivity of the different organs and the brain itself, and steps can be taken to rectify any overstimulation or malfunctioning. This is the best method of treating disease, stop it before it occurs. Half an hour of meditation every morning helps to bring quietude and to thereby improve external activities. Our ability to perform our daily work and play depends entirely on our inner being. If our inner being is not in harmony, then our interaction with the external environment cannot possibly be harmonious.

Meditation is the sure way to counteract pessimism, depression, tension and so on, states of mind which most people have accepted as a normal part of life. Even psychologists now believe this and modern progressive thinkers in the field of psychology have stated this idea. They now believe, like yoga, that the normal state of man should be a continuous expression of joy. Meditation can be utilized by everyone for mood control, to switch off negative states and to replace them with states of well-being.

One of man's greatest problems is his inability to adapt to change. A hundred years ago and before, and even now in countries that have not developed a technological society, this was no problem for there were virtually no changes from year to year, let alone from day-to-day. Technological societies, however, are in a continual state of change. The changes occur faster that the mind can adapt to them. The result is mental disorder, in a minor or major way depending on the individual. Psychology has recognized this problem and is recommending meditation as the sure way to develop the capacity to face change.

Psychology has always recognized the need to know the extensive inner workings of the unconscious mind. It has tended to be concerned with the part of the unconscious that contains our complexes and phobias. This is, of course, necessary in order to purge the deep-rooted conflicts that tend to dominate our lives. The method used by yoga, and also increasingly by modern fields of psychology, is meditation. Yet at the same time it is important to explore the vast regions of the mind, the higher unconscious, to use psychological terms, in which are contained our hidden capacities, abilities, our inner potentialities. Many of us have a true vocation in life, a natural flair to do certain things, yet because we don't know them, we never do them. In a sense we are in a state of continual frustration. If we could express this potential, then we would start to live self-actualizing, creative and happy lives. The method is through meditation. In this way we can find our inner being and then start to fulfil its innate nature. We can start to do what we are best at.

Biofeedback: a modern trend in yoga

Biofeedback techniques have been utilized in relation to meditation. Biofeedback is concerned with measuring and monitoring electrical waves emitted from the brain. Let us first of all discuss the cause and nature of these brainwaves. The existence of brainwaves, though perhaps brain rhythms is a better description, was noticed at the end of the nineteenth century during research into the brains of monkeys. In the early part of the twentieth century, this field of research spread to humans. It was found that the frequency, voltage and amplitude of the waves varied quite appreciably. Steady research into this phenomenon has been going on ever since and the pattern of the brainwaves has been used in pathology to show the existence of malfunctions in the brain, such as tumours and general mental disorders.

What are these brainwaves? Medical researchers are not absolutely sure, but the following is a brief description of their cause and nature. The brain is made of millions and millions of cells, called neurones. There are countless connections between these individual cells and other cells. In fact, we say tentatively that every cell in the brain is directly or indirectly connected to every other cell. Nerve pulses continually travel along these complex neurone circuits. Each neurone consists of a central body, an axon and various dendrites. It receives nerve impulses from other neurones via the axon, a long strand-like fibre. The individual neurone in turn transmits nerve impulses to other neurones through branch-like fibres called dendrites, which connect to the axons of other neurones. The nerve impulse is only transmitted when the electrical charge in the neurone builds up to a certain level. At this predetermined level there is a sudden burst or impulse. It is these pulses that give the brainwaves.

Researchers have found that a distinct relationship exists between the frequency, voltage and amplitude of the brainwaves and the state of the individual. For convenience, the waves have been divided into four types: beta, alpha, theta and delta. The reader must remember that these brainwaves are not the states of mind; they are merely a manifestation which allows one to know one's state of mind. Though much is still to be discovered regarding the relationship between these waves and the state of mind, the following is a brief summary of present-day knowledge regarding these waves.

Beta waves are the patterns that we predominantly emit from our brain during everyday, wakeful states. They are related to external activities, extroversion. When we utilize the brain for rational thinking, when we use the senses, when we are anxious, tense and in 'normal' frames of mind, beta waves are emitted. They are of low amplitude and high frequency with over 13 cycles per second.

Alpha waves are most noticeably emitted during milder states of meditation. They are related to a relaxed state of mind, passivity and a non-anxious and tensionless state. They are very much related to creativity, so that during periods of creativity alpha waves are profusely emitted. They manifest when the rational mind and senses become inoperative. Studies on yogis and Zen Buddhists while in states of meditation have confirmed these generalizations about alpha waves. They are associated with passive awareness, a distinctive characteristic of meditation. Alpha waves have frequencies ranging from 8 to 13 cycles per second.

Theta waves are profusely emitted during sleep. They are associated with the unconscious mind and occur when deep unconscious data or impressions bubble to the surface and to conscious awareness. Theta waves are manifested during deep states of meditation, during intense creativity, ecstasy and receptivity of extrasensory perception. Many children emit this type of wave during the waking state, though this is more rare in adults. Theta waves have a frequency range of 4 to 7 cycles per second.

Delta waves are high amplitude waves with frequencies below 4 cycles per second. Less is known about this type of wave emission, though it has been closely linked with deep, dreamless sleep. In this state there is great receptivity to learning. In other words, people in this kind of state can absorb learning, perhaps from a tape recorder, even while asleep. Knowledge seems to be directly absorbed into the unconscious mind, bypassing the sense organs.

The reader should appreciate that this classification is arbitrary. The classification should not be considered as a rigid and natural division. A person who has sufficient mental control, such as an advanced yogi, can move progressively from one state to the next at will. He can start off in the beta range of 'normal' wakefulness, then by willpower he can proceed to the state of mind characterized by alpha waves. At first beta waves are present, then eventually all the beta waves disappear and after some time theta waves will start to appear. If there is no sleep, then deep states of meditation will be attained, progressively becoming deeper as the theta waves predominate more and more. Eventually he can manifest delta waves, which are normally associated with deep sleep. However, we will speculate, and it is only supposition, that during meditation the predominance of delta waves corresponds to very high states of meditation and perhaps even samadhi.

These wave patterns can be detected by means of an electrical system known as electroencephalograph (EEG). This is an amplifier system that detects electrical activities that occur within the brain, which are picked up by means of electrodes fixed to the side of the head. These electrical patterns can then be recorded on a graph by means of a pen-recorder, which immediately indicates the type of wave being emitted. In turn, the states of mind of the person can be read from the shape of the waves. This type of instrument is used mainly for research and in pathology but is, however, out of the question for the person in the street. To cater for his need, various companies have manufactured, at very reasonable prices, simple instruments that will allow anyone to detect the wave form being emitted from his brain. The most common, and also the simplest, consists of a headphone and an instrument that gives audible and variable sounds that correspond to the fluctuations in brainwave activity. Another type only emits a sound when one starts producing a certain type of brainwave. Various other types are available and many more are sure to be developed.

How does biofeedback help one to meditate? By knowing one's particular brainwave activity at any given time, one can take conscious steps to change the wave pattern to the desired state. In this way one can change one's state of mind. However, great practice is required; one is unlikely to be able to pick up a biofeedback instrument and immediately change one's state of mind, but with practice one will be able to attain states of meditation.

How can one consciously change the brainwave emissions? At first this seems impossible, for the wave form is a function of the mind itself. It might seem surprising that all that is required is practice and perseverance, but this is exactly the same thing that we do with everything in life. We learn to walk, to speak, to read, all by persistent effort. Research has shown that all body processes can be controlled, even the so-called automatic or vegetative functions, such as heartbeat, respiration, etc. This is something that yogis have been doing for thousands of years. Yet it is only recently that it has been taken seriously by modern science.

Scientific tests, some also utilizing biofeedback, but measuring emissions from particular organs, have shown that the heart and other organs can be slowed down or speeded up by mere willpower. It is only a matter of practice. It is the same with the control of brainwaves. Each person must work out his own method. For example, one person may try too hard to change the brainwaves from say beta to the more relaxing alpha state. The very intensity may cause more tension, and perhaps more prominent beta waves. Some people find that the best method is merely to think about the change and the change automatically takes place, but each individual must find his own technique.

One can of course attain high meditational states without biofeedback, as people have done throughout history. Great yogis, Zen Buddhists, etc., hardly need the aid of biofeedback instrumentation, for they can change their state of mind almost at will, such is their sensitivity. However, the biofeedback technique holds great potential for beginners and for those people who even after constant practice are not making any noticeable progress in meditation. Most of us are so insensitive that we lack the ability to feel whether we are becoming more relaxed, more tense, or whether we are remaining in the same frame of mind. Biofeedback will indicate to the meditator whether progress is being made or not. So useful is this system that some yoga teachers are already using it for themselves and their students.

To sum up, we can say biofeedback is in its infancy, yet it seems to promise great possibilities for the future. A further point is that it is increasingly being adopted by young people who have been using large amounts of drugs for their glimpses of the beyond. It will give the same results with practice but without the damaging effects associated with most drugs. It will complement meditation and will bring meaningful meditational experiences into the range of all people. Meditation coupled with biofeedback could do much to raise the level of mind, or the level of consciousness in the world.

The reader might be interested in the differences that exist between the brainwaves emitted during meditation and the other states which are often closely related to meditation, namely trance and hypnotism. There is little or even no correlation. During trance and hypnotic states, wave emission actually takes the form suggested by the hypnotist. These states are usually typified by beta emissions which are characteristic of our normal extroverted state of mind, and are certainly not related to meditation.

Every cell contains infinite knowledge

Scientists have developed an appreciation of the complexity of each and every cell in the body. They have been able to build a model of the so-called DNA molecule, the molecule of life. This is the molecule that transmits all the characteristics of the mother and father to the son and daughter. It is contained in the sperm and in the ova. Not only this, it is contained in every cell of the body.

Scientists have only formulated its physical shape and confirmed that it is concerned with moulding individual characteristics such as hair colour, height, size of feet and the pattern of growth from childhood to adulthood. It is the blueprint, the underlying plan of life. It is this molecule that fixes our basic mode of life and we must obey its orders throughout our lives. Of course there are other things that affect our lives: the environment, our circumstances, our interactions with other people. Yet it is the DNA molecule which fixes much of the mode of our lives.

Now this scientific viewpoint is moving very close to the yogic viewpoint. Yoga has always regarded each and every cell in the body as having consciousness. In other words the underlying existence of each and every cell is consciousness. Its manifestation can be regarded as the physical nature of the cell, the DNA molecule being the blueprint for human life. The primordial pattern of human existence is fixed and directed by the consciousness of the cell; the molecular structure discovered by scientists is merely the executor, the thing that implements the will of the cell consciousness. Scientists have taken the pattern of the DNA molecule as being the instrument that guides life along certain directions; they have missed the underlying principle behind the DNA molecule itself, that is, consciousness.

Great thinkers now begin to exclaim in awe that each cell contains, inherent within itself, the total knowledge of our evolutionary past. In other words, each cell contains a memory of everything that has happened in each individual's past: when he was a germ plasma, struggling to emerge from the primordial mud during the birth of life; when he was a fish; when the fish struggled onto the land to start the line of land animals; when he was a monkey; when he was a Neanderthal man; when he became a human of the same type that exists today, a few thousand years ago; when he was in his mother's womb. All this information is stored in every single cell in the body. The immediate reaction to this idea is that it is impossible. Our conditioned mind cannot accept or grasp it, yet this has been frequently described by progressive thinkers, including many great scientists.

This is what has always been said by great spiritual giants throughout history. They have said that infinite knowledge exists within. What is outside is also inside. The human is the miniaturized version of the universe. They have said that as you dive into the depths of your being you are able to gain knowledge of your past lives. And now science is starting to prove the truth of these statements. Religion and science, which only a few years ago seemed so far away from each other, are starting to merge into a higher form of knowledge.

Scientists have mapped out the physical form of the DNA molecule. They have explored it with electron microscopes. The next stage is to investigate the inherent nature of the DNA molecule, the property that science cannot explore at present because its nature is a subjective experience, beyond the realms of science. Is it too much to suggest that the method of exploring these DNA molecules is meditation? Because meditation is all about exploring the inner nature. Meditation should become the tool of scientific investigation into the nature of the DNA molecule or anything else that needs to be investigated internally.

The white matter ego

The reticular activating system is located at the top of the spinal cord. It is the valve that controls the information that actually reaches our conscious perception. It is the part of the brain that regulates man's depth of consciousness, e.g. sleeping, conscious, superconscious states, etc., and it allows only a refined trickle of information to seep through the consciousness, preventing other data which it considers unsuitable from reaching conscious perception. It is the censor of the human mind.

Some people have called this system the ego, which is the central theme in psychology. Through its activity we are aware of only certain aspects of perception, and totally unaware of most of the information reaching the brain. It is in fact an essential part of the brain, for without it we would be flooded with sense data. For example, while we write a letter our consciousness is concerned with thinking what to write and the writing process itself. If we simultaneously received an influx of sounds, smells, skin sensations and information on organic activity in the body, we would find it impossible to write the letter. The reticular activating system shuts out all irrelevant information from the senses, allowing information which is concerned with the work in hand to reach consciousness. It allows us to concentrate on our work.

How does the system act as the ego? The reticular activating system allows information to reach consciousness if it has intensity. In other words, information about the outside world reaches our awareness if, and only if, it reinforces our mental programming, if it agrees with our prejudices, if it fits our mental pattern. It is in this way that it acts as the ego. It identifies with complexes, inhibitions, likes, dislikes, etc., which make up the egotistical nature of an individual, and feeds the individual consciousness with the information which tallies with or will satisfy these facets of the individual's taste or desires. Therefore, if we fear something, then information which reinforces this fear will be most likely to rise to conscious perception. It is the same with other emotional and rational programming. For this reason we can never see the world as it is. We see a blurred picture of the world and the people around us.

If we remove these fears, phobias, complexes, likes, dislikes and any other prejudices, we will start to see a clearer picture of the world. The reticular activating system will have less of a bias, less of a tendency to let us be aware only of the things that reinforce our complexes, etc. It will allow information to flow to consciousness which is less determined by our negative mental programming. If our mind is reasonably untroubled and loving, then we will see the environment in the same light. If our mind is habitually relaxed, then we will see the world in a similar way, where everything is harmonious.

Eventually, in the highest stages of the spiritual path, even love in an emotional sense disappears. In this case the feeling of love is transcended, so that even love doesn't colour the mind. The consciousness now identifies with everything; the oneness is experienced; now there is no intermediate censor between consciousness and the environment. In this condition even the ego has disappeared. It becomes superfluous, for there are no preferences in the mind to be satisfied. The centre of consciousness now operates from the self instead of the ego.

Purification of the mind is the aim of yoga in general, of meditation in particular, as well as the techniques given in this book. Thus the aim is to break down the existing complexes, phobia and prejudice-riddled mental program and replace it with a purified mental program. Meditation, highest meditation, then becomes a spontaneous process. Thus the barriers that have long kept separate the fields of science and spirit are fast being broken down. The dichotomy between them is lessening. Even now science presents possibilities of helping people to tread the spiritual path, and meditation offers great potential in helping science to understand the mind systematically and to gain a deeper insight into existence.

3

Meditation and Health

Meditation implies relaxation, both physical and mental, at a level which few of us experience even during sleep. For this reason meditation brings excellent health and can alleviate and cure many types of disease.

Before discussing this we would like to emphasize the non-duality that exists between body and mind. For too long it has been assumed that a physical ailment is devoid of mental content, and that a mental ailment is devoid of any physical content. Only comparatively recently has the intimate relationship between the physical and mental spheres been realized. They are really one whole. For example, physical relaxation will surely also bring mental relaxation and conversely, mental relaxation will also bring physical relaxation. The reader must have realized this for himself. So when one discusses any disease, it must be seen as involving both mind and body.

Meditation acts as a holistic, or whole, treatment for disease. It is a more widely encompassing method of treatment than is provided by drugs, which tend to 'cure' the disease of an organ but can have unforeseen negative repercussions on other parts of the body. Many cases of this can be cited. Meditation takes the treatment back to the sufferer. The patient will be able to exercise more power himself over his health for the removal of his ailment. The treatment will concern the whole mind-body complex. Through meditation the mind can be trained to cure the ailment, but first one must know how to meditate and exercise a greater control over the mind-body. When one becomes aware of the inner processes of the mind and body, one can direct energies where they are most needed. People with diseases will know how to direct their inner energy to the diseased organ.

The physiological effects of meditation

Meditation is a most powerful way of controlling physiological processes and also of controlling physiological reactions to psychological events. One of the most profound changes that takes place in the body during meditation is the slowing down of the metabolism, the rate of breaking down and building up the body, for there is a sharp reduction in oxygen consumption and carbon dioxide output. Experimenters have measured up to a 20 percent decrease in oxygen consumption, which is because the respiration rate is slower. The reduced metabolic rate is due to the control over the involuntary nervous system which one develops through meditation.

Meditation has a noticeable influence on blood pressure, which drops much lower than normal both during and after meditation, and, therefore, meditation can be particularly recommended for those people suffering from high blood pressure. The heart rate also slows down to a few beats every minute. Another interesting discovery regarding the blood system is the fact that the blood flow increases during meditation. To explain this we must again bring in the autonomic nervous system and, in particular, the sympathetic nerve network. This network, as one of its many functions, constricts the blood vessels and in turn the blood flow. The greater the constriction, the less the blood flow. During meditation the activities of the sympathetic system are reduced and therefore constriction of the blood vessels is automatically decreased, resulting in a greater flow of blood.

This increased blood flow greatly benefits the meditator. For example, let us consider lactate production. Lactate is a substance produced mainly in the muscles when there is no free oxygen. It is profusely produced during periods of intense activity when the muscles are performing extensive work. A so-called energy debt is incurred because the muscles must expend more energy than the oxygen supply to the muscles allows for. Now lactate is produced to provide for the much required extra energy.

During periods of rest, lactate is slowly broken down into other substances, since enough oxygen is now being supplied to the muscles. In meditation, the increased blood flow ensures that oxygen is more efficiently delivered to the muscles and that lactate is more quickly and effectively removed. The reader should note that in meditation, total intake of oxygen is actually less; what is increased is the distribution of available oxygen to the muscles where it breaks it down the lactate. At the same time, intake of oxygen into the cells during the metabolic process is reduced. Production of lactate is stimulated by the sympathetic nervous system; inhibition of the sympathetic nervous system during meditation automatically reduces production of the lactate.

Why is the subject of lactate production so important? Because medical tests show that persons suffering from anxiety, neuroses or tension have a high level of lactate compared to when they are calm and tranquil. When lactate is injected into the body in scientific experiments, there is a sudden and marked increase in the level of anxiety. Also, people suffering from high blood pressure have markedly more lactate in the body than people with normal blood pressure and those who meditate regularly.

Meditation is the perfect method of reducing the lactate level and consequently reducing blood pressure and all types of anxiety symptoms. Remember also, that anxiety is the cause of many of the so-called physical ailments, as well as innumerable mental diseases. Meditation is the method of treating these diseases, by doing away with their root cause. This is far preferable to the present widely adopted cures which treat the symptom and not the underlying cause.

How do these physiological changes compare with other forms of relaxation, such as sleep and hypnotism? There appears to be little or no correspondence whatsoever. During hypnotism there is little or no change in the metabolic rate, and in sleep the physiological changes take place normally after some hours. In meditation the ratio of oxygen to carbon dioxide in the blood (not the quantity) remains reasonably constant. During sleep there is a noticeable build-up of carbon dioxide in the blood.

The fight or flight body defence mechanism

The fight or flight defence system of the body is the sympathetic nervous system and the adrenal glands. The activities of the sympathetic nervous system and adrenal glands have been known for quite some time; these two systems complement each other. During times of stress, danger or fear, the adrenal glands secrete a hormone called adrenaline, which prepares the body for fight or flight. It makes the body more efficient. It increases the heart rate, increases the respiration rate, improves eyesight, hearing, etc., as well as inhibiting the digestive functions so that the energy can be more usefully employed to face threatening situations. This system is for short-term dangers. For threats that last a longer period of time, the sympathetic nervous system takes over and keeps the body at a continuous higher level of intensity. Eventually, however, when the threat has disappeared the body functions return to their usual level of activity.

The stressful, competitive, modern way of life is such, however, that many people almost continually operate at a high level of preparedness for fight or flight. It may be from fear of the boss, fear of losing respect in the eyes of friends and neighbours, fear of not being able to pay all the hire purchase bills, and so on. Under these conditions, the individual is always tense, liable to large fluctuations of moods and is almost in a continual state of dissatisfaction and general unhappiness. The body also loses its ability to resist disease.

Many persons may say or think that they are relaxed for most of their lives. For some this may be true but for many, scientific tests will conclusively show that they are almost constantly tense, though they are not aware of it. In reaction to various situations, even of an inconsequential nature, they tense their muscles, squint their eyes, bite their nails or whatever. This type of action is so habitual that they are not aware they are doing these compensatory activities.

These habitual reactions are the forerunner of psychosomatic diseases. When a person is manifesting these tensions, whether he knows it or not, he is really preparing himself for the fight or flight reaction; the reaction that the sympathetic nervous system and the adrenal glands are designed to bring about. These actions are small and insignificant in external appearance, but they indicate that changes in heart rate, blood pressure, etc., are taking place internally. This prolonged stimulation of the adrenal and sympathetic system can lead to the so-called civilized ailments such as high blood pressure, diabetes, coronary thrombosis, peptic and duodenal ulcers, together with a large number of mental diseases, as well as backache, skin problems, muscular twitches and a host of other ailments.

The only sure method of counteracting, preventing and curing these ailments is to completely relax the whole body and mind every day. Sleep, of course, is the usual way, yet most people are so tense that they don't even relax during sleep. They are still trying to solve their daily problems while sleeping. Sleep is generally insufficient to relax, balance and eradicate the damaging effects of the overuse of the adrenal and sympathetic systems. It is only during deep relaxation that the body processes can finally recuperate themselves and return to their normal level of activity. Meditation is a means to do this. In a sense, meditation can be regarded as the counterpart or the counterbalance to the sympathetic nervous system and the adrenal glands. It is a panacea for modern life. It is the sure means of attaining positive health of the whole mind-body complex.

Not only must we learn to relax, we must also change our response to our surroundings. The happiness of each person depends on harmonization and integration with the environment, not on being in perpetual fear of the environment. The mind-body system must be reprogrammed so that the adrenaline is not squirted into the blood at every possible situation. We must reprogram our body and mind so that the reaction is different, so that the individual can relax, be happy and start to raise the level of his awareness.

So that the reader can appreciate the importance of changing the mind, we will give a brief explanation of the mechanism of the brain which is concerned with making us tense or relaxed. An important part of the brain is the limbic system. This system, which is situated at the top of the brain stem, has the function of comparing sense data from the sense organs with the information that is already in the brain from previous experiences in life. In other words, the limbic system compares data stored in the brain (our memory) with the incoming sense data; it analyzes them in terms of previous experiences.

The limbic system also intensifies emotional responses to data that do not harmonize or fit in with previous conditioning or memory. Thus if something happens to us that is unexpected or different from our previous experiences, the limbic system immediately creates an emotional reaction such as anger, stress etc. This eventually triggers off the adrenal glands, which release the hormone adrenaline into the blood system. This then makes the whole body tense; the heart beats faster, the respiration rate increases, and so on. It is in this state that many modern day people spend much of their lives, and this prolonged tension leads to all types of disease.

Yet, at the same time, a part of the limbic system called the septal region acts in the opposite direction. It reduces our emotional responses; it releases tension and creates relaxation of the whole body and mind. By meditation we can make the septal part of the limbic system operate for the predominant part or even all of our life. Under these conditions we live a life of relaxation, not laziness, enjoy life more, do our work more efficiently and are free of disease.

If one wants relaxation and a happy life, one must change the mind, not the outside world or other people. A happy and healthy life comes from changing the mind and its reactions to the outside world. One can spend the rest of one's life seeking happiness in the outside world, but if the mind retains its present programming one will never find happiness; one will be chasing the pot of gold at the end of the rainbow. Meditate and reprogram your mind if you want a healthy and disease-free life. Modify the mental program that was put into your brain by faults in your upbringing, as this is the cause of all your unhappiness.

4

Yoga's Psychic Physiology

The psychic realm of existence is a subject which generally causes great confusion to the average man, because most people cannot view it and at present the language contains very few precise, technical terms which can correctly be used to describe it. Happily, however, many first-line scientists in numerous countries are presently making constant breakthroughs in their research concerning the subtle realms, and with their discoveries the English terms for the phenomena which are being uncovered are, out of necessity, being created. We are certain that the day is not far off when psychic matters will form an important part of every man's general knowledge, and when the psychic world will be commonly viewed by all people, using machines which are in prototype stage in many of the forward-looking research institutes around the world.

One of the basic premises of the system of yoga is that the universe exists simultaneously on a number of different levels of subtlety. Every object or being which exists on the physical plane has a corresponding form on the more subtle planes, and life and activity go on there in a manner which has many similarities to events of the 'solid' physical world.

It is said that matter which is made up of particles which are smaller than protons, electrons and neutrons and which has a basic rate of vibration faster than the speed of light, is psychic in nature. Additionally, there are said to be planes which are more subtle than the psychic, but these cannot presently be defined using the terminology of the science of physics. The two most well-known of these higher planes are the mental and causal planes, which are experienced only by a person in the state of meditation before he transcends all existence whatsoever and enters into samadhi.

The plane directly above the physical level is the psychic realm of existence. It has many things in common with the physical world with which we are familiar, and most people naturally experience events from time to time which are taking place on the psychic plane. This occurs most often during the state of sleep or when a person passes out or experiences a severe physical or emotional shock. This spontaneous viewing of psychic events also takes place through the use of certain dangerous drugs, and spontaneous psychic awakening is the basis of intuition, so-called 'spiritual experiences' and visions.

The system of kundalini yoga, which is based on the teachings of the ancient tantric scriptures, encompasses many techniques which are intended to bring about a controlled awakening of psychic experiences within the practitioner. Although the psychic awakening is never considered to be a goal of sadhana by the serious practitioner of yoga, for he is more interested in spiritual unfoldment, it is an important level through which all aspirants must pass.

Many of the practices of kundalini yoga require the aspirant to view events taking place on the psychic plane. In most cases, what these kriyas require is that one must view certain centres, known as chakras, which exist in his own psychic body, and also view the flow of subtle energy which takes place in the pathways (called nadis) connecting the psychic centres. Of course, not all people can view these psychic occurrences at will, and so the practices of kundalini yoga alternately allow the practitioner's awareness to follow (or imagine) a group of specified physical centres and passages which are interrelated with and can trigger off the actual psychic centres.

The following is a description of the different psychic centres located within the psychic body of man, and energy passages in the physical body which are utilized in the practices given in this book for the awakening of psychic centres themselves.

The psychic centres

There are very many psychic centres, or chakras, although only eleven are of the utmost importance to the practitioner of yoga. Of these eleven centres, which we will now describe, the first eight are the major chakras located along the sushumna nadi and the last three are subsidiary trigger points used to stimulate the chakras. In the following descriptions we have first described the chakras as they appear in the psychic body, along with the mantras, animals and sensations associated with them. Additionally, we have also shown the physical areas which act as the 'trigger points' for these chakras, where the awareness must be placed during the yoga practices.

Mooladhara: Mooladhara chakra is positionally the lowest of the chakras and is known as the root centre. It is associated with the earth element in nature, and is the seat of the primal energy in man known as kundalini shakti or sexual/ spiritual energy. Mooladhara is visualized in the form of a deep red lotus flower having four petals. On the petals the Sanskrit letters *Vam, Sham, Sham,* and *Sam* are written in black. In the centre of the lotus is an equilateral triangle pointing downwards, and within the triangle is a smoky coloured shivalingam encircled by a golden coloured serpent with three and a half coils.

Mooladhara chakra is presided over by the god Brahma, the creator of the universe and the goddess Dakini, who controls the element of skin in the body. The beeja (seed) mantra of the chakra is *Lam* and the animal or vehicle is the elephant, symbolic of the solidarity of the earth. By far the most important aspect of mooladhara chakra is that it is the seat of the primal energy, symbolized by a coiled serpent which unravels and travels upward through all the chakras via the sushumna nadi at the time of spiritual awakening.

The physical trigger for mooladhara chakra is different in men and women. In males this point is located at the perineum, the point directly between the genitals and anus. In females mooladhara is located at the back of the cervix, where the uterus and vagina join.

Swadhisthana: The literal meaning of *swadhisthana* is 'one's own abode'. It is the second chakra, associated with the unconscious mind, storehouse of the collective consciousness, of all samskaras and remote genetic memories. It is the centre of the most primitive and deep-rooted instincts, those animal drives which cause modern man so much pain and confusion. Swadhisthana chakra is visualized in the form of a vermilion lotus with six petals, upon which are written the Sanskrit mantras *Bam, Bham, Mam, Yam, Ram, and Lam.* In the centre of the lotus is a white crescent moon, and also the chakra's beeja mantra *Vam* written in black.

Swadhisthana is presided over by Lord Vishnu, the preserver of the universe, and the goddess Rakini, controller of the element of the blood. The sensation of this chakra is that of drowsiness and it is related to the physical organs of reproduction and excretion.

The trigger point for swadhisthana is located at the level of the pubic bone or coccyx. It is generally visualized as being in a column, though for certain practices it is also felt in the front of the body at the pubic bone.

Manipura: *Manipura* literally means the 'city of jewels', and this chakra is the centre of heat, the fire pit. It is associated with vitality and energy, and is symbolized by the ram, a most fiery and aggressive beast. The deity of manipura is Rudra, the consumer or destroyer of the universe, and the goddess is Lakini, controller of the flesh element. Manipura chakra is visualized as a bright yellow lotus with ten petals on which are written the Sanskrit mantras *Dam, Dham, Nam, Tam, Tham, Dam, Dham, Nam, Pam* and *Pham.* Within the lotus is an inverted red triangle with the beeja mantra *Ram.*

The physical point used for meditation on manipura is located at the level of the navel. It is usually felt as being centred on the spine, though in some rare cases it is also experienced in the front of the body at the navel.

Anahata: The word *anahata* literally means 'unstruck'. This chakra is the seat of the psychic sounds which are experienced in meditation and which are said to be unstruck because they are not created by physical friction. Anahata is the heart centre, root of all emotions, where love for God and man can become divine. Anahata chakra is visualized in the form of a blue lotus with twelve petals inscribed with the Sanskrit mantras *Kam, Kham, Gam, Gham, Nam, Cham, Chham, Jam, Jham, Nam, Tam* and *Tham*. In the centre of the lotus are two interlaced triangles forming a Star of David, with the beeja mantra *Yam* written inside. Anahata is symbolized by a swift black antelope and the presiding deity is Isha, the Lord in an all-pervading form, and the goddess Kakini, ruler of the fat element of the body.

In the physical body, anahata chakra is felt to be located at the level of the heart behind the breast bone. It can be visualized inside the spine and also just inside the front of the chest.

Vishuddhi: Vishuddhi chakra is the centre of purification and is best known as the nectar and poison centre. It is visualized as a violet lotus with sixteen petals inscribed with the mantras *Am, Am, Im, Im, Um, Um, Rim, Rim, Lrim, Lrim, Em, Aim, Om, Aum, Am, and Ah.* In the centre of the lotus is a white circle with the beeja mantra *Ham* written therein. The animal of this chakra is the elephant, symbolic of ether, and the presiding deity is Ardhanarishwara, the form of Lord Shiva and Parvati combined in one body. The goddess is Sakini, who presides over the bones.

Vishuddhi is visualized in the physical body at the throat in the region of the Adam's apple, centred around the spinal cord. The sensation which is related to this chakra is that of cold, sweet drops of nectar dropping down into it from above, causing a feeling of blissful intoxication.

Ajna: This chakra is known as the third eye or the command centre. It is the point in the psychic body where outside information is received, and during higher sadhana the guru guides the aspirant by issuing commands to him through this centre. It is the famous eye of intuition, through which one who is psychically awakened can view all events on both the physical and psychic planes. Ajna chakra is depicted as a silver blue lotus having two petals with the mantras *Ham* and *Ksham*. In the centre of the lotus is a bright yellow beeja mantra *Om* with three red lines running from top to bottom and a white crescent moon near the top. The deity of ajna is Paramshiva, the formless consciousness, and the goddess is Hakini, who controls the subtle mind.

In the physical body ajna is visualized directly behind the centre of the eyebrows at the top of the spinal column. Its sensation is that of formless drifting, beyond all awareness of time and space.

Bindu: Bindu is the moon chakra, the point where psychic sounds manifest to those who are ready to hear them. It is visualized in the form of a tiny crescent moon on a moonlit night. It is considered as perhaps the most important centre in practices of kundalini yoga. The physical trigger point for bindu chakra is at the rear top corner of the head, where Brahmins traditionally allow a long tuft of hair to grow.

Sahasrara: This is the highest of the psychic centres, which symbolizes the threshold between the psychic and spiritual realms. Sahasrara is said to contain all of the other chakras within itself, as it is infinite in dimensions. It is like a huge radiant dome, inside of which all psychic forms exist. Sahasrara is visualized as a shining red lotus of a thousand (or infinite) petals containing all the letters of the Sanskrit alphabet twenty times over, with a shining shivalingam located in the centre. In the physical body its point is at the very crown of the head, from where it is visualized to extend outwards in all directions as far as the inner eye can see.

Lalana: Lalana chakra is not one of the major chakras, yet it is very important to the practitioner of kundalini yoga as the point from which amrit, or nectar, emanates and drops into vishuddhi chakra. Its physical point of concentration is located in the upper palate, just at the root of the tonsils.

Bhrumadhya: Bhrumadhya is not a chakra in itself. It is merely a trigger point for ajna chakra. The word *bhrumadhya* means eyebrow centre, and this is where this point is located.

Unknown point: This again is not a chakra but merely a trigger point, and is located in the centre of the head directly between the ear orifices.

Chidakasha: This literally means the 'space of knowledge'. It is a psychic space where all psychic events are viewed. Chidakasha is visualized as a jet black room directly behind the forehead. In the rear of the room at the centre of the bottom side is a small hole, from which sushumna nadi travels downward.

Hridayakasha: *Hrid* means heart. Hridayaskasha is the space of the heart, visualized and experienced in the centre of the chest region.

Psychic pathways and nadis

The word *nadi* literally means a flow or current. In the ancient texts it is written that there are seventy-two thousand nadis in the psychic body of man, which are visible as currents of light to a person who has developed psychic vision. These nadis connect the different chakras and psychic centres in the subtle body. A few are important to the practitioner of yoga because in certain practices of kundalini yoga the awareness, often in the form of a serpent, nectar, an arrow, a trident or a sprouting lotus bud, is visualized as moving through these passages. The nadis and psychic passages which are used in the practices given in this book are explained below.

Sushumna: This is the most important nadi in the psychic body, and it is also the most important psychic passage visualized in the mortal frame of man. Its base is at mooladhara chakra (experienced in the perineum, exactly between the genital root and the anus in men, and the cervix, or base of the uterus in women). From mooladhara, the sushumna travels slightly rearward and upward to swadhisthana chakra, which is the point in front of the coccyx where the sushumna enters the spinal column. From there it travels upward through the spinal column via manipura, anahata and vishuddhi chakras. From the point in the lower brain where the spinal column ends, sushumna travels directly upward passing through ajna and bindu and terminates at the centre of sahasrara.

Pingala and ida nadis: These are two of the most important psychic channels, though only pingala nadi is utilized as a psychic passage. The reason for this is that when ida is utilized in this manner, the mental forces in a person become dominant, which subjugates the pranic vitality and causes one to lose physical and mental stability. The passage of pingala starts at mooladhara and extends in a semicircular curve on the right side of the body. It crosses sushumna nadi at swadhisthana chakra and then proceeds in a similar curve on the left side, again joining sushumna at manipura. In this way it continues upward, travelling on the right side to anahata, crossing and going left up to vishuddhi and then right to ajna, the termination point of pingala nadi.

Frontal passage: This is visualized as extending up the front of the trunk from the navel to the centre of the throat. It is used extensively in the preliminary practices of kundalini yoga, such as vishuddhi shuddhi and ajapa japa.

Windpipe passage: This is actually a continuation of the frontal passage. It extends from the middle of the throat, near the Adam's apple, up to an unknown point in the centre of the head at the level of the temples, slightly above ajna chakra.

Arohan and awarohan passages: These form an irregularly shaped circle in the body, which somewhat resembles the shape of an egg under great lateral pressure. The passage of *awarohan*, or descent, starts at bindu chakra and extends through sushumna nadi to mooladhara, its terminus. The passage of *arohan*, or ascent, on the other hand, starts at mooladhara, travels forward to the pubic bone and then follows the curve of the lower belly to the navel. From there it joins the frontal passage, travelling to that route's end point in the middle of the throat, and then it cuts directly through the skull up to bindu chakra.

An alternate arohan passage is also mentioned in the tantric texts describing the practices of kundalini yoga. As it is traditionally explained, this passage is the same as the regular arohan passage up to vishuddhi, from where it goes straight up to lalana chakra at the root of the palate near the tonsils. From there it goes upward and forward to bhrumadhya, the eyebrow centre, then follows the curvature of the skull to sahasrara, and then down sushumna to bindu.

Ajna's tube: This is the psychic passage which runs from the eyebrow centre straight through ajna chakra to the back of the head.

Conical passages: These are the only passages which actually extend outside of the physical body. They both start together at a point just behind the eyebrow centre, and extend downward and outward at angles, each passing through one of the nostrils and terminating a short distance outside of the body. The distance beyond the nosetip to which these two passages extend varies with the strength and grossness of the breathing.

Nectar passage: This passage starts at vishuddhi chakra and extends directly upward to lalana chakra at the root of the palate, near the tonsils, where it terminates.

5

Reprogram Your Mind

Inside your head you have the most remarkable computer ever devised. It is a biocomputer that is so complex that we cannot even imagine its complexity. According to scientists, it consists of something in the region of ten to thirteen billion neurones which analyze, interpret, compare, store and transmit information that comes from the outside world, including our own body. It is capable of handling millions of bits of information in the form of audible and visual sensations, together with sense data from every part of the body every second. Remember, every hair has a connection to the brain. Every square inch of the body has a vast number of connections to the brain.

Yet you are never aware of most of this activity; it happens in the subconscious realms of the mind. This unawareness is absolutely necessary, otherwise we would be aware of so much that we would become completely overpowered by the continual flow of information. In this context, it is imperative that we are totally unaware of most of the activity of the brain so that our consciousness is left free to follow things other than body sense data and so on. The human mind is in a way similar to a modern electronic computer. If a computer programmer wants a solution to a problem, he is interested in the answer, not the intermediate calculations. The programmer will only become interested in the intermediate workings if something goes wrong, i.e. the output is not in an acceptable form, or the program will not pass through the computer. In this case either the program or the computer itself is wrong. This is the topic of this section.

Most of us live a life that is like a faulty computer output. Now, it is not the brain itself that is wrong, apart from a few cases; it is the program in the mind. In other words, if we are to live meaningful lives we have to reprogram our minds. It is the incorrect mental program that we have slowly developed since birth that is causing us all our unhappiness and anguish in life. Reprogram the mind and you will start to live a life that has deep meaning and that is happy. A well programmed mind can make this world a veritable heaven on earth. A badly programmed mind can make this world a hell on earth.

The reason for our unhappiness is our mental programming. This makes us seek happiness through making money, obtaining a nice new car that is bigger and better than any other, obtaining status, drinking and chasing after so many other things that give a flush of transitory pleasure. In short, we can say that we try to gain happiness through satisfying or boosting the ego. What's the result of this method of seeking happiness? It makes us use other people for our own selfish ends. If they get in our way we use all kinds of gross or subtle ways of bypassing or pushing them out of our way. The result is hatred, fear, jealousy, anxiety, tension and so on. Our continual chase after these ways of attaining happiness actually causes the opposite result; we become mentally tense and thus unhappy. If we don't obtain our objectives, our objects of desire, then we suffer mental tension, boredom and unhappiness.

Though these things don't give us happiness, we continue to chase after them. Why? The answer is that we are following the program that we have constructed for ourselves. We have programmed ourselves to chase after these things, even though they don't bring any kind of lasting happiness. Now a computer program can be changed. In the same way, the mind program can be changed if we make the necessary effort. We can reprogram ourselves so that we react in a different way to our environment, so we don't depend on 'ego trips' and desires for happiness.

Meditation is almost impossible when we are continually fighting life and the people who surround us. Meditation will occur almost spontaneously if we flow with life instead of fighting it. If we can reprogram our mind, we will start to tune in with our environment and meditation will take place automatically, without effort. Our consciousness will start to expand. When we harmonize our mind with the pattern of our surroundings, then we will automatically become happy. Happiness lies in the mind, not in manipulating the world to suit our desires. By reprogramming our mind we will be able to find permanent happiness in our own being.

It is our present likes and dislikes, hatreds, jealousies, etc., which distort our interpretation of the outside world and also ourselves. Our mind accepts and acts on only that information which is compatible with our present programming. In other words, if we now feel, if our mental program dictates, that everyone outside hates us, then our mind will only accept and give access to information that reinforces this attitude. Other information will be suppressed. If we feel our mental program dictates that everyone loves us, then again our mind will interpret information to reinforce this belief. This is a gross oversimplification, but it illustrates how our mind colours the outside world to suit our programmed mind. The outside world and other people are never seen as they really are because of our conditioning, because of our desires, attachments and so on.

We are not saying that desires are bad. All we are saying is that they are blocking your spiritual evolution and path towards meditational experience. Indescribable happiness and a higher awareness are waiting for us, all we have to do is to reprogram our minds and meditate.

Points to note

The first point to remember is that we do not want you to change your lifestyle in any way. What we want you to change is your relationship with the outside world by reprogramming your mind.

Secondly, you must realize is that the chase after outside happiness is futile. If, even after years of experience of trying to find happiness from the outside world, you have not come to this conclusion, then you will have no incentive to change your mind. You will only try to change your mind when you have realized the impossibility of getting happiness and peace from the external world. One only needs to look at people who have gone to extremes in seeking happiness through outside interests, they never seem to find what they want. In fact they tend to become despondent and cynical; they start to believe that permanent happiness and peace is a myth.

The third point to note is that the mind can be reprogrammed. There is a saying: as we think, so we become. Our present programmed mind is no more than the result of our previous thinking. The mind is like a piece of wax, it moulds itself to suit the impression imposed on it. If we start to try to think in a new way, then the mind will gradually but surely reprogram itself. Let's take an example of how the mind has already programmed itself, so that we are now forced to follow its dictates. A child might live in a home where the husband gets everything his own way by acting almost like a tyrant. At the same time, the child might find that he is always at the mercy of the whims of others. For example, he wants to go and play with his friends, but his father says no. His mind starts to program itself so that he thinks that power is the way to do what you want to do in life. When he becomes older he therefore seeks power as a means to attaining happiness.

It is the same with nearly all our external motivations in life; they start in essentially the same manner. At the same time we have the ability to remove this existing program so that we no longer have to follow its commands, and to replace it with a program which allows us a harmonious way of life and allows us to expand our consciousness. We can build a future that is consciousness orientated, positive and awake, merely by altering the mind that we now have. We can eventually aim at experiencing the hidden truth and beauty that exists inside us.

Autosuggestion

All people have phobias, complexes, emotional stresses and so on which make the mind continually tense, whether consciously or unconsciously. All these prevent the mind from becoming tranquil and peaceful, and act as obstructions to meditation. We should remember the cliché, as you think, so you become, for this tells us the way to remove these mental symptoms. The power of suggestion is very great. If we think negatively in life, then our life will become negative. If we think positively, then we will surely become positively inclined. If we think that we will suffer from cancer with sufficient intensity and belief, then surely we will eventually suffer from cancer, such is the power of suggestions or belief.

These suggestions don't only come from the mind; they also come from the external environment. In fact they occur almost continuously. Our mind is continually influenced by outside events. We read a book and it suggests ideas to us which influence our behaviour. We talk with someone and though we are not always conscious of it, we are constantly being given suggestions. Everything comes to the mind in the form of suggestions. Suggestions come from the way people look at you, the way they move their hands, the way they speak and in so many other subtle ways. Using this power of suggestion in the form of autosuggestion is the simplest way to remove all the aspects that keep our minds tense, and to prevent negative outside influences from disturbing the mind further.

At the same time we should use autosuggestion to prepare ourselves immediately before meditational practices. The essential requirement for effective autosuggestion is the deep need to see the aims and suggestion translated into the desired results. Without a strong need or will, the object of the autosuggestion is unlikely to succeed or materialize. One must want to make a change. If the need is only half-hearted, it can be built up to a higher level of intensity by continually dwelling on the subject. As the reader treads the spiritual path, he will become more and more aware of things that cause him mental disturbance. The more he progresses, the more they will manifest and rise to the field of consciousness. As soon as they show themselves, they should be negated by replacing them with their opposite or else by autosuggesting that they are not really so very important.

As each individual will always have different problems, the reader must work out for himself and should develop his own technique for removing them. For example, consider a person who has a fear of the dark. Since he must spend much of his life in darkness, this is bound to cause mental disturbance. His mind will always be tense, consciously or unconsciously. The way to remove the phobia is to realize how ridiculous this fear really is; to realize that darkness is only the opposite of light; to realize that many other people are not afraid of the dark, so therefore why should he have a fear of the dark, and so on. Constant autosuggestion in this way will surely remove the fear. These kinds of suggestions are most powerful when the individual is in a state of relaxation. Even a deep-rooted fear is amenable to this type of treatment, providing the individual devotes himself wholeheartedly to its removal. Eventually a new, indifferent attitude, to the dark in this example, will penetrate the subconscious and the fear will disappear.

Autosuggestion can work for all types of complexes, conflicts and phobias. All that is required is the need to remove the problem. Now how can a person find out the deeper problems that adversely influence his life, that cause him unhappiness and tension, the ones that he doesn't even know about? The practitioner will find that his or her problems, phobias, fears, etc., slowly show themselves as more awareness is developed through yoga and meditation.

A particularly good method of exposing these deep-rooted emotional and mental tensions is to regularly perform the meditational technique antar mouna, and to make a mental or written record of what is revealed during practice periods.

The next thing to be practised in the attempt to remove mental and emotional problems is to prevent outside occurrences and crises from having adverse repercussions on the mind. In other words, the mind must be made stronger so that it is not greatly influenced by external events. The method is to slowly develop detachment (*vairagya*) to everything and every person. This does not mean that you should become a vegetable or not involve yourself with the ups and downs of life and with personal relationships. It means that though you react to external activities in the form of love, hate, argument, etc., these should not influence you in a deeper sense. On a human level they must influence you, but in a deeper way they should have no effect.

It is a matter of identification; if you see yourself as the body or the mind, then painful or undesirable physical and mental manifestations will greatly influence your life. In a similar way, on the other hand, if you don't identify yourself with the body-mind, but with the centre of consciousness, then the physical and mental sorrows of life will have little effect on you. We can compare external stimuli to ripples on a pond. Ripples disturb the surface of the pond, but they have relatively little influence on the bottom of the pond. The same should apply to the spiritual seeker; negative mental vibrations and physical ailments ideally should not disturb his being. This is easier said than done, but with continuous practice of self-awareness one can attain the state where one is calm and tranquil among the tumultuous events of the outside world.

Another important usage of autosuggestion is in the cure and prevention of disease and bodily upsets. By consciously willing the body to become whole, strong and balanced, even the most serious terminal diseases such as cancer or leukaemia can and have been remedied by aspirants with strong willpower. The best times to make the autosuggestions are after meditational practices, or when just waking up in the morning and just before going to sleep at night. At these times the mind is particularly receptive to suggestion. Repeat the autosuggestion with intensity and feeling for a few minutes. Believe wholeheartedly that the autosuggestions will bring about the desired change. If this is done then the suggestion can only be successful. Half-hearted suggestions will surely fail.

Self-identification

This is intended to show the reader that a process of re-identification is necessary with regard to ourselves and to our surroundings. Much unhappiness in life arises because we identify ourselves with our body, our mind, our job or any other role in life. We identify ourselves with transitory facets of existence, instead of with that in us which is permanent and unchangeable, namely, the very core of our existence. If and when we can dissociate ourselves from our role in life, our body and our mind, and accept these as merely manifestations of our inner being, the self, then meditation will almost be a constant and spontaneous process. Even a limited degree of detachment from our manifested aspects: mind and body, etc., will greatly help us to attain meditational experience because we will be released from the meditational impediments of bodily disturbances, mental disturbances and emotional disturbances. When all the physical, mental and emotional aspects of our being are calmed, then meditation will become a natural, simple and automatic process.

It is strange that if someone is asked what they are they will reply, "I am a doctor" or "I am a plumber" or "I am a housewife" or "I am a footballer". They will answer in various ways, depending on what they consider their main role in life. They might give various answers; a woman might say that she is a mother, a wife and also a typist during the daytime. Yet really these things are not what they are, but what they do.

Let's take an extreme example of how this kind of identification can lead to much unhappiness. Consider an actor. He sees himself as an actor, an actor with a fine physique, a handsome face and a manly voice. He takes great care to keep himself in good physical shape. Yet as the years pass he will progressively and very critically notice that he is becoming older. His handsome features start to fade, his body loses its strength and his voice loses its depth. He might even spend many hours every day despondently looking at himself in a mirror. He becomes depressed and unhappy because his conception of himself is disappearing. His self-identification with a transitory phenomenon is taking its toll. In many cases, especially with actors, this crisis has often led to an emotional breakdown or even suicide.

The situation exists with a mother; eventually her children will leave her. Again much unhappiness can result because of her self-identification as a mother. It is the same with a doctor, a plumber, a housewife, a typist. They are not permanent realities. Over-identification with them by the individual will surely lead to much strife and emotional upset. Identification with our body, mind and emotions is so common and widespread that we automatically assume its truth. For example, someone says, "I am thirsty." This statement is said with no thought of its significance. It is not realized that the 'I' signifies our self-identification, and the 'I' refers to a temporary phenomenon, the physical body. A more realistic statement should be, "My body is thirsty". In this way it will be implied that the body is merely a temporary manifestation of the permanent self, the inner core of existence.

The same applies to our emotions and thoughts. We say "I am angry" or "I am depressed" and so on. Yet it is really the emotional system of the mind that feels these things. These are temporary emotional states which disappear as quickly as they arise; one moment there is friendship and then later there is a feeling of enmity. They are not permanent, even though we habitually identify ourselves with these states. We say "I think this" or "I think the sky is blue" or "I think that one plus one equals two". Yet it is not really 'I' that thinks, it is the mind, and the mind is changing from day to day. It also is not permanent, so how can it be the permanent reality that is 'I'? One day our mind can think one thing and the next day it can think something else. It is in a state of flux. How can we really identify ourselves with it? What we should say is "my mind thinks" or "my mind feels", for the mind is not the real 'I'.

We have the ability to watch the activities of the mind and the body. How can something that we watch possibly be our true identity? There must be something that is watching. The body and the mind are only instruments of action, of perception, of thought. Nothing else. Our real identity, the real 'I' is the centre of our consciousness. It is that which illuminates and witnesses everything that we do in life, the self. Though this is our core of existence, the essence of our being, very few of us operate from or identify ourselves with it. As we have already explained, most people identify with its manifestations and instruments, the mind and body. If we operated from the self, if we knew the self to be our true identity, then we would be able to use our body and mind to their fullest capacity. Our mind and body would be able to work at peak efficiency. We would be healthy, for we would not impede the operation of our mind-body by our complexes and prejudices. From this viewpoint of identification, meditation would be a spontaneous activity.

How does one start to operate from the centre of consciousness, the real 'I'? This is the whole aim of the spiritual path. It is a long and arduous path, yet the following is a great help in itself. Also, as already explained, even partial identification with the self and dissociation with the body-mind and roles in daily life are great assets in attaining meditational experiences. And meditation is itself a powerful tool in eventually reaching the centre of one's being.

The first point you must realize is that the actions in life are only roles which you are fulfilling. They in no way represent your being or your true identity. They are merely a manifestation. This does not mean that you will cease to perform your roles; you will still do them, but you will now see yourself in the position of an actor. You will be able to witness yourself performing and acting your roles. You will see your true self as being in the audience, and the body-mind acting out its role.

The next point you have to realize that you are not the body and its sensations, you are not your emotions, you are not your intellect, you are not your mind in any way whatsoever. At first this will have to be done intellectually, but after some practice you will cease to identify with all these manifested aspects of yourself, and you will know yourself as your true inner being, a part of the whole, the manifest and unmanifest existences which we know as God.

The experience of dhyana

During meditation one experiences a feeling of no anxiety. One's normal self-interest seems to disappear and one feels the same, if not more, for other people as for oneself. Life no longer seems fragmented by opposing ideas and opinions. Everything merges into one composite whole. External events enter the mind, are absorbed, yet without causing the usual disturbances or reverberations. All things take their normal course of action, without any unnecessary hustle or bustle. Fear, the biggest troublemaker in life, no longer exists. Even fear of death disappears, and the idea of death seems almost superficial, non-existent and unimportant. The usual ups and downs of life are replaced by a continual and elevating feeling of the joyfulness of life. Everything seems to fit together like a jigsaw puzzle. Even normally opposing religious, philosophical and cultural ideas seem to be in unison with one another. Everything fits. The past and future seem to be unimportant. They lack meaning. What is important is the eternal now. Living and experiencing the totality of the present seems to be the only important thing to do.

The present is so absorbing that the mind automatically fixes itself on the work or action being done. Efficiency and perfection become the natural course of life's events. The normal impediments to efficiency, such as worry or anger, no longer block the total absorption of the mind. Under these conditions work becomes play and play becomes work. There is no differentiation. Life becomes so joyful so that it needs no ambition, no justification, no reason; it is sufficient just *to be*. Remember that it is through frustration, dissatisfaction and unhappiness that we try to find a reason for life, or follow modes of life that are unnatural or contrary to our very being.

One does not lose one's zest, nor does one lose one's interest in the activities of the world. One merely ceases to worry about things. There may be superficial worry, but internally there is perfect peace. All the preliminaries associated with preparing oneself for meditational experiences no longer seem important or necessary. In other words, all the rules laid down in the yamas and niyamas (see the chapter on raja yoga), for example, detachment, renunciation and so on, are no longer necessary. The experience of meditation stands way above these rules. The rules no longer apply. These rules are designed to eliminate the mental disturbances. But now the individual can do anything: exciting activities, be angry, be happy, all the multifarious actions in life. These actions no longer adversely affect his inner being. He goes through life as a witness. Sense enjoyments are not diminished; in fact they are heightened.

Everything unites to become *one*. The faculty of intuition is the medium of knowledge. Objects show their deeper and essential characteristic. Everything assumes an attitude of friendliness and the universe assumes a state of helpfulness; opposition to one's nature no longer exists. Every atom shimmers with life and vitality. The progress of time and immensity of space lose their fixed meaning; they are seen as nothing more than a manifestation of the universe. Time begins to stand still and the outer depths of space no longer seem so far away. The stars come within grasping distance. Infinity and eternity become almost tangible. Existence is seen as the permanent aspect of everything. One realizes that one's being is intimately bound up with everything that is. As such, the ego no longer seems important or even a reality.

One normally sees oneself as a small, insignificant part of the universe, as a small cog in a large wheel, a small particle in unending space and time. One often feels completely isolated and often alienated from other parts of existence. One feels alone, and very mortal. One never even suspects that one can overcome this situation. Most people merely shrug their shoulders and fatalistically accept their fate. Meditation changes all this. One realizes through meditation that one is a necessary, intimate and important part of the universe. One starts to relate deeply to everything that exists. They are no longer separate entities. You are *That*. This is a mystical state of meditation.

There will be different descriptions of the experiences depending on the depth or height of the meditation. Also each person will use his own language, religious terms, symbolism and personal feelings in an attempt to express the inexpressible. One doesn't suddenly experience the highest stage of meditation. It is a progressive intensification of spiritual experience that shows itself in small ways in the beginning. It might initially show itself in visions, in various tangible and intangible ways. Most of these visions will seem strange at first, for they don't seem to relate to everyday life. You may wonder how such weird and wonderful visions can come from your being. One may see dazzling visions of Buddha or psychedelic, multicoloured energy patterns. One may experience intensification of feelings and emotions. One may hear various sounds which come from the very depths of one's being.

Finally, let us take an example where a transcendental experience has almost flashed into existence, given illumination of an intense form for a very short time. The following is an extract from *The Varieties of Religious Experience* by William James: "All at once I, without wrapping of any kind, found myself wrapped in a flame coloured cloud. For an instant I thought of fire, an immense conflagration somewhere close by in that great city; the next instant I knew that that fire was in myself. Directly afterwards there came upon me a sense of exultation, immense joyousness, accompanied or immediately followed by, an intellectual illumination quite impossible to describe. Among other things, I did not merely come to believe, I saw the universe is not composed of dead matter, but is on the contrary a living presence; I became conscious in myself of eternal life. It was not a conviction that I would have eternal life, but a consciousness that I possessed eternal life. Then I saw that all men are immortal; that the cosmic order is such that without any peradventure all things work together for the good of each and all; that the founding principle of the world, of all the worlds, is what we call love, and that the happiness of each and all is in the long run certain. The vision lasted a few seconds and was gone, but the memory of it and the sense of reality of it has remained during a quarter of a century which has since elapsed. I knew that what the vision showed me was true. That view, that conviction, I may say that consciousness has never, even during periods of deepest depression, been lost."

Large numbers of classical books have been written which attempt to show spiritual growth and experiences in symbolic or allegorical terms. The writers have realized the futility of trying to describe the spiritual experiences directly. They therefore use indirect methods which will only be understood by those people who have already started to have some kind of experiences. Other people will understand the contents of the books in a literal sense. Examples are the *Ramayana* and *Srimad Bhagavatam* giving the life stories of Lord Rama and Lord Krishna, Dante's *Divine Comedy,* Goethe's *Faust* and numerous other books and poems. They all try to appeal to people on a deeper level than the rational mind. In the same line of thought wc therefore ask the reader to try meditation for himself and not to get attached to reading about other people's experiences and spiritual paths.

6

Yoga Philosophy

Although yoga is more concerned with practice than with theory, a basic idea of the philosophical aspects will help the practitioner to know what he is trying to do and achieve in yoga and how he will attain meditational states. The reader will find that the yogic philosophy, though containing great insight, is always relating to how the practitioner can proceed to his own self-realization. Many philosophies, especially western varieties, tend to lose themselves in their own words. They tend to make their conceptions fit the facts around them, to make a nice word picture of reality. The philosophers become so attached to their words that they eventually assume that their picture is an exact representation of the truth. They don't seem to realize that their conception is no more than a model, just as a plan of a house is only a plan, it is not the house itself. Eastern philosophies, particularly yogic, Zen and so on, accept the inadequacy of their ideas and try to show the aspirant how he can realize the truth by his own efforts. They acknowledge that understanding of a verbal or written picture of reality does not and is probably unlikely to express the truth itself. Yogic philosophy applies to and is for everyone; it is not reserved for the few people who like to play with words. It is practical.

The first necessity of a useful philosophy is that it should try to relate to human life. It should formulate or at least throw some light on the human condition and how to raise mankind above suffering and pain. Buddha realized this, for he refused to answer questions on the existence of God, not because he didn't have any opinion, but because he didn't consider the question relevant to man's condition. He could have answered, "Yes, there is a God" or "No, there isn't". In either case people would not have gained anything from the answer. It would have been mere words to them, without any change in their being or happiness. Buddha's main aim was to help people to raise themselves above unhappiness; when they had raised themselves above their existing condition, the answer they were seeking would come of itself They wouldn't need to ask the question.

The kleshas

This is also the aim of yoga, to alleviate man's suffering so that the spiritual aspects in man can spontaneously reveal themselves. Yoga specifies that there are definite causes of human suffering and pain. These can be classified into five groups and are known as *kleshas* in Sanskrit. These are not based on obscure theories, but on a careful and practical study of man, his life and actions. These five kleshas were postulated by sages who had experienced them personally and transcended them; therefore, they were able to see the overall picture and not just a fragmented picture. Most of us are so bound up in the causes of our unhappiness that we cannot recognize them. Human suffering is caused by:

1. ignorance, or unawareness of reality
2. the ego
3. likes or attraction towards objects
4. dislikes or repulsions towards objects
5. the strong aversion or fear of death.

Actually these kleshas are not separate; one leads to the next. Ignorance of the true reality is the root cause. Because of this, each individual thinks only of himself. He becomes aware of his identity, his ego, and automatically feels different from the other people and objects around him. He becomes the ego moving among other things. In gross or subtle ways everything outside himself becomes subservient to him, to be used to bring more happiness, comfort, etc., to him. In this way likes and dislikes arise. Things or people who make him feel good, happy, who inflate his ego, attract him. Things that tend to make him feel unhappy, uncomfortable, etc., become things of repulsion or dislike. Of course it is not always as clear cut as this; some objects or people might bring about both feeling of dislike and like at different times, some might appear to be neutral, causing no like or dislike; given the right conditions, however, these neutral things can easily turn into objects of like and dislike. From one's attachment to objects and people and one's feeling of egoism comes the deep attachment to life and the aversion to death. One doesn't want to lose one's identity and the things or people who make the ego happy.

Kleshas cause suffering by making the individual identify with things that are transient. The individual identifies himself with his body, mind and ego and as such he is always consciously or unconsciously unhappy because he knows these things will eventually disappear at death. He doesn't identify with the eternal self. It is the same with objects that give rise to like; they are not permanent and will eventually disappear. They will cease to give satisfaction. What about dislikes? Well, of course they cause unhappiness superficially by not feeding the ego in a way that gives man pleasure. But actually dislikes are not very different to likes, they are merely different sides of the same coin. We are bound equally to both likes and dislikes. There is a lot of truth in the saying, "One's greatest love is also one's greatest hate". A person we hate can easily, under the right circumstances, turn into someone we love.

Kleshas continually cause unhappiness because we are trying to protect their present condition. We are very attached to a new car. Someone steals it and we become unhappy and depressed. Someone tells you that your work is not very satisfactory. You become unhappy because the work is an extension of yourself, it is part of your ego. And so on in all the things we do in life. If the reader carefully thinks about everything he does in life and why he is unhappy, either permanently or temporarily, he should come to the conclusion that in fact the five kleshas cover every aspect of suffering in life.

The word *vasana* can be roughly translated to mean 'desire'. Vasanas or desires continually attract us to our surroundings where they can be satisfied. If we carefully analyze all our mental and physical activities, the conclusion will surely be reached that they are prompted or stimulated by desire in one form or another, sometimes subtle, sometimes gross. These are the driving force behind our every thought and action in life. Our mind and body, therefore, go only in that direction in which the inherent desires of the individual can be satisfied. In this way, the consciousness that illuminates the mind is also fully enmeshed and forced to follow the never ending chase after the fulfilment of desire. All the different desires, of course, cannot be satisfied at the same time and are expressed when the suitable opportunity shows itself.

What are the causes of these desires? The causes are the kleshas that we discussed in the previous section. If there were no kleshas then there would be no desires. It is the attraction and repulsion towards objects, the feeling of egotism, the attachment to life and ignorance of reality that cause all our desires. How do these desires adversely influence our meditational practices? They continually distract our mind away from the object of meditation. They tend to make the mind wander here and there and dwell on external things that need satisfaction. A wandering mind is completely unable to concentrate and therefore unable to meditate.

It is impossible to remove the kleshas completely until one has attained self-realization. The best that one can do is to slowly and systematically reduce them. This can be done in various ways; some very effective ways are given in this book. One can first of all brood over their manifestation and realize that they do indeed bring about unhappiness and suffering. Then one can become aware of how they operate to bring about this suffering. We have already briefly explained this process in the section on kleshas, but the individual must deeply realize it for himself. Then the individual can take definite and intensified steps to remove his likes and dislikes, egoism, etc., by consciously putting into practice the methods given in the previous chapter.

At the same time, wrong identification with the body-mind can be slowly removed by following the advice given in the section 'Self-identification'. This will help very much to reduce the ego and to help the individual identify more with a permanent reality, the self. Simultaneously, the yamas and niyamas described in the chapter on raja yoga can be practised to attenuate the kleshas; karma and bhakti yoga, are also excellent methods of reducing the influence of the kleshas in one's life.

As one advances along the spiritual path the kleshas automatically become less of an influencing factor. The reader might say that the removal of the kleshas will mean that life will lose its flavour and almost its whole meaning, for likes and dislikes, etc., are the features which give life its distinctive character. Without them, something would be lacking in life. This, of course, proves the truth of the fifth klesha, that we are over-attached to life as we know it. However, in answer to the question, we must point out that this form of life, as we know it at present, is life in its most gross manifestation. As one progresses and evolves along the spiritual path, one will realize this truth and understand that what we think is life in our present state of consciousness, is nothing compared to the more subtle essence of life which slowly unfolds itself. We will find that our attachment to life in its present form is attachment to something that is not worthy of this attachment. In this way we will also automatically start to reduce the influence of the kleshas.

7

The System of Raja Yoga

The most systematic method of attaining states of meditation is raja yoga. It is not the only method, and in fact all other types of yoga such as bhakti, karma, jnana yoga, etc., are equally important and all aim at eventually bringing about meditational experiences, and ultimately gaining self-realization. In fact, all the different systems should be practised as much as possible in conjunction with each other, for they don't oppose each other. The other systems of yoga are discussed in the following chapter.

Raja yoga is explained in the *Yoga Sutras,* written by the ancient yogi Patanjali some time before the birth of Christ. It is worth discussing this system in some detail, for it throws much light on the obstacles that must be overcome before successful meditation can be attained. The first stages have little direct connection with meditation but are of the utmost importance, for they prepare the practitioner's mind and body for the higher stages. Without some practice of the first five stages few people will have success in meditation. Of course they are not absolutely necessary and some people will be able to meditate without even knowing of their existence, but these are the few lucky people who have no mental or physical disorders, and who from birth have been inclined to looking inwards and toward the meditational way of life. Raja yoga is for every person, whatever his or her nature. It starts with the very basic requirements for higher spiritual life. It begins by moulding a person's character in the way necessary for spiritual progress.

Stages of raja yoga

Patanjali divided the path of raja yoga into eight stages, starting from the basic rules of character change in the individual and ending with the final stage of samadhi, samadhi being also divided into four stages, culminating in self-realization. The first five stages are the preparatory practices and stages six to eight are the higher stages.

1. Yamas (social code)
2. Niyamas (personal code)
3. Asana (postures, states of being)
4. Pranayama (control of prana, life-force, cosmic energy)
5. Pratyahara (withdrawal of the senses)
6. Dharana (concentration)
7. Dhyana (meditation)
8. Samadhi (transcendental consciousness)

The first five practices are *bahiranga* (external) yoga and the last three are *antaranga* (internal) yoga. The inner and higher practices become easier to perform when the external and preliminary practices have been developed to a reasonable degree of perfection. The reason for this is that most of us are totally unable to concentrate and meditate because of the continual wandering and rational thinking of the mind. Only a person with a tranquil mind can meditate. Let us look at the types of disturbances that prevent concentration and meditation:

- Emotional disturbances due to mental conflicts and moral imperfections, which are eliminated or at least reduced by developing the yamas and niyamas (stages 1 and 2).
- Physical discomforts such as pain, illness and uncomfortable posture which are removed by practising asanas (stage 3).
- Irregularities in the pranic flow in the body which cause disturbances. Prana is energy in the body that can be loosely defined as vital or bioenergy (see the chapter on

pranayama for details). The techniques of pranayama (stage 4) remove any mental disturbances which arise from this source.

Outside distractions such as sounds which cause mental disturbance. How can we possibly perform the inner techniques when our mind is absorbed and continually distracted by the outside environment? Pratyahara (stage 5 in raja yoga) eliminates this source of disturbance by disconnecting the association of the sense organs, eyes, ears, nose, etc., from external happenings. The outer occurrences are still there, of course, but the sense organs no longer send messages to the mind, or if they do the mind does not become aware of them.

The reader should now realize how important Patanjali's first five stages are in order to successfully practise the higher stages. Though the first five stages have been systematically explained in other books on this subject, we will briefly deal with them here.

Yamas or self-restraints

These are five in number, and the reader on first impression may wonder what these seemingly socially inclined codes have to do with yoga. They are closely connected with higher yoga, however, for as has already been explained, these rules seek to remove all emotional disorders from the individual. It does not take much thought to realize that these topics cause most of our guilty feelings, inner conflicts and general mental disturbances. The way to tackle the symptom is to root out the cause. In this way the mind will be rendered more peaceful and ready for the higher practices.

Patanjali actually was an idealist and intended the practices of raja yoga for people who devoted their life to seeking realization and who probably isolated themselves from society. This becomes obvious when he writes in one of his sutras (verses) that they are inviolable and should be followed no matter what circumstances arise, even if the result is serious injury to oneself or others. This, of course, is not practical for the modern person in society, for sexual relations are a natural part of life, and sometimes one needs to tell a lie under certain circumstances, perhaps to safeguard another person from undesirable knowledge.

We therefore ask the yoga practitioner to exercise his own discretion with regard to the yamas. However, we must point out that the more the yamas are followed, within capacity and individual circumstances, the more likely it is that the mind will be calm and stable. This only occurs when there is no conflict between one's conscience and one's actions or thoughts. The five yamas are as follows:

Ahimsa (non-violence): Non-violence should be practised as far as it is possible. This does not only mean physically, but also in thought and words. Of course, if someone causes you trouble and you have to fight, then do so, but without hatred or malice if it is possible. Just accept it as something that you must do. As one evolves and practises the higher stages of meditation, etc., the less one wants to hurt anyone, and the more one will feel compassion towards everything and everyone, including so-called enemies. Yet at the same time a highly evolved person will do his duty (dharma) even if it means harm to others.

Satya (truth): One should be as truthful as is possible, for lies and the covering up of lies involves much mental strain. Most people who tell lies are also under a constant fear, perhaps unconsciously, that their lie will be revealed to others. This subject covers various forms of lies such as pretending to be more than you are, richer than you are, hiding facts by only telling half the truth and so on. A further point is that we will eventually practise meditation to seek truth. How can we do this if we are not truthful to ourselves and our dealings with life?

Asteya (honesty and non-theft): Little explanation is required here regarding this rule of conduct. There are very few people, especially those who are inclined to do yoga, who will not feel mental or emotional disturbances, manifest or unmanifest, as a result of dishonesty.

Brahmacharya (sexual control): This is a code which people do not take very seriously in this reasonably liberated modern world. "Why shouldn't we have sexual relations?" most people will say. "It's natural, isn't it?" Yes, it surely is, and in fact more people have suffered emotionally throughout history by suppressing their natural desires, often in response to strict rulings proclaimed by various religions which have forgotten the real reason why the rule was originally made. People of today should interpret this rule to mean that they should reduce their sexual activity as much as possible, after fulfilling obligations to partners, if they want to have great success in meditational practices, real success that is. Why? What is the relationship between sex and meditation? The need for sexual intercourse is nothing but the build-up of energy, vital energy. When one completes the sexual act the body is drained of this vital force. Energy can manifest in different ways, and sexual energy is no exception to the rule. If this energy is redirected towards spiritual or meditational experiences, they will be highlighted and expanded. The reader must, however, find this out for himself.

Aparigraha (non-possessiveness): The idea here is that you can have belongings, but you must try not to be attached to them. Think of the unhappiness in your life that has been caused by the loss or damage of a prized possession. Consider also the continual fear you have that you might lose or damage your possessions. The overall result is that your mind is continually plagued by some kind of tension, perhaps consciously, though probably subconsciously. You can be a very rich person, yet if you have this attitude of non-attachment you will be unburdened of many worries and tensions of the mind.

Niyamas or observances

These, like the yamas, are five in number. They are more concerned with the personal discipline of the practitioner. They are intended to prepare the spiritual aspirant for the arduous yogic path that lies ahead. Like the yamas (which are ethically inclined), the niyamas reduce mental and emotional conflicts and render the individual's mind tranquil for concentration and meditation.

Shaucha (purity): This rule needs little explanation. One should keep the body as pure as possible by regular bathing and also by eating food that is as pure and nutritious as possible. If you don't, then you will be more susceptible to diseases both internal and external and this is a great hindrance to meditational practices, for how is it possible to direct the mind inwards to the deeper realms when one's attention is continually distracted by indigestion or any other ailment?

There is also another factor. One's meditational capacity is related very much to the type of food one eats. If one eats impure and coarse food, then the mind is unlikely to be sensitive enough to respond to the subtle vibrations and experiences of meditation. The subtle states of meditation need a clear and pure mind in which to manifest. This rule also applies to the purification of the mind from disturbing thoughts and emotions. Since this is the whole reason for the yamas and niyamas, it implies that yamas and niyamas must be practised.

Santosha (contentment): It is essential to develop the ability to withstand daily problems without being deeply affected, to be contented no matter what circumstances beset one. Most people have a continually changing mood because of the ups and downs of life. One moment they are happy, then something occurs and they suddenly become very unhappy. A mind that is continually fluctuating in this way is not suitable for meditation. For this reason contentment is of the utmost importance. Not external contentment to impress other people, but inner contentment. Easier said than done, you might say. This is true, but by continual development of the other yamas and niyamas and a conscious effort to accept what comes to you, no matter what, this contentment will surely come.

Tapas (austerity): This is intended to strengthen the willpower, by undergoing small austerities such as fasting, maintaining a vow of silence for a few hours and so on. This can help to discipline the mind. This tapas should not, however, involve suppression of the mind for this can do more harm than good. Willpower is absolutely necessary in yoga, for the mind is like a kitten which wanders here and there without purpose. It will try to make you do things you don't want to do. In this way, it will bring more disturbances to the mind and thereby hamper your meditational practices. Willpower is the only way to bring it under control.

Swadhyaya (self-study): This has various interpretations, the most likely being that you should continually watch your actions and reactions with more awareness. See how you react to different situations and why you become happy in one situation and unhappy in another situation. If you become angry, ask yourself, "Why did I become angry?" If you are attached to certain things, ask yourself why you are attached to that thing and so on. By this continual self-analysis you will gradually find out how your mind works, at least on a superficial level, and you will become more aware of the things that disturb your mind.

Self-study should also extend to your meditations, however deep, so that you progressively understand more about yourself. In other words, if you see visions in your meditations, let them come. Don't suppress them for they will tell you more about the things that are embedded in your subconscious mind, your memories, your deep-rooted problems and other things, many of which are causing persistent tension in the mind, in many cases without your knowledge. It is only when you know them that you start to remove them and further improve your ability to experience deeper meditations, which these deep-rooted tensions hamper.

Ishwara pranidhana (self-surrender): This means to surrender your actions to God, the supreme consciousness, existence, or whatever name you have for that which drives you through life. Your every action should be a dedication of worship. You should try, by constant practice, to lose your individuality, your ego, and realize that your actions are nothing but a manifestation of the supreme consciousness. Remember, it is our ego that causes much of our emotional and mental problems. It is our ego that makes us hate, fight, become attached to objects and so on. If we reduce our ego a little, our mind becomes correspondingly less disturbed and more tranquil. If we can totally lose our ego, which is not easy, then our meditations will automatically take us to reality. Karma and bhakti yoga, selfless action and divine devotion respectively, are a great help in this respect.

Yamas and niyamas – a summary

An objection might be raised that perhaps it is a person's true nature to be dishonest, untruthful, etc., and so therefore any attempt to practise the yamas or niyamas could be contrary to his nature and could therefore cause more mental problems instead of reducing them. This is of course a controversial and philosophical question. However, all the great sages have emphasized that the intrinsic nature of all human beings is to be truthful, honest, to do good and so on. Anything done to the contrary, though appearing to be a manifestation of the individual's true nature, is therefore really a shield or an act which has arisen through circumstances in life, poverty, mistreatment by other people and so on. Consciously the individual may feel he is only doing what comes naturally, but subconsciously it is a different story. Conflict occurs in the subconscious realms and these cause mental disturbances of the type that the individual feels consciously but does not know what the cause is. It is in this form that most mental problems occur in our modern society. There is a conflict between what one actually does and what the subconscious really wants to do.

The yamas and niyamas are therefore applicable to everyone without distinction. The reader may find these yamas and niyamas a little impractical, perhaps even a little 'heavy'.

But remember, your aim is transcendence and the path to perfection. Even if you abide by them to the slightest extent this is a definite step in the right direction. Even a small step will be helpful. Don't aim further than you are able, tread slowly and gently.

Asanas or yogic postures

In traditional raja yoga, as enumerated by Patanjali, asanas are briefly mentioned as suitable sitting poses which give a steady and comfortable position of the body. This enables one to practise concentration and meditation without physical disturbance. In view of the close relationship between mind and body, this is a most essential part of every meditative session. Any position of the body which is even slightly uncomfortable will prevent any serious progress in meditation, for the mind will be preoccupied with the body to the exclusion of all else.

However, as the reader is probably aware, there are numerous other asanas which are not generally suitable for meditation practice. These we will call therapeutic asanas, as opposed to meditational asanas. The therapeutic asanas, sirshasana, halasana, etc., are nevertheless very useful in allowing the aspirant to gain success in meditation. These asanas, if performed regularly, remove and prevent diseases of the body and mind. They loosen up the muscles and tone the nervous system. They help to induce tranquillity of mind. In this respect, they encourage successful meditation by eliminating a large number of factors which tend to prevent meditation. They also allow one to perform one's daily duties with more zest and less emotional upsets, which greatly helps one to meditate.

These asanas are discussed in a wide selection of books on yoga (such as *Asana Pranayama Mudra Bandha,* published by the Bihar School of Yoga). The reader is sincerely advised to refer to one of these books for details of their practice and benefits and to do them on a daily basis. He should particularly refer to the chapter on meditative poses in this book.

Pranayama or vital energy control

The word *prana* is often used in yoga, yet it is not well understood by the majority of people. It can be defined as vital or bioenergy. The reader is referred to the section on pranayama for full details. It is the medium through which matter and mind are linked to consciousness. Without this vital medium, consciousness could not express itself in the external world through the mind. It therefore seems logical that control of the flow of prana helps to control the mind and therefore leads one along the path to meditation. It is this control that the many techniques of pranayama attempt to achieve.

Many people, especially those new to yoga, assume that pranayama is not more than regulation of breath. This is partly true, for breath is indeed modified during the practice of pranayama. Yet this is only half the story and it is not the prime motive of pranayama. The aim of pranayama is control over the flow of prana, which is intimately related to the breathing process. So close is this relationship, that any manipulation of the breath will automatically cause manipulation of the prana.

One can meditate without doing pranayama, but its regular practice is a great help in achieving success in meditation. For example, the stage before dhyana (meditation) in raja yoga is dharana (concentration). Without being able to concentrate on one object for some time, dhyana is impossible. The usual method is to visualize an internal object with closed eyes. This in itself is not so simple, for any mental image is either blurred or fades from view within a short time.

Pranayama is extremely useful in encouraging the appearance of clear mental images which remain visible for longer periods of time. This is caused by redistribution of prana in the body, which renders the mind more able to perceive and control the images. Pranayama and its techniques have been discussed in depth in *Prana, Pranayama, Prana Vidya* and the reader is advised to refer to this Bihar School of Yoga publication for more information.

Pratyahara or sense withdrawal

Most of us spend the majority of our waking life with our mind externalized. In other words, our mind is predominantly concerned with events which occur outside the body. To gain any success in meditational techniques, we need to withdraw the mind from association with the outside world, and forget this external environment. This is easier said than done, for the mind has been habituated since birth to looking outside, and like all habits it is difficult to overcome. Most people find it difficult to close their eyes and forget the outside world, even for a minute or so. During meditation lessons we ask the practitioners to try and keep their eyes closed for the duration of the practice. We tell them that they should resist the temptation to open their eyes by asking themselves the question, "What is outside that can possibly interest me? I am in a room and certainly nothing is happening outside." All of us have this conditioned reflex always to think of external things. Our awareness is drawn outside in the same way as iron is attracted to a magnet.

The biggest problem is that our mind is continually receiving data about the outside world via the sense organs: the ears, the eyes, etc. Our mind can not really dissociate itself from the outside world until it is trained or encouraged to ignore this never-ending stream of stimuli from the sense organs. This is a natural process, for the mind does not assimilate or take note of all the messages it receives from the sense organs. If it did, it would be unable to make decisions or obtain knowledge of the outside world, for it would be inundated with so much information that it would be powerless to act. The situation would be similar to having fifty radios in a room emitting fifty different radio stations with equal intensity. Sitting in the middle of the room, one would be unable to perceive any one station and comprehend any one program. The mind selects some of the data and then makes decisions.

What we must do is to reduce the selection of sense impressions which are communicated to the mind to zero.

Actually we do this more that we think. If we are absorbed in an interesting book we automatically lose awareness of the surroundings; we forget the sound of the clock or the voices of people in another room or the crackling of a fire in the room. What we must try to do in meditation, concentration and pratyahara is to lose awareness of our environment, but without the help of an exciting book or any other external object that absorbs the intellectual faculties of the mind. The mind should be absorbed; one should be concentrated, but without intellectualization.

The mind is like a naughty child; it does the opposite of what you want it to do. So if you try to shut out sense impressions, the mind automatically makes them more intense. If, on the other hand, you force the mind to think of external things while the eyes are closed, it will after some time tend to lose interest in the external sounds, etc., and will not associate with sense impressions. This state of mind, called pratyahara, is exactly what we want for meditation. This idiosyncrasy of the mind is utilized in the yogic process called antar mouna, which is an excellent method of attaining pratyahara and preparing for meditation. This method is described in the section on meditational practices.

The degree to which a person can do pratyahara successfully depends very much on his ability to sit in a comfortable asana for the duration of practice. If he feels continual physical discomfort, then of course his mind will be continually aware of stimuli from the sense organs giving information about pain, stiffness and so on. Pratyahara, and consequently meditation, will be out of the question. It is therefore necessary that the practitioner trains the body so that it can maintain one position for a prolonged length of time, without any discomfort whatsoever.

Many of the techniques given in this book involve a systematic rotation of one's awareness around different parts of the body, awareness of the breathing process, of sounds uttered either mentally or verbally, etc. This is used partly to concentrate the mind, but also to keep the mind engrossed internally, so that it automatically forgets the surroundings, thereby inducing a state of pratyahara. This satisfies the wandering tendency of the mind, but in a controlled manner, and avoids the problems encountered in the practice of pure one-pointed concentration, during which the untrained mind tends to rebel against the forced restraints and all progress may be lost.

Dharana or concentration

By the time one is ready to practise this stage all external disturbances to the mind should have been eliminated. However, the mind is still in a state of turmoil; it is still plagued by thoughts. These thoughts are not concerned with the present time, for all outside stimuli have been shut off. They can be classified into two groups: memories of the past and projections of future events. How can we remove these activities of the mind? The method of elimination is through dharana or concentration.

Concentration in this context means fixing the mind totally on one object to the exclusion of all others. When this is achieved then the mind automatically does not think of other things or ideas. It becomes totally absorbed in the object of concentration. The object of concentration is usually an internal image kept in front of the closed eyes, though it can also be an external object. However, the mind tends to wander more easily if it is concentrating on an external object, but concentrating on an external object is very useful for those people who have difficulty in visualizing an internal object. If one concentrates on an external object (for example, in trataka,) for a reasonable length of time daily, it will eventually be possible to close the eyes and visualize the image of that object internally. Concentration on one idea to the exclusion of all other ideas can also be practised, but this is more difficult and is usually done when one has developed the powers of concentration to a very high level.

In yogic concentration the mind is not held completely rigid; the processes of the mind are not curtailed. The mind is held so that it is aware of one object, but it should move in the sense that it realizes deeper aspects of the object. It realizes aspects of the object that were not perceivable before when the mind was continually wandering from one object to the next. This may be compared to a person visiting an art gallery. If he quickly glances at each picture, he sees little of the fine detail. If, on the other hand, he spends half an hour studying one picture, the finer and more subtle points will be revealed.

Even people who think they have highly developed powers of concentration will find concentration on one object difficult. This is because concentration is normally of a wider type, where one concentrates on a train of ideas while reading a book for example, or on a large number of objects. To hold your mind on one object is far more difficult and its benefits in the form of deeper insight into the object of concentration are also correspondingly greater. Concentration on one object is not impossible. It requires persistent practice and annihilation of all mental disturbances by the practice of the lower five stages of raja yoga, and when the mind has been completely purified by these basic practices, concentration will come by itself, naturally, without any special effort being required.

Dhyana or meditation

Dhyana is really an extension of dharana and has been defined by Patanjali as the uninterrupted flow of concentration of the mind on the object of meditation or concentration. There is a fine difference between dharana and dhyana. In dharana the mind continually tries to think of things other than the object, and the practitioner has to bring the awareness back to the object; distractions still exist in one form or another. In dhyana, however, the mind has been subjugated and is totally and continually absorbed in the object. It is in meditation that the deeper aspects of the object start to manifest themselves. The depth of concentration in dhyana is far greater than in dharana. It is through the regular and continual practice of concentration that dhyana spontaneously manifests itself.

Samadhi or illumined consciousness

Samadhi is the fullest extension of dhyana. It is the climax of meditation. It is divided into four stages, all of which must be transcended before one eventually reaches the culmination of yoga and of life itself, self-realization or oneness with reality. These four stages will not be discussed in this book, for they are so far above normal experience that words are today inadequate to describe them. We would merely be playing with words, even more so than when we tried to describe meditation on the lower levels. Anyone, however, who is interested in the technical aspects of samadhi should refer to Swami Satyananda's commentary on Patanjali's *Yoga Sutras*, called *Four Chapters on Freedom.*

Patanjali described samadhi as that state during meditation where there is only consciousness of the object and no concurrent consciousness of the mind. This needs some explanation. During lower states of meditation the object's deeper reality slowly shows itself. Yet the ultimate essence does not show itself, something seems to prevent it revealing itself. This something is, in fact, the mind of the meditator. It acts as a screen between the object and consciousness. The self-conscious nature of the mind veils the reality of the object from consciousness. We can compare this to a person who is singing. If he is singing without awareness of himself, his singing will be much better than if he is self-conscious and aware that people are listening to him. One only needs to look at all great people to see that they have produced their greatest work when they have lost this element of self-consciousness. When the mind removes its impediment, higher inspiration can shine through. It is exactly the same in high states of meditation.

In samadhi the self-consciousness of the mind disappears. The quality of object and perceiving subject disappears so that the object and subject become one. It is only under these circumstances that the ultimate essence of the object reveals itself, for if the object and subject are no longer different but the same, then the subject must know everything about the object, the object of perception, the person perceiving and the perception that takes place all become one entity. This situation is difficult to explain in words, for it transcends normal experience.

Let us take a very gross analogy. A man sees a large crowd of people from a distance. He feels that he is separate from the crowd and of course he is. This is like our normal relationship to the things around us. The crowd is discussing something but it is too far away for the man to hear. A large fence exists between him and the crowd, preventing him from discovering what is being talked about. The fence is the mind. It must be overcome or climbed if he wants to find out what the crowd is talking about. He climbs the fence, joins the crowd and finds out what it is talking about. In a crude sense the man becomes one with the crowd and also the knowledge that keeps the crowd together, the reason for the formation of the crowd. The viewer joins with the viewed and the point of view held by the viewed. They become one. It is the same in samadhi. Of course the unity obtained during samadhi is indescribable and far transcends any of our day-to-day experiences.

A person looking at a man in samadhi will have no comprehension of what that man is experiencing. The spectator might even feel that the man in samadhi is asleep if he is in a sitting position, or else acting completely normally, with 'normal' thought processes if he is performing his daily duties. Not even the man in samadhi consciously knows the height of the experience he is undergoing. When he leaves the state of samadhi and returns to normal awareness, or perhaps we should say normal non-awareness, he maintains the deep wisdom and peace and expresses it in everyday activities. A man who has experienced samadhi even once is a completely changed man. He has raised himself above the average and he sees everything in a totally new light.

The stages from dharana to samadhi are really different names for different degrees of attainment. One automatically leads to the next when the aspirant has reached a certain level of development. They are not totally different practices as are the lower stages such as asanas, pranayama, for example. There is no abrupt change from one stage to the next. The progress of the aspirant in these realms is natural and spontaneous. It is at these stages that the guru is said to become an absolute necessity, for while the aspirant's awareness is fully engrossed in the experiences he is passing through, only the guru can provide the guidance needed to carry him safely on the path to the goal.

8

Other Forms of Yoga

It has already been explained that all forms of yoga aim at bringing about the state of meditation. The reader should not assume, however, that one type of yoga should be practised to the exclusion of all others. Though they are usually regarded as the different paths of yoga, a more realistic description would be to call yoga the path, and its various forms different lanes of that path. This can be compared to a piece of rope composed of various smaller strands. The different strands have separate identities, yet together they form the rope. In the same way, the different strands of each type of yoga, when performed in conjunction with each other, form the composite whole which takes one to meditation.

Bhakti yoga

Bhakti is the yoga of devotion. It is generally devotion to God or the supreme consciousness in one of its manifestations. These manifestations may be one of numerous avatars, divine incarnations who have existed at various times throughout history, such as Krishna, Rama, Buddha, Christ, Mohammed and so on. It may be one's guru or anyone or thing that provokes strong emotional feelings. The important point is that the object of the bhakta's devotion has strong emotional ties for him, so strong in fact, that all his emotional energy is directed to serving his personal form of the supreme consciousness. Instead of directing his attention to an impersonal form of consciousness, as in raja yoga and jnana yoga, he directs his love to something more tangible and concrete.

All of us are emotional to a greater or lesser degree; it is part of the human constitution. Most people, however, suppress this emotion and this force becomes bottled up inside them. It has to manifest somewhere and it often does so in the form of diseases or mental problems. Other people express their emotional feelings, but do so in so many different directions that it lacks force. This also causes mental disturbances for the many different objects of emotional attention do not hold the devotion of the individual. As such the individual is continually trying to find someone or something to which he can totally direct his emotion and devotion. This search carries on continually throughout an individual's life. Once we find a worthy object of devotion, then we no longer have emotional problems and we start to live life and not half live it.

How can we find an object that we can devote ourselves to? Actually we don't find it; it spontaneously reveals itself. Bhakti yoga is almost unique among different types of yoga in that it cannot be consciously developed. The powerful and overwhelming devotion occurs spontaneously. It might be something we have inherited from childhood. But one thing is certain; as one lives the yogic way of life and slowly reduces the mental distractions and disturbances which hold the awareness from perceiving the true directions of one's destiny, devotion will increase and the object of devotion will definitely manifest itself spontaneously from within.

How does bhakti yoga bring about states of meditation? The answer is that a person who feels devotion automatically concentrates his mind. The degree of concentration depends on the level of devotion. A person who is continually thinking of his object of devotion has a highly concentrated mind. The ups and downs of life are less likely to cause disturbances in his mind, which becomes calm and steady. Also, a person who continually thinks of something else, i.e. his object of devotion, automatically starts to lose awareness of 'I-ness'. He loses the awareness of his ego. If this process continues for a long enough period of time, the individual essentially loses his personal identity. In this way he will automatically reduce the kleshas and desires which make meditation so difficult. That is, providing that the object of meditation itself is not someone or something which will cause new distractions and pain by instability or fickleness.

Ideally, bhakti yoga alone can be sufficient to induce high states of meditation and even self-realization. No other practice is necessary; raja yoga, karma yoga, etc., are all superfluous. This, however, is only true if, and only if, the individual has total and untiring devotion. Few of us have this capacity. Most of us might be able to devote ourselves for a short time, but tend to be distracted or lose faith in our object of devotion. If this happens, bhakti yoga alone will not take us to meditational states. We must then supplement it with other forms of yoga.

Stages of bhakti

Bhakti yoga is most powerful if the object of devotion is spontaneously in the mind and one forgets one's ego. However, there are specific methods by which the devotion can be enhanced and expressed, as has already been explained. The object of bhakti is generally God in any of his traditional manifestations, though this need not always be the case. However, for the sake of argument, we will assume that this is the case so that we can easily explain the different methods of expressing bhakti. These methods are applied in all religions as a means to lift the emotions from the mundane to the transcendental. They include the following:

1. *Sravana*, which includes hearing stories about the glories of God and reading the different scriptures such as the *Bible, Koran, Srimad Bhagavatam,* which relate stories about personal forms of God.
2. *Nama sankirtan*, continuous repetition of the different names of God in song form.

3. *Smarana,* continuous remembrance of God by performing japa.
4. *Vandana,* prayers to God.
5. *Archana,* which is worship in its ritualistic form. All religions have a large number of rituals of this type.

In higher stages of bhakti yoga, the bhakta feels as though he is the servant of God and totally surrenders himself to the will of God. Even still, however, this love is a projection of the ego, a highly spiritualized and purified projection, but nevertheless still of the ego. The bhakta loves because he has an inherent need to love, in a way that a brother would love a sister or a lover would love his beloved. It is still a relationship based on the individual and something else. There is still a gap between the devotee and the object of devotion. This gap, this seemingly uncrossable separation, must be overcome if the bhakta is to attain self-realization.

When the bhakta attains self-realization he becomes the oneness, he becomes God and can utter from the depths of his being *Aham Brahma Asmi* (I am God). He can say, "My Father and I are one", as did Christ. Through his devotion the bhakta reaches the stage before the ultimate goal. To attain the final goal this very devotion has to be transcended. At this point the bhakta has expanded his love so much that the love no longer exists in the normal sense of the word, which by definition implies love between two things. He has become *one* and so he becomes love itself. At this point he has reached the same realization as a raja yogi, jnana yogi or any other person who attains supreme enlightenment. The path of love takes one to ultimate knowledge.

The spiritual aspirant is aiming for meditational experiences and should realize that bhakti or devotion is one of the most powerful means. Devotion brings about a state of mind in which meditation naturally manifests itself. If you do not know your object of devotion, your ishta, wait for it to show itself, for it surely will as you do yoga and slowly evolve. It will surely show itself one day, probably at a time when you least expect it.

Karma yoga

Karma yoga is not merely work. Karma yoga is doing work with complete awareness, but without attachment to the fruits or outcome of the work. The work is the end in itself, not the means to attaining some reward, payment, etc. It is selfless work. It is work in which one loses identity with one's ego. One merely becomes an instrument. Of course karma yoga in its early stages is only work, for the individual still possesses his strong sense of ego, and consciously or unconsciously he longs for the fruits of his efforts, or at least recognition of his work in the form of praise or respect. By constantly losing oneself in work and by mental effort one will gradually but surely bring about a continuous dissociation from one's personality and consciousness of the ego.

In karma yoga, the individual aims at becoming the perfect instrument of the supreme consciousness in the manifested universe in which we live. This manifestation is usually obstructed in its perfect fulfilment by the whims and ego of the individual. When the individual no longer considers himself the doer but merely as the instrument, the work becomes spiritualized. The individual becomes very efficient and expert in his actions. The individual develops equanimity of mind under all circumstances, for how can he be upset or angry when he is only an instrument? It is only from desire and egocentricity that one reacts adversely towards other people.

One of the greatest examples of a karma yogi in this century was Mahatma Gandhi, who lived up to all the ideals of karma yoga. He performed actions in life and yet he was unaffected by likes and dislikes, personal fancies and so on. He saw that every action he did was nothing but a role in the divine process of the universe in accordance with the will of the supreme consciousness. He was only an instrument, a mere witness of his actions. He offered all the fruits of his actions to the service of humanity and to God.

How does karma yoga relate to meditation? In its lower stages it is a most powerful way of removing one's identification with the ego. The desires and mental problems automatically disappear. Likes and dislikes gradually melt away. All these are obstacles to meditation and so their removal or even their reduction allows the individual to progressively attain higher states of meditation. Mental problems cannot be removed by doing nothing or living in seclusion. They only tend to fester or lie dormant in the deeper recesses of the mind. Activity in the form of karma yoga is the means to expose all these inner conflicts. Interaction with people during karma yoga is the sure way to show up any personality problems. When they are exposed, the individual can take active steps to remove them through introspective awareness and positive use of autosuggestion.

Another important point is that the constant practice of karma yoga develops the faculty of concentration. The ability to concentrate is essential before one can meditate in all forms of yoga. Therefore, the development of concentration during karma yoga can automatically lead to meditation. The cultivation of the powers of concentration is of indispensable value if one wishes to attain transcendence through raja or kundalini yoga. In the higher stages of karma yoga, the very performance of actions becomes a form of meditation in itself. In a sense the actor, the objects which are acted upon by the karma yogi and the performed actions become one and the same thing. In this state of mind the karma yogi is truly meditating.

Another aspect of karma yoga which is often missed is that it develops the will. The importance of the will is often overlooked by most people. Briefly, the will can be defined as the ability to harmonize, motivate and mobilize all one's abilities and actions to achieve a definite aim. In karma yoga a man sets out to achieve results through his work in a most efficient manner. This develops the power of an individual's will, and it is through the will that an individual experiences and expresses his unique nature. In fact it is the capacity of an individual to express his will that identifies his personal existence. The more his will harmonizes with his nature, the nearer he will move to identification with the centre of his existence, the self.

The essence of karma yoga can be summed up by the following extract from the *Bhagavad Gita*: "The world is imprisoned in its own activity, except when actions are performed as worship of God. Therefore, you must perform every action sacramentally and be free of your attachments to the results."

Tantric kundalini yoga

This system of yoga is concerned with awakening the psychic centres or chakras which exist in every individual. To understand the basic operation of the chakras, the reader will have to remember that the mind of every individual is made up of various levels of subtlety, each higher stage of mind progressively allowing consciousness to illuminate closer approaches to reality. Each level of mind is associated with a psychic centre or chakra, located throughout the psychic body of man. There are numerous chakras, including ones associated with planes below the average human level of mind, and others associated with higher psychic and superconscious states. In other words, within us we have chakras that can connect us to animal levels of mind, to the instinctive realms of being or to the sublime heights, far beyond the scope of our normal mundane awareness.

The chakras which are utilized in kundalini yoga are the chakras that lead to the higher levels of the mind.The aim and object of kundalini yoga is to bring the unawareness of the aspirant to these higher centres of mind, and in so doing to activate or awaken the subtle faculties with which these higher centres are associated. The reader should not think the awakening of these chakras is abnormal and something that is beyond normal experience. All of us spend our lives in the various realms of mind that are connected with a few of the chakras.

Most of us spend part of our lives in the frame of mind where we are concerned with manipulating other people for the gratification of our own needs. Some people spend most of their time in this attitude of mind, some a small part and others none. This level of mind is associated with manipura chakra in the region of the navel. Each of us at some time or other has experienced the feeling of great love for all humanity; for most, however, it comes on rare occasions. For other people it is almost a continuous state of mind. This level of mind is associated with the anahata chakra in the heart region. When we have a feeling of love for all, then it means that our anahata chakra is in operation and the individual is thinking from the corresponding level of the mind.

It is the fundamental aim, the only aim of kundalini yoga, to overcome the normal inactivity of the higher chakras so that they are stimulated and the individual is able to experience higher levels of mind. The basic method of awakening these psychic centres in kundalini yoga is deep concentration on the centres and willing their arousal.

Asanas, pranayama, mudras, bandhas and mantra repetition are also used to stimulate the awakening of the chakras. Actually, all the methods of yoga eventually awaken these chakras, for as the spiritual aspirant ascends to higher levels of mind, the chakras automatically manifest. Most of the other forms of yoga have the added safeguard that the individual progresses more slowly along the spiritual path and is, therefore, more likely to have removed many of the impurities from his mind. In these cases, undesirable experiences associated with the premature awakening of the chakras, which can be dangerous to persons practising kundalini yoga without the direct guidance of a guru, are avoided.

Hatha yoga

Hatha yoga is primarily concerned with bodily purification practices which tranquillize the mind and discipline the body. Traditionally, it consists of the following six groups of techniques called the shatkarmas.

1. *Neti*: methods of nasal cleaning
2. *Dhauti*: methods of cleansing the alimentary canal

3. *Nauli*: practice of abdominal massage
4. *Basti*: methods of cleaning the intestines
5. *Kapalbhati*: method of purifying the frontal portion of the brain
6. *Trataka*: methods of developing the powers of concentration.

Technically, asanas (postures), pranayama (bioenergy control), mudras (body gestures and mental attitudes) and bandhas (energy locks) can also be classified as part of hatha yoga, because they are mentioned in the classical texts on hatha yoga. The asanas included in hatha yoga are far more numerous than the meditational asanas in raja yoga. They include a large number of asanas which beneficially influence the whole mind-body complex.

Hatha yoga is based on the principle that one can become aware of higher states of mind by manipulating the different forces and systems in the physical body. Any stimulation or manipulation of the nervous system will surely have some effect on the mind, for all the nerves in the body are directly or indirectly connected to the brain, of this there is no doubt. For example, the techniques in hatha yoga bring a balance between the sympathetic and parasympathetic nervous systems, which have a large influence on the working of almost every organ in the body. Both these systems are connected to the different organs such as the heart, lungs, digestive system, etc.

Each system opposes the operation of the other, so that the operating condition of the organs at any given time is a compromise between the two opposing forces. The sympathetic system tends to mobilize the whole body so that it can perform external activities. The parasympathetic system, on the other hand, tends to make the individual become introverted to encourage him to think and reflect. Neither of these extremes is good for meditation. If one thinks too much, then meditation is impossible. If one's attention is continually directed to the outside environment, meditation is again impossible. The ideal condition is where the two systems are balanced and it is this that hatha yoga does. This is one example; hatha yoga has numerous other effects.

In the word *hatha*, *ha* stands for the ida or lunar nadi and the *tha* stands for the pingala or solar nadi. In the pranic body, the bioenergy body that is finer than the physical body, there are large numbers of psychic passages or nadis through which the prana or vital energy flows along within definite channels, just as blood flows inside the blood vessels. These two particular nadis, ida and pingala, each connect mooladhara chakra to ajna chakra, criss-crossing each other and passing through each of the intermediate chakras.

Travelling directly from mooladhara to ajna chakra is the most important nadi in the body. It is called sushumna and it is in this nadi that the kundalini flows when it is awakened. It is found that when the flow of prana in ida is equal to the flow of prana in pingala, kundalini automatically starts to rise. Hatha yoga, as its very name suggests, is concerned with the two nadis, ida and pingala. It aims at balancing the flow of prana in each nadi. In this way the kundalini is activated, which starts to stimulate the chakras, and meditation automatically takes place.

Many of the hatha yoga practices also attempt directly to stimulate the chakras which are the intermediaries between the different and progressively subtle levels of mind. The lowest manifestations of the chakras are connected with various physical organs in the body. Hatha yoga tries to stimulate, clean and generally improve the condition of these organs so that the chakras can more easily awaken. For example, the practice of kapalbhati physically purifies the frontal lobe of the brain, and the practice of neti stimulates nerve connections in the olfactory bulb of the brain above the nostrils, which is considered to be a major stimulation point for ajna chakra. The methods of dhauti physically clean the whole alimentary canal and stimulate the nerves in the chest region, thereby affecting anahata chakra. Similarly, the practice of nauli massages the abdominal region, which influences manipura chakra. These chakras are directly connected to the different levels of mind; their awakening will surely lead towards meditation.

We can say that hatha yoga considers the body the temple of the soul and as such it should be kept in good condition. Hatha yoga helps to remove many diseases and body ailments, all of which are serious impediments to meditation, for how can one attempt to still the mind or forget the body when there is pain or discomfort? Meditation is much easier for those persons who have good physical health. If you suffer from any kind of illness such as diabetes, high blood pressure, constipation and so on, we recommend that you begin your practice with hatha yoga, including asanas, pranayama, etc., not only as an effective way of gaining health, but as a preliminary stage on the path to meditation.

The sixth hatha yoga practice, trataka, is often considered out of place in hatha yoga, for all the other techniques require physical action and are directly concerned with the cleansing of the body. Trataka, however, is concerned with developing the power of concentration by gazing fixedly at an external or internal object. However, if we remember that hatha yoga is often regarded as a preliminary to the higher stages of raja yoga, we can see the reason for the inclusion of trataka in hatha yoga. Concentration is absolutely necessary before meditation can manifest and without it meditation is impossible. Hatha yoga can also be considered as a preliminary for the practices of kundalini yoga, for it tunes and stimulates the chakras which are later to be opened and awakened by the kriyas of kundalini yoga

In summary, we can say that hatha yoga itself does not lead to stages of meditation. However, it is most useful and usually utilized to prepare the practitioner for the higher stages of meditation attained through other forms of yoga.

Mantra yoga

Mantra yoga is concerned with the audible chanting or silent repetition of combinations of sounds. These are more than mere sounds; they are sound combinations that were received by realized sages and rishis during states of deepest meditation. The mantras, the names given to these special collections of sounds, have since been handed down from generation to generation.

During the early stages of yogic practice, the chosen mantra (often given to an aspirant by a guru or spiritual preceptor) has to be repeated over and over again with effort of will and full awareness. This awareness or concentration prevents the mind from thinking of other things. Eventually, after continuous and dedicated practice, the mantra is repeated automatically without strain or effort. The mantra spontaneously manifests itself and becomes an integral part of the mind. The mind vibrates with the sound of the mantra. It becomes an integral part of the individual's being and needs absolutely no conscious effort. It repeats itself spontaneously with every breath and continues spontaneously day and night. This is a very powerful way of approaching meditational states, for the mind is rendered calm and concentrated. The mantra acts as a pathway between normal states of consciousness and superconsciousness.

The best known mantra is the monosyllable *Om*, which is regarded as the root sound from which all other sounds emanate. The sounds *Amen* and *Amin* in Christianity and Islam respectively are derivatives of *Om* and, similarly, the ultimate God in Egyptian religion was known as *Amon*. For this reason *Amon* frequently formed a part of the names of pharaohs: e.g., *Tutankamon, Amenhotep*. In Hinduism there are similarly many well known mantras such as *Ram, Om Namah Shivaya, Om Shanti* and so on. Each of these mantras can be most powerful in inducing transcendence if repeated with constant devotion and concentration.

Tantric yoga

Tantra is an ancient system that is very closely affiliated with yoga, and in fact it is widely accepted that yoga was initially an offshoot of tantra. As most of the yogic practices such as asana, pranayama, trataka, yoga nidra and kriya yoga are described in the ancient tantras, which precede the *Upanishads* and *Yoga Sutras* by many centuries, we can say that the great yogic innovators such as Guru Gorakhnath and Rishi Matsyendranath had in fact simply integrated the philosophy of the *Upanishads* with the practices of the tantras to create the system that we now call yoga.

In practice, both yoga and tantra have the same aim, the transcendence of the material world in which we now live. They both aim at giving the practitioner meditational experiences. However, in many ways their methods are very different and often seemingly contradictory. For example, most forms of vedantic based yoga advise the practitioner to sublimate sexual energy into spiritual energy. It does not advocate suppression of the sexual energy, but says that one definitely should reduce and control sexual activities as much as possible. Not only will this save the wastage of energy, allowing it to be transformed and utilized to attain transcendence, but it also helps, if no suppression is involved, in removing or at least reducing the great attachment that people have to sex.

Freud preached that the two prime motivating forces in life are sex and self-preservation. This may be a great oversimplification, but it does show how much of our time we devote to thinking about sex, putting ourselves in sexual situations and actually performing sex. This time could be more usefully utilized in spiritual directions, the yogis say, and though sexual union is a transcendental experience, it is far inferior to high states of meditation. Therefore, the ideal of yoga is that if you can leave sex you will attain a far greater degree of transcendence, bliss and union in the long run. If possible, leave sex behind, divert your mind to treading the spiritual path, and greater things will come. Sex is regarded as a necessary part of mundane life but a hindrance to spiritual evolution.

What does tantra say? It says almost the opposite. It says that the transcendental experience of sexual union should be utilized in your path to spiritual awareness. Does this mean that one system must be wrong? No, absolutely not! It just means they are tackling the problem of attaining transcendence in different ways. Their aim is the same, only their basic method differs. Tantra can be used by people who do not want to leave sexual activities, either through their very nature or because they are deeply involved in family life. It says don't suppress your sexual inclinations, but utilize the power of sex to gain transcendence. Don't just have sexual interplay; use it to climb the spiritual path. Be conscious of your heightened awareness during sexual acts, using it as a stepping stone to higher awareness. Through the experiences gained by tantric sexual union and through other tantric practices, the aspirant will naturally evolve and then he will automatically lose mundane interest in sex. Of course sexual activity will not stop the continual distraction of one's mind in life, but when the urge is strong it is far preferable to try to utilize it for spiritual purposes rather than to suppress it.

However one point must be remembered, and that is that tantra does not preach indiscriminate sexual interplay. It actually lays down specific rules about how the sexual energy can be utilized. For example, people who practise tantric union, known as *maithuna,* in its uncorrupted form, perform the sexual act without allowing the occurrence of a physical orgasm, which requires an enormous amount of willpower and nervous control. Additionally, persons who practise this aspect of tantric sadhana must do so under the guidance of a guru, who will surely lay down strict guidelines on how they must conduct their lives and what course their spiritual sadhana must follow.

General summary

There are various other types of yoga, but generally they are only modifications of the systems we have already mentioned. For example, jnana yoga is the yoga of knowledge; it is the means to attain high meditational states, and eventually samadhi, through reason. Actually it means reasoning in a particular sense, namely, discrimination between what is real and what is unreal. It is very close to raja yoga except it does not utilize the preparatory stages of raja yoga such as yamas, niyamas, asanas and pranayama. Raja yoga uses these as methods of stilling the mind. Jnana yoga tries to still the mind by reasoning.

All religions, whether the adherents know it or not, aim at attaining meditation or transcendence. We will not deal with this subject in detail, but to give a few examples, Christianity, Islam and Judaism are all basically bhakti or devotional faiths that aim at attaining oneness with a personal form of God. In this endeavour prayers, rituals, hymns, contemplation, etc., are utilized to purify and concentrate the mind, thereby inducing transcendental experiences.

Buddhism has much in common with raja and jnana yoga, but gives an emphasis on attentiveness. Every action must be viewed from the standpoint of a witness. Awareness of every action and thought must be heightened. Samkhya, which provides the philosophical background to yoga, also utilizes the same system. The idea is to de-automate our actions. Many, if not most, of our actions are entirely automatic; on attention, no concentration is required. By being more aware of our every action, our consciousness is opened up to new spheres of being. Further, continual attention to the task or action in hand prevents the mind becoming absorbed or brooding over problems, dislikes, fears and so on. With continual awareness, complexes and worries disappear of their own accord; they no longer play a large role in the individual personality. All this leads to meditation as a continuous process throughout every minute of life.

Hinduism is not really one religion; it actually encompasses all types of religion and yoga. It is a compendium of religions. All the different facets lead to meditational states. Thus we can say that meditation is a common aim of all religions, including the many that we have not mentioned, eventually leading to self-realization.

Preparation for Meditation

9

General Instructions and Suggestions

The importance of making preparations for meditation cannot be over-emphasized. Though there are a few evolved people who can merely sit down and start their meditation, and even fewer who are continually meditating anyway, adequate preparations are necessary for most people. Without making suitable preparations their progress will be seriously impeded. It is for this reason that the reader is advised to carry out the following instructions. As he progresses he will find out for himself the best preparations. The following is a guide applicable to most people.

Calming the mind

Sometimes it is possible to sit down for meditation and the mind spontaneously concentrates, no effort is required, yet at other times the mind wanders here and there like a wild elephant. Even autosuggestion doesn't seem to work. An excellent method to calm the mind, to tame its wandering tendency and to gain the ability to concentrate during the meditation practice is to chant *Om* loudly for as long as you can. Chant *Om* from your heart and not from the mouth; say it with intensity and feeling. Lose yourself and your ego in its sound. Feel its vibrations in your whole body and mind. If this doesn't still the mind, then nothing will. Incidentally, *Om* chanting alone can be considered an extremely powerful meditation technique.

Regularity and dedication

Don't expect meditational experiences to occur the first time you meditate. Just do your practices regularly and persevere. In fact, at times one may become disheartened and will wonder whether meditation is a waste of time or even a myth. With dedication, transcendental experiences must come to you. The eventual aim is for the meditation to be a spontaneous, unrestrained flow of bliss or joy. One's whole life becomes a meditational experience. This is the culmination of your practice of sitting down at a particular time and place every day.

Suitable place of practice

When you decide on a place to practise meditation, try to use the same place daily. It should be clean and conducive to tranquillity. It should be well ventilated but not breezy, and it should be dry. Place a blanket or rug on the floor. During meditation it is desirable to reduce outside stimuli as much as possible; therefore a quiet corner of a room is recommended where you cannot see out of a window. Don't meditate under a fan, and try to ensure that there is no furniture or other objects within a radius of about two yards.

Time

It is best to meditate in the early morning and in the evening before going to bed. The best hours are from 4 to 6 in the morning. This is the period of brahmamuhurta and it is particularly conducive to meditation. Allow at least one to one and a half hours before meditation after taking light refreshment, and four hours after a meal. This is because attention is drawn to the stomach and the digestion process. Try to eat moderately, not heavily.

Regularity in meditation is very important. Set fixed times for yourself, say between 4 to 6 in the morning and 8 to 10 in the evening, and keep firmly to these times. Start with perhaps half an hour's meditation daily and slowly increase the time.

Overcoming sleepiness

People who are not accustomed to getting up earlier than usual will probably find they fall asleep. Don't sleep, for you are merely wasting your time getting up early. If you want to sleep, it is better to stay in bed. There are various methods of combating sleep: one is to go to bed earlier at night, another is to go for a shower or wash either before you start to meditate or when you start to feel sleepy during your practices, or both. Another method is to use autosuggestion. Suggest to yourself that you will not sleep before you start the practice, and at various times during the day you can repeat the resolve so that the idea goes deep into the subconscious mind.

If you find that you are more tired after meditation than when you started, it is a sure indication that you are trying too hard, perhaps fighting the mind. Remember, meditation should be a source of joy, and anything that gives joy cannot possibly result in tiredness. It is only things that cause unhappiness, which are out of tune with our nature, that can result in fatigue. So if you feel lethargic or tired after meditation, check that you are not practising incorrectly.

Relaxation

One of the biggest obstacles to meditation is physical tension. If there is pain, stiffness or general tension in the body, the awareness will tend to dwell on the body. The ability to transcend the body to attain meditation experience will be impossible.

An excellent and simple method of systematically relaxing the body is to tense it as much as possible for some time and then release the tension. This appears contradictory, but if the reader tries it for himself he will indeed find that he can attain greater states of relaxation. Compare this with an elastic band. If you fully stretch an elastic band and then release it, it will reduce to a length that is even shorter than its normal unstretched length. All tension in the rubber is reduced to a minimum.

It is the same with muscles; tense them as much as possible for a short time and then release the tension. They will relax more than they are normally able. After experiencing extreme tension in the muscles one then experiences the extreme opposite. All the different parts of the body should be tensed in turn. It is best to lie flat on your back. Start with your legs and tense each in turn for as long as you are able without strain. Relax each completely for twenty seconds. Repeat the same procedure with the arms, fists, feet, abdomen, shoulders and finally the whole body. Then relax your body for a minute or so and start your meditation practice.

General obstacles

There are various obstacles to meditation. As already explained, the main impediments are physical and mental disturbances. Many physical ailments can be removed or relieved by practising asanas and other yogic techniques, as well as by trying to meditate. Asanas are not described in this book and the reader is advised to refer to a book on asanas, such as Swami Satyananda's *Asana Pranayama Mudra Bandha.*

Mental disturbances of all types: jealousy, hatred, pride, selfishness, irritability, etc., can all be rooted out by a number of methods. The methods we have given in yamas and niyamas, together with autosuggestion, will be found very useful. Mental problems will also automatically disappear if the reader develops the method fully described in chapter 5, where self-identity is removed from one's role in life and the mind-body, to the centre of consciousness. In this way external events as well as bodily and mental disturbances will have little or no effect on the individual, depending on the degree of perfection of the new identification.

What about states such as depression? This can be rooted out by the above methods. Another good method of removing it, if only on a temporary basis, is to chant *Om* as loudly as you can for half an hour or so, or walk in the countryside or the mountains and commune with nature. These are all excellent therapies.

Anger is another common hindrance to meditation. Its root lies in egoism and identification with the trivial things in life. Practise the method of 'self-identification' (see chapter 5, 'Reprogram Your Mind'), or try to feel that you are part of existence as a whole.

Doubt is another hindrance to meditation. One often wonders, before attaining any kind of transcendental experience, whether or not meditation might be a hoax, something that will never measure up to its high claims. If one feels in this frame of mind, read books on great saints or by people who are trying to describe their meditational experiences. You will find such enthusiasm and awe in their writing, that you cannot fail to reinstate your belief in the great transcendental experiences that lie ahead.

Use the methods given in this book to remove your mental disturbances or develop your own techniques. In this way you will remove the biggest obstacles to meditation. Often we have disturbances which we experience without knowing what the cause might be, due to an unconscious conflict, complex, fear, etc. Meditation is a method of recognizing and eventually expelling these problems. Yet at the same time it is difficult to meditate in the first instance when one is disturbed by these deep problems. To overcome this hurdle, one should first try to remove the known mental disturbances by autosuggestion. This will make the mind a little more relaxed.

Though meditation itself might be impossible, the practitioner will start to recognize manifestations of the deeper part of his mind coming to the field of consciousness. Many of these manifestations will be deeper conflicts. Once the conflicts, phobias, etc., are recognized, they can be removed through autosuggestion. It is a linked process; the more you purify your mind, the more you are able to meditate; the nearer you approach meditation or start to see the deeper aspects of your mind, the more you are able to remove your deeper, ingrained complexes. The deeper you delve into the mind, the less your problems will become.

Eventually transcendence will take place, perhaps even remain on a permanent basis, not only when you sit down for meditation practice.

Thought

The aim is eventually to transcend rational thought. When this occurs, meditation will take place. The aim of meditation is to dive deeper into the mind, beyond the realms of rational thought. Therefore, when performing meditation practices, try to reduce intellectualization as much as possible. Merely let the mind follow the mental actions necessary for execution of the practice. The practice of antar mouna is an exception in that in certain stages one actually uses the rational mind, but again the eventual aim is to transcend the intellect.

Object of concentration

Although any object can be chosen for meditation, it is generally found that objects with some deep meaning or significance for the individual are most conducive to attaining deep concentration. The mind is more likely to be riveted to the object and thereby less tempted to wander onto other thoughts. If the object of concentration has little or no significance to the practitioner, then the mind will surely wander and perhaps there will be a temptation to strain the mind by forcing it to concentrate. This will give mental tension, which is definitely not conducive to meditation.

The object should be chosen with discrimination. The practitioner might want to meditate on a form of God. If he was born in a Christian country, it is more likely that he will attain success in meditation if he concentrates on Christ or any other figure associated with Christianity. If the individual comes from Asia, it is more likely that one of the incarnations associated with Hinduism or Islam will be more auspicious. This is not a hard and fast rule and there will be many exceptions, such as an Englishman who finds that Buddha is the ideal object of concentration. The reader must find out what is best for him by experience, by knowing his own background, and if he feels any identity with a particular manifestation of God.

The object of concentration need not be an incarnation. It can be anyone or anything, but again it is preferable that it is something that the mind automatically identifies with. For example, it can be a cross, the yin and yang symbol, *Om* in its symbolic form, a flower, the moon, a candle flame. It is important, we emphasize again, that it is something the mind is automatically attracted to, that the mind spontaneously wants to concentrate on without effort.

Often people consider that they are not really attracted to any particular object. Yet, after practising various other forms of meditation which do not require any special object, they suddenly find that while watching their mind a manifestation in the form of a vision or image shows itself. This symbol arises to the field of consciousness from the deeper realms of the mind. The awareness of this image will strike one with its intensity. He will find immediately that it has great significance for him, even though perhaps the same object previously had absolutely no meaning for him. He might be very surprised at the form of the object, for it might seem very alien to his culture or way of life. When this happens, and it is a very common occurrence, this symbol should be adopted as the object of concentration. If necessary a drawing can be made of it and trataka performed on it, to develop the ability to eventually see a clear internal image.

Remember that it might be difficult initially to keep the mind on the chosen object. With practice, however, it will become easier. Only patience and perseverance are required. As pathways or habits are made in the mind, so the practitioner will find it progressively easier to concentrate on the object of choice. The mind will eventually automatically centre itself on the object, it will go in no other direction. Though a concrete object is the most useful in general for concentrating the mind, sublime ideas can be utilized for purposes of concentration. A few possibilities are love, compassion, infinity, eternity, existence and consciousness.

10

Meditation Poses

The main object of all meditation poses is to enable the practitioner to sit completely still for extended periods of time. For advanced stages of meditation it is necessary to remain in one position for a few hours without physical discomfort. In fact, only when the body is steady and still can deep meditation take place. The asanas listed are such that after practice they can be maintained without strain and discomfort for a long time. Other asanas do not have this virtue. Furthermore, these meditative asanas keep the spinal column straight (a prerequisite for deep meditation) and they keep the body locked in a steady position without conscious effort. This counteracts the effect of deep meditation, where the practitioner loses control over the muscles of the body.

Beginners to meditation practices can first sit in sukhasana (the easy posture), but they should slowly progress to the classical meditation asanas such as padmasana and siddhasana. Persons with very stiff legs or who are infirm from any debilitating disease can practise meditation sitting on a straight backed chair or lying on a hard bed, if necessary. When sitting in a posture, imagine yourself as firm as a rock. The steadier you are in your asana, the better your concentration and the more one-pointed the mind will be.

After one year of regular practice, you will surely be successful and will be able to sit for three hours at a time.

Even people with very stiff bodies should eventually be able to sit in padmasana if they persevere and do not slacken in their practice. For these people, the practices of *Pawanmuktasana* 1, 2 & 3 and the pre-meditation asanas illustrated in the book *Asana Pranayama Mudra Bandha* are recommended to quicken the limbering process. One should progressively prolong the duration of sitting by one minute daily. The ability to sit in padmasana does not only depend on the flexibility of the body, but also on the state of mind. If the practitioner believes in his own mind that he will eventually be able to sit in padmasana with perfect ease, the mind itself will help to prepare the body.

The classical meditation asanas are: padmasana (lotus pose), siddhasana (accomplished pose for men), siddha yoni asana (accomplished pose for women) and swastikasana (auspicious pose). Simplified meditation asanas for beginners are: sukhasana(easy pose) and ardha padmasana (half lotus pose). Subsidiary asanas which can also be usefully employed for meditation practices are: vajrasana (thunderbolt pose), bhadrasana (gracious pose) and shavasana (corpse pose). We have additionally included vipareeta karani asana (inverted pose) and nadanusandhana asana (discovering the psychic sound pose) in this section because they are used in certain specific meditation practices, although they are not suitable for most of the basic techniques of meditation.

The classical asanas are generally practised in conjunction with chin or jnana mudra which are illustrated in the following section on mudras.

Precautions

Do not on any account use undue force or strain to sit in an asana. If you find severe pain in the legs after some time in a meditation asana, slowly unlock the legs and massage them. The classical and simplified meditation poses should not be practised by persons suffering from sciatica or sacral infections. For these people only vajrasana, bhadrasana or shavasana should be employed.

Sukhasana (easy pose)

Sit with legs stretched in front of the body.

Fold the right foot under the left thigh.

Fold the left foot under the right thigh.

Place the hands on the knees in chin or jnana mudra.

Keep the head, neck and back upright and straight, but without strain. Close the eyes.

Relax the whole body. The arms should be relaxed and not held straight.

Benefits: This is the ideal meditation pose for beginners who have difficulty sitting in any of the classical meditation poses. Once the practitioner can comfortably do any of the other meditation asanas, sukhasana should be disregarded.

Practice note: Sukhasana is a relaxing posture which may be used after extended periods of sitting in siddhasana or padmasana.

Although sukhasana is said to be the simplest meditation posture, it is difficult to sustain for long periods of time unless the knees are close to the ground or on the ground. Otherwise most of the body weight is supported by the buttocks and backache develops. The other meditation asanas create a larger and steadier area of support.

Variation: For those who are extremely stiff, sukhasana may be performed sitting cross-legged with a belt or cloth tied around the knees and lower back.

Hold the spine upright.

Concentrate on the physical balance and equalising the weight on the right and left side of the body. A light, spacey feeling may be experienced.

While maintaining the posture, place the hands on the knees in chin or jnana mudra (see chapter 11).

Ardha Padmasana (half-lotus pose)

Sit with the legs straight in front of the body.

Bend one leg and place the sole of the foot on the inside of the opposite thigh.

Bend the other leg and place the foot on top of the opposite thigh.

Without straining, try to place the upper heel as near as possible to the abdomen. Adjust the position so that it is comfortable.

Place the hands on the knees in either chin or jnana mudra.

Keep the back, neck and head upright and straight.

Close the eyes and relax the whole body.

Benefits: As for padmasana, but at a reduced level.

Practice note: This meditation asana can be practised by people who can nearly do padmasana, but who have difficulty in attaining the final pose. It is to be practised in preference to sukhasana.

Padmasana (lotus pose)

Sit with the legs extended forward.

Fold one leg and place its foot on the top of the opposite thigh. The sole of the foot must be upward and the heel should touch the pelvic bone.

Fold the other leg and place its foot on the top of the other thigh.

Benefits: Padmasana allows the body to be held completely steady for long periods of time. It holds the trunk and head like a pillar with the legs as the firm foundation. As the body is steadied the mind becomes calm. This steadiness and calmness is the first step towards real meditation. Padmasana directs the flow of prana from mooladhara chakra in the perineum, to sahasrara chakra in the head, heightening the experience of meditation. This posture applies pressure to the lower spine which has a relaxing effect on the nervous system. The breath becomes slow, muscular tension is decreased and blood pressure is reduced. The coccygeal and sacral nerves are toned as the normally large blood flow to the legs is redirected to the abdominal region. This activity also stimulates the digestive process.

Siddhasana (accomplished pose for men)

Sit with the legs extended forward.

Fold the right leg and place the foot flat against your left thigh with the heel pressing the perineum, the area between the genitals and the anus.

Fold the left leg and place the left foot on the top of the right calf.

Press the pelvic bone with the left heel directly above the genitals.

Press the toes and the other edge of this foot into the space between the right calf and thigh muscles. It may be necessary to move and replace the right leg.

Grasp the right toes, either from above or below the left calf and move them up into the space between the left thigh and calf.

The legs should now be locked with the knees on the ground and the left heel directly above the right heel.
Make the spine steady, straight and erect, as though it were planted in the ground.

Benefits: Same as for siddha yoni asana.

Practice note: Siddhasana can be practised with either leg upward and is done in conjunction with jnana mudra or chin mudra. Many aspirants, especially beginners, find it easier to assume and maintain siddhasana for long periods when their buttocks are slightly elevated by a cushion.

Siddha Yoni Asana (accomplished pose for women)

Sit with the legs extended in front of the body.
Fold the right leg and place the sole of the foot against the upper left thigh.
Place the heel inside the labia majora of the vagina.
Fold the left leg and place its foot on the top of the right calf and thigh.
Pull the right toes up into the space between the calf and thigh.
Make the spine fully erect and straight, feel as though it were planted in the earth.

Benefits: Siddhasana and siddha yoni asana are meditation poses in which one can maintain the spinal steadiness necessary for long, productive meditation. They automatically activate two sexually related psychomuscular locks (moola bandha and vajroli mudra) which redirect sexual nervous impulses back up the spinal cord to the brain. They give the practitioner control over the sexual function, which he/she can use either for the maintenance of brahmacharya and the redirection of sexual energy upward for spiritual purposes, or to gain greater control over the sensory sexual function. Siddhasana and siddha yoni asana have a calming effect on the entire nervous system.

Practice note: This pose can be practised with either leg uppermost and is best practised without underwear. It is always used in conjunction with jnana or chin mudra. Many practitioners, especially beginners, find this pose easiest to assume and to maintain for long periods if they place a low cushion under their buttocks.

Swastikasana (auspicious pose)

Sit with the legs stretched in front of the body.

Fold the left leg and place the foot near the right thigh muscle.

Similarly bend the right leg and push the foot in the space between the left thigh and calf muscles.

The toes of both feet should lie between the thighs and calves of the two legs.

The hands can be placed on the knees in jnana mudra or in chin mudra, or they can be placed on the lap.

Benefits: As for siddhasana and siddha yoni asana, but at a lesser level since moola bandha and vajroli mudra are not automatically performed.

Practice note: This is the easiest asana to do among the classical meditation asanas. Outwardly this asana resembles siddhasana. It is, however, different in that the perineum is not pressed by the heel.

Vajrasana (thunderbolt pose)

Stand on the knees with the feet stretched back and the big toes crossed.

The knees should be together and the heels should be apart.

Lower the buttocks onto the insides of the feet. The heels will be at the sides of the hips.

Place the hands on the knees with the palms downwards.

Benefits: Vajrasana alters the flow of blood and nervous impulses in the pelvic and visceral regions. It increases the efficiency of the entire digestive system. It is the best meditation pose for people with sciatica or sacral infections.

Note: *Vajrasana is the prayer and meditation posture of Moslems and Japanese Buddhists.*

Bhadrasana (gracious pose)

Sit in vajrasana.

Separate the knees as far as is possible while keeping the toes in contact with the ground.

Then separate the feet just enough to allow the buttocks to rest flat on the floor, between the feet.

Try to separate the knees further but without strain.
Place the hands on the knees, palms downwards.

Benefits: This is predominantly a pose for spiritual aspirants as it has a stimulating influence on mooladhara chakra. It is an excellent meditation pose. The benefits are basically the same as for vajrasana.

Practice note: If necessary, a folded blanket may be placed under the buttocks. Whether a blanket is used or not, it is important that the buttocks rest firmly on the ground in order to stimulate mooladhara chakra.

Vipareeta Karani Asana (inverted pose)

Lie flat on the back with legs and feet together, arms at the sides with palms on the floor.
Use the arms as levers and raise the legs to a vertical position, but the back should be at an angle of 45° to the floor, with the trunk and neck slightly bent.
Use the hands to support the buttocks.

Breathing: Retain the breath inside while assuming and returning from this asana.
Breathe normally in the raised position.

Duration: Practise for a few seconds at first, gradually increasing to a few minutes over a period of weeks.

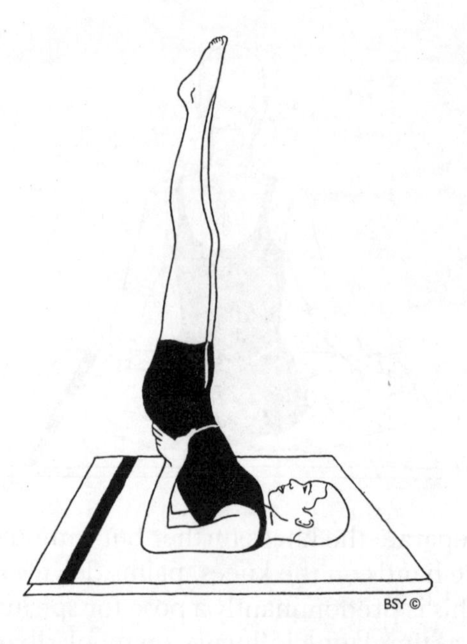

Contra-indications: Not to be practised by sufferers of enlarged thyroid, liver or spleen, high blood pressure or heart ailments.

Note: *Vipareeta karani asana provides the basis for vipareeta karani mudra, which is one of the important kriyas of kundalini yoga, used for awakening the flow of amrit, nectar, at vishuddhi chakra.*

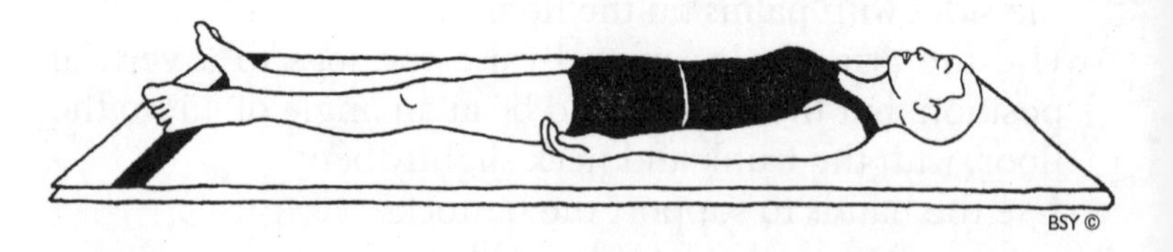

Shavasana (corpse pose)

Lie flat on the back with the arms beside and in line with the body and with palms facing upwards.

Move the feet slightly apart to a comfortable position.

Close the eyes and relax the whole body.

Do not move any part of the body even if discomfort occurs.

Benefits: Shavasana gives relaxation to the body and mind of the practitioner and is the best pose for yoga nidra and any other practices which require complete relaxation. It is an excellent pose for sleeping. This is, however, the one drawback of shavasana as a meditation pose. Many aspirants, especially beginners, tend to sleep if they attempt to practise meditation in shavasana.

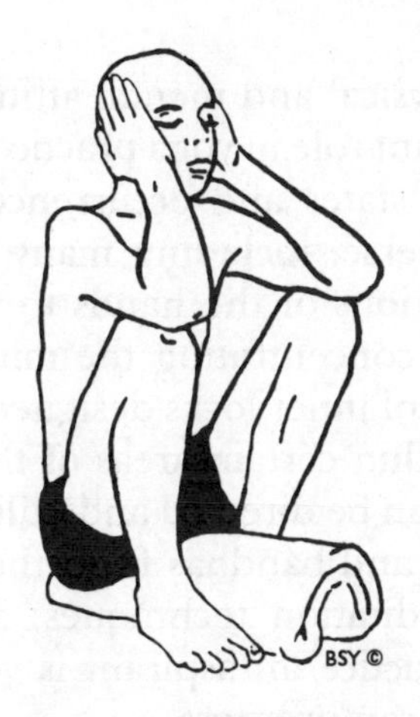

Nada Anusandhana Asana (discovering the psychic sound pose)

Squat on a rolled up blanket or cushion, keeping this beneath the buttocks and between the legs. The cushion should be high enough so that the back is not cramped. The head and spine must be straight.

Rest the elbows on the knees, and place the fingers on the top of the head and the thumbs in the ears.

Alternately, the index fingers can be used to seal the ears.

Note: *This pose is used in the practice of* nada yoga, *the yoga of psychic sounds.*

11

Mudras and Bandhas

Mudras are physical and mental attitudes which have a very important role in yoga practice in bringing about controlled psychic states and occurrences. The system of mudras is very diverse, including many types of practices ranging from positions of the hands to very complex and subtle methods of concentrating the mind. The system of bandhas is a group of inner locks designed to hold prana, or psychic energy, within certain areas of the body so that its pressurized force can be directed and utilized. Together the systems of mudras and bandhas form the basis of many of the important meditation techniques, and without their knowledge and practice an aspirant is very limited in the extent to which he can progress.

There are very many mudras and bandhas. In this chapter we have included only those which are preliminary to the meditation techniques given throughout this book. Many other more complex mudras will be listed in the later sections. However, these complexes or compound mudras are for the most part made up of combinations of the different primary mudras which we are taking up now.

Most of the mudras and bandhas are very powerful practices; they are intended to be so, for power is necessary for progress. They should, therefore, be learned very gradually and carefully so that they are not able to harm the body or mind of the practitioner. If any difficulty is experienced while attempting to practise the mudras or bandhas, or if any minor physical imbalance is noticed after practice has been initiated, then you should stop the practice and seek expert guidance.

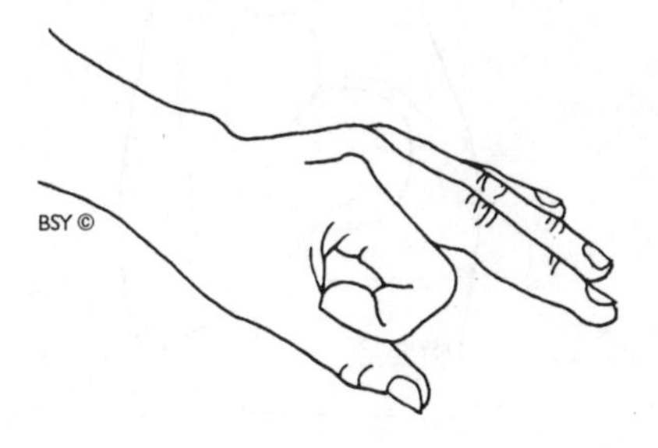

Jnana Mudra (psychic gesture of knowledge)

Assume a meditation asana.

Fold the index fingers of both hands so that they touch the inside roots of their respective thumbs.

Spread the other three fingers of each hand so that they are lightly apart.

Place the hands on the knees with the palms downwards and the three unbent fingers and thumb of each hand pointing towards the floor in front of the knees.

Variation: Some people prefer to practise jnana mudra with the tips of the thumb and index finger touching.

This is also correct.

Chin Mudra (psychic gesture of consciousness)

Chin mudra is performed in the same way as jnana mudra except that the palms of both hands face upwards while placed on the knees.

Benefits: Jnana mudra and chin mudra are simple but important psychoneural finger locks which make the meditation asanas such as padmasana, siddhasana, siddha yoni asana, sukhasana, vajrasana and others, complete and more powerful by redirecting the nervous impulses from the hands upwards to the body.

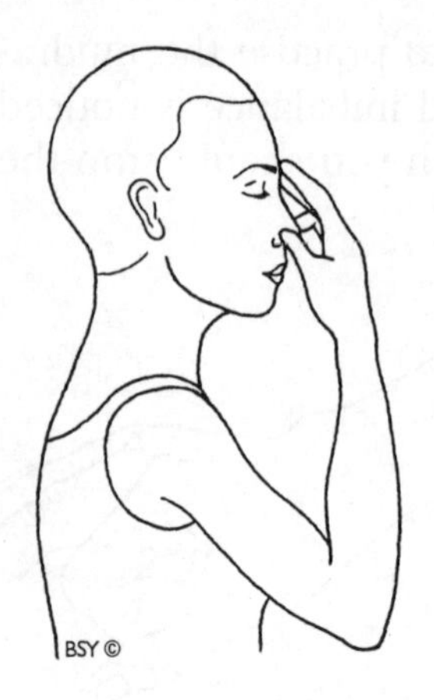

Nasagra Mudra (nosetip position)

Sit in a comfortable meditation posture.

Place the left hand on the left knee in jnana or chin mudra.

Hold the fingers of the right hand in front of the face.

Rest the tips of the middle and index fingers on the forehead at the eyebrow centre. These two fingers should be straight.

In this position the thumb should be beside the right nostril and the ring finger beside the left nostril.

These fingers are used to close off the nostrils. The little finger is not utilized in any way. The elbow of the right arm should preferably be in front of and near to the chest. The forearm should be nearly vertical.

Practice note: Some practitioners who do a lot of pranayama use a strip of cloth tied around their neck to support the right elbow. Nasagra mudra can also be practised with the hands reversed.

Note: Nasagra mudra *means 'the attitude of the nose'. Its purpose is to enable the practitioner to close off one nostril in order to inhale through the opposite one, as instructed by the rules of pranayama.*

Shanmukhi Mudra (closing the seven gates)

Sit in padmasana, siddhasana or siddha yoni asana.
Close the eyes and place the hands on the knees.
Inhale slowly and deeply.
Retain the breath inside and raise the hands to the face.
Close the ears with the thumbs, the eyes with the index fingers, the nostrils with the middle fingers and place the ring and small fingers above and below the lips to seal the mouth.
Retain the breath inside for as long as is comfortable while concentrating on bindu chakra.
Then release the middle fingers from against the nostrils and slowly exhale and inhale.
Reseal the nostrils and continue in this way.

Precautions: This mudra involves kumbhaka (breath retention) so it should be taken up very gradually and carefully.

Benefits: Shanmukhi mudra is most useful in inducing the state of pratyahara, or sense withdrawal. It helps the mind to turn inward to see itself.

Note: *The word* shanmukhi *is comprised of two roots:* shan *meaning 'seven' and* mukhi *meaning 'gates' or 'faces'. It is utilized in the practice of kundalini yoga.*

Khechari Mudra (tongue lock)

Technique 1: Raja yoga form

Close the mouth.

Roll the tongue backwards so that the normally lower surface touches the upper palate. Try to bring the tongue tip as far back as possible without strain.

One may optionally perform ujjayi pranayama in this position.

Perform for as long as possible. Beginners may find discomfort after a short time. They should relax the tongue for a few seconds and then repeat the tongue lock.

With practice, the tongue will automatically ascend into the sinuses to stimulate many vital nerve centres in the brain.

Breathing: Beginners can breathe normally during the practice of khechari mudra. Over a period of weeks and months they should gradually try to reduce the respiration rate, until after about two months or more the number of breaths per minute is only five to eight.

With further careful practice, preferably under expert guidance, the respiration rate can be further reduced.

Precautions: There are two forms of khechari mudra: the hatha yoga form and the raja yoga form.

The hatha yoga form should never be attempted without the direct guidance of an experienced guru, so whenever khechari mudra is referred to in this book the reader should understand it to mean the raja yoga or natural form of khechari mudra.

If khechari mudra is performed during physical exercise, a bitter secretion may be tasted. This can be harmful. The practitioner is therefore advised to discontinue this mudra if this bitter secretion is tasted.

Technique 2: Hatha yoga form

This form of khechari mudra should never be attempted without the guidance of a qualified guru, as the effects are irreversible.

The tendon beneath the tongue must be slowly cut week by week. Surgical methods or a sharpened stone can be utilized for this purpose.
The tongue is massaged for long periods daily by milking it. Butter, oil or any other type of lubricant may be used to make this action easier. This process should be continued for many months until it is possible to touch the eyebrows centre with the tip of the tongue.
When the tongue has reached the required elongation, full khechari mudra can be practised. The tongue is turned backwards towards the back of the mouth and carefully inserted through the back and upper cavity in the palate, as far as it will go. In this way, the air passages are effectively blocked, and the centre known as lalana chakra is awakened.

Precautions: Once the tongue is cut, control over the faculties of speech and swallowing are impaired, which cannot be reversed. Therefore, the hatha yoga technique was traditionally done only by those yogis who were totally dedicated to spiritual awakening and no longer involved with worldy life, as the effects make it unsuitable for interaction with the outside world.

Benefits: Khechari mudra has a very subtle influence. In the back of the mouth and the nasal cavity there are various pressure points and glands which are stimulated by this practice. These points influence the whole body. A number of glands are also massaged, stimulating the secretion of certain hormones and of saliva. This practice reduces the sensations of hunger and thirst, and induces a state of inner calm and stillness. It preserves the vitality of the body and is especially beneficial for inner healing. Ultimately, this mudra has the potential to stimulate prana and awaken kundalini shakti. In its full form this practice can cause the astral body to detach itself from the physical body. The consciousness thereby dwells in akasha, the space between the astral and physical planes. Khechari mudra was regarded as very important in the ancient yogic texts.

Note: *The name* khechari mudra *literally means 'the attitude of flying upward'. It is one of the most basic practices used in the advanced techniques of meditation, and its mastery is a prerequisite for anyone wishing to practise kundalini yoga.*

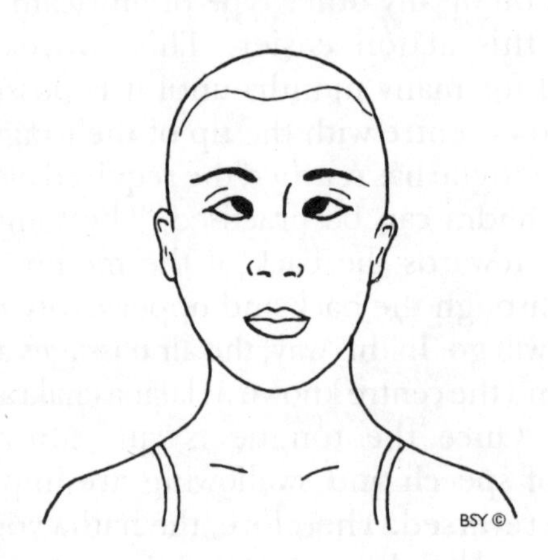

Shambhavi Mudra (eyebrow centre gazing)

Sit in any comfortable meditation pose.

Keep the back straight and place the hands on the knees in chin or jnana mudra.

Look forward at a fixed point.

Next, look upward as high as possible, without moving the head. Concentrate and focus the eyes on the eyebrow centre.

Benefits: Shambhavi mudra is a powerful technique for awakening ajna chakra, the seat of union between the lower and higher consciousness.

Physically it strengthens the muscles of the eyes. Mentally it brings about calmness of the mind and removes stress and anger.

Note: *The name* shambhavi mudra *literally means 'the attitude of Lord Shiva'. It is also known as bhrumadhya drishti, or eyebrow centre gazing.*

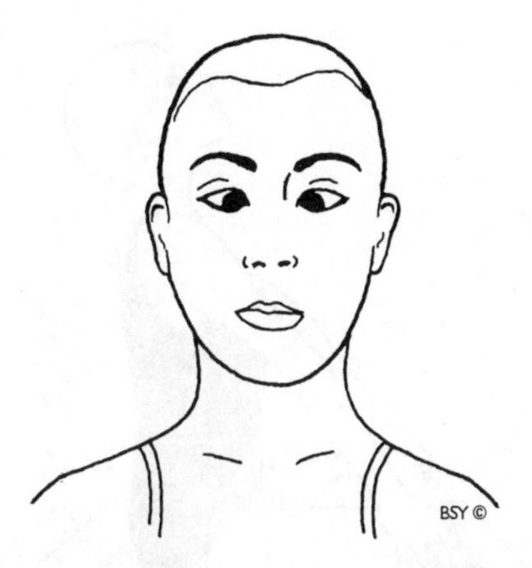

Agochari Mudra or Nasikagra Drishti (nosetip gazing)

Sit in any comfortable meditation pose.
Hold the spine erect and the head facing forwards.
Focus the two eyeballs on the tip of the nose.

Precautions: Do not strain the eyes. Slowly increase the duration over a period of weeks and months.

Benefits: This mudra, like shambhavi mudra, develops the powers of concentration. If performed with awareness for a long period, it helps to awaken mooladhara chakra and induce meditative states. It takes the practitioner into the psychic and spiritual planes of consciousness.

Note: *The name* agochari mudra *literally means 'the unknown attitude'. This practice is also known as nasikagra drishti or nosetip gazing, and is used in many meditation techniques.*

Akashi Mudra (awareness of inner space)

Sit in any comfortable meditation pose.
Fold the tongue back against the upper palate in khechari mudra.
Practise ujjayi pranayama and shambhavi mudra.
Simultaneously bend the head backwards, but not to the fullest extent; the head should not lean on the top of the shoulders behind the head.
Breathe slowly and deeply.

Benefits: This practice brings about calmness and tranquillity in the mind. When perfected, it arrests the thought processes and induces higher states of consciousness.

Practice note: At first ujjayi pranayama may irritate the throat in this inclined position of the head, but with practice it will become more comfortable.

Note: Akashi mudra *literally means 'the attitude of inner space'. It is a very powerful practice, and must be learned slowly and carefully.*

Vajroli/Sahajoli Mudra (thunderbolt/spontaneous psychic attitude)

Technique I: Simple form

Sit in siddha/siddha yoni asana or any comfortable meditation posture with the head and spine straight.

Place the hands on the knees.

Close the eyes and relax.

Take the awareness to the urethra.

Inhale, hold the breath in and try to draw the urethra upward. This muscle action is similar to holding back an intense urge to urinate.

The testes in men and the labia in women should move slightly due to this contraction.
Hold for as long as comfortable.
Exhale while releasing the contraction and relax.

Technique 2: Advanced form

The advanced form should never be attempted without the guidance of a qualified guru, otherwise permanent injury may result.
A silver tube about 12 inches or 30 cms long is inserted into the urethra. Through this water is drawn upward. When this is perfected, milk is drawn through the tube. After this is developed, honey and then mercury are drawn up.
After prolonged practice these liquids can be drawn into the urethra without the tube. At first the tube or catheter should only be inserted for 1 inch or 2½ cms. The distance should be slowly increased to 12 inches or 30 cms.

Precautions: There are two forms of vajroli mudra. The advanced form is only for male aspirants and can be dangerous if practised incorrectly. For this reason, whenever vajroli mudra is referred to in this book, it is the simple form which is intended.

Benefits: Vajroli/sahajoli mudra regulates and tones the entire uro-genital system and helps overcome psychosexual conflicts and unwanted sexual thoughts.
Through the practice of vajroli mudra the sexual energy gate in the body is controlled, allowing the aspirant to control his prana and to utilize it for spiritual awakening.

Note: *The word* vajroli *is derived from the Sanskrit root* vajra *which means 'thunderbolt', and* sahajoli *from the root* sahaj, *meaning 'spontaneous' and* oli *which means 'to cast up' or 'to fly up'. Vajroli is therefore the force which moves upward with the power of lightning, and sahajoli is the psychic attitude of spontaneous arousing. Vajra is the name of the nadi which connects the reproductive organs with the brain.*

Ashwini Mudra (horse gesture)

Technique 1: Rapid contraction

Sit in any comfortable meditation pose.

Relax the whole body and close the eyes.

Contract the sphincter muscles of the anus for a few seconds, then relax them for a few seconds.

Repeat the process as many times as possible.

Technique 2: Contraction with Antar Kumbhaka (inner retention)

Sit as for technique 1.

Inhale while simultaneously contracting the anus.

Practise antar kumbhaka (internal breath retention) while holding the contraction of the sphincter muscles.

Exhale while releasing the contraction of the anus.

Repeat for as long as you have time available.

Duration: Practise for as long as is comfortable. Do not strain.

Benefits: This practice strengthens the anal muscles and alleviates disorders of the rectum. By practising this mudra one is able to gain control of the sphincter muscles of the anus. Perfection of this mudra prevents the escape of pranic energy from the body. This energy can therefore be conserved and directed upwards for higher and more valuable purposes.

Practice note: Ashwini mudra is a preparatory practice for moola bandha.

Note: *The name* ashwini mudra *means literally 'the horse gesture'. It is so-called because the anal contraction resembles the movement a horse makes with its sphincter immediately after evacuation of the bowels.*

Moola Bandha (perineum contraction)

Sit in siddha/siddha yoni asana so that pressure is applied to the perineal/vaginal region.

Place the hands on the knees in jnana or chin mudra.

Close the eyes and relax the whole body.
Concentrate on the trigger point of mooladhara chakra.
Try to touch this point with your awareness, and then contract it.
Hold this contraction for as long as is possible, then slowly release it.
Relax for a few seconds, and then practise it again.

Precautions: Moola bandha must be perfected gradually and with great care. Do not strain while attempting it.

Benefits: In this bandha the region of mooladhara, located between the urinary and excretory organs, is contracted and pulled upwards. This forces the apana vayu (vital energy in the lower parts of the body below the navel) to flow upwards and thereby unite with the prana vayu (vital energy in the region between the larynx and the heart), thus generating vitality. The perfection of this practice leads to a spontaneous realignment of the physical, mental and psychic bodies.

Practice note: In the basic practice of moola bandha the aspirant is instructed to exert muscular contraction in the area associated with mooladhara chakra. Later, however, when the exact root point of mooladhara has become familiar to the practitioner, then the muscular contraction need not be employed and the aspirant can merely touch the correct point lightly with his awareness. If mastered completely, this subtle technique is far more powerful than the physical contraction, however all aspirants should utilize the muscular contraction in the initial stages of practice.

Note: *The word* moola *means 'root', and* bandha *means 'to lock'. This technique locks the psychic energy in the upper part of the psychic body and does not allow it to descend into the lower limbs. It also stimulates mooladhara chakra through mental compression, which helps in the awakening of kundalini.*

Ashwini-Vajroli/Sahajoli-Moola Alternation

Stage 1: Sit in a meditation pose, preferably siddhasana or siddha yoni asana. Practise jnana or chin mudra.
Perform the simple form of vajroli/sahajoli mudra.
Hold for a slow count of ten.
Release vajroli/sahajoli.
Then perform moola bandha, hold for a count of ten.
Release moola bandha.
Continue in this way for as long as possible.
On subsequent days increase the count from ten to fifteen or more.

Stage 2: Practise vajroli/sahajoli mudra.
Add moola bandha to vajroli.
Now practise ashwini as well.
Hold all three for a few seconds, then release ashwini, moola and vajroli/sahajoli, respectively.

Practice note: This practice is very important in assisting the aspirant to distinguish between ashwini mudra, vajroli/sahajoli mudra and moola bandha. It should be attempted only when one has learned the three basic techniques separately. Often aspirants do not learn to sense the subtle difference between these three kriyas in the early stages of practice, and they simply tense all of the muscles in the region no matter which technique they are attempting. This can destroy the efficacy of the three techniques when used as part of the advanced kriyas of kundalini yoga. The concentration should be on distinguishing the three separate areas of contraction. Practise daily until the three can be distinguished clearly from each other.

Jalandhara Bandha (throat lock)

Technique 1: Raja yoga form

Sit in a meditation pose which allows the knees to firmly touch the floor. Sukhasana is not suitable. Persons who cannot sit in padmasana, siddhasana, etc., can do jalandhara bandha while standing.

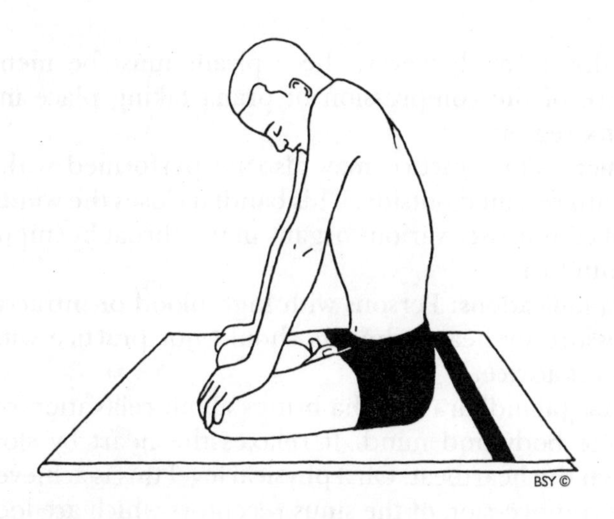

Place the palms on the top of the knees.
Relax the whole body and close the eyes.
Inhale deeply, retain the breath inside, bend the head forward and press the chin tightly against the chest at the sternum.
Straighten the arms and lock them in a fixed position.
Simultaneously hunch the shoulders upwards and forwards; this will ensure the arms remain locked.
The palms should remain on the knees.
This is the final pose.
Stay in the final pose for as long as the breath can be held comfortably.
Then relax the shoulders, bend the arms, slowly release the lock and raise the head.
Slowly exhale.
Repeat when the respiration returns to normal.

Technique 2: Kundalini yoga form

This is the same as the raja yoga form, except it is practised very subtly and without any tensing of the shoulders or arms.
The head is simply dropped forward till the chin touches the sternum.

In this form, however, the aspirant must be mentally aware of the compression of prana taking place in the trunk region.

Breathing: The practice may also be performed with the breath retained outside. This bandha closes the windpipe and compresses various organs in the throat by imposing a chin lock.

Contra-indications: Persons with high blood or intracranial pressure or heart ailments should not practice without expert advice.

Benefits: Jalandhara bandha brings about relaxation of the whole body and mind. It relaxes the heart by slowing down the heartbeat. On a physical level this is achieved by the compression of the sinus receptors which are located in the throat region. These receptors are sensitive to the blood pressure in the jugular vein which supplies blood in the brain. If the pressure is high the receptors send messages to the brain and heart, which are slowed down. If the pressure is low then the heart is speeded up in the same way. The receptors are pressure sensitive and so the compression they receive during jalandhara bandha slows down the heart and brings tranquillity to the mind.

The thyroid and parathyroid glands are massaged and their functioning improved. These glands, especially the thyroid, have wide influences on the human organism, growth, sexual functions and so on. The whole body consequently benefits from their enhanced efficiency.

This is a good practice for reducing and removing stress, anxiety and anger.

Practice note: Do not inhale or exhale until the chin lock and arm lock have been released and the head is upright.

Note: *The name* jalandhara bandha *means 'throat lock'. It is an important technique which compresses the pranic force in the trunk region of the body, which is useful in stimulating the kundalini energy.*

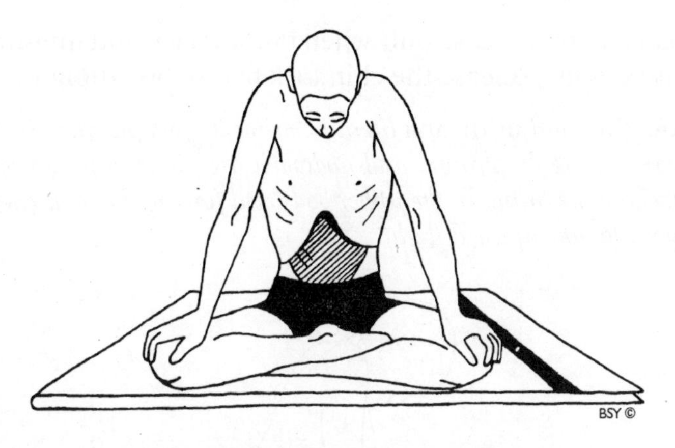

Uddiyana Bandha (abdominal contraction)

Sit in siddha/siddha yoni asana or padmasana with the spine erect and the knees resting on the floor.

Place the palms on the knees. Close the eyes and relax the whole body.

Exhale deeply and retain the breath outside.

Perform jalandhara bandha.

Then contract the abdominal muscles as far as possible inwards and upwards. This is the final position.

Hold this lock for as long as is comfortable.

Then slowly release the stomach muscles, followed by jalandhara bandha and inhale.

When the respiration is normal the process may be repeated.

Contra-indications: Not to be practised by persons suffering from heart disease, high blood pressure, colitis, stomach or intestinal ulcer, hernia, glaucoma and raised intracranial pressure. It should also be avoided by pregnant women.

Benefits: Uddiyana bandha stimulates the solar plexus which has many subtle influences on the distribution of energy throughout the body. It creates a suction pressure which reverses the flow of the sub-pranas, apana and prana, uniting them with samana and stimulating manipura chakra. Then there is an explosion of subtle force which travels upward through sushumna nadi.

Practice note: Practise only when the stomach and intestines are empty. Release the chin lock before breathing in.

Note: *The word* uddiyana *literally means 'to fly upwards'. In this bandha the diaphragm and abdomen are made to fly upward, locking the prana in the upper body and forcing the vital energy itself to take upward flight.*

Maha Bandha (the great lock)

Sit in a meditation asana, preferably padmasana, siddhasana or siddha yoni asana with the hands on the knees and the spine straight.

Close the eyes and relax the whole body.

Exhale slowly and completely.

Retain the breath outside.

Perform jalandhara bandha, then uddiyana bandha followed by moola bandha.

Hold the bandhas and the breath for as long as is comfortable.

Alternately the awareness may be centred on the three bandhas as they are retained.

Then release moola, uddiyana and jalandhara bandhas in this order.

Exhale a little more and then slowly inhale.

Exhale and inhale once or twice and repeat the practice.

Precautions: Maha bandha is a powerful combined practice. It should not be attempted until one has mastered the three bandhas individually and the preliminary stages of nadi shodhana pranayama.

Benefits: Maha bandha gives the benefits of all the three bandhas. It is a very powerful method used for stimulating the flow of psychic and spiritual energy, and for making the mind introverted in preparation for meditation.

Note: *Maha bandha, or the great lock, is really the combination of moola bandha, jalandhara bandha, uddiyana bandha and bahir kumbhaka (external breath retention) as they are practised in the techniques of pranayama.*

12

Pranayama

The control of vital and psychic energy is a matter of great concern to any practitioner of yoga, whether he be interested in it for therapeutic, health or spiritual purposes. The science of yoga is itself the science of life energy, and pranayama is the most direct method which has yet been found to adjust the energy flows within the human body.

Many people consider pranayama to be a physical practice of breath control, but this is not so. The main effects of pranayama manifests in the nervous system and in the subtle psychic energy body, and the control of breath is only the means of manipulating these finer processes. The breath is known as the 'thread of life', and depending on its actions the entire life process is refined, balanced, or else thrown out of proper order.

Pranayama serves as a basis for many types of meditation. It is used within the practices themselves; it prepares the aspirant's body and mind for the safe and successful practice of meditation, and it serves as a system for introverting the mind prior to sitting for meditation. It is of the utmost importance. We sincerely suggest that all persons intent on attaining success in meditation should first master the techniques of pranayama. It will help them greatly. However, a warning must be given. Pranayama is very powerful. Persons with any physical imbalance should never attempt it without expert guidance. This goes especially for those who are aged or who have coronary ailments. Additionally, if any irregular effects are noticed after one has started pranayama, then the practice should be immediately stopped and expert guidance sought. Furthermore, the techniques must be learned very slowly and gradually. Development of nadi shodhana is intended to take place over a long period of time. Never rush on to a new stage of practice until you have completely mastered those which precede it. If these suggestions are followed, the practice of pranayama will bring you many great benefits.

Nadi Shodhana Pranayama

Basic breath control on inhalation (pooraka), inner retention (antar kumbhaka), exhalation (rechaka) and outer retention (bahiranga kumbhaka) are the most important prerequisites for the successful practice of pranayama sadhana. Progressively practise each of the following techniques of nadi shodhana until they can be done without any strain or shortness of breath being felt. If any difficulty is encountered during your practice, stop until you can gain the advice of a competent yoga teacher. Nadi shodhana, if practised properly and without strain, is the greatest of pranayamas for purifying the body and stilling the mind.

Nadi Shodhana Pranayama (psychic network purification)
Technique 1: Preparatory practice

Sit in any comfortable meditation asana, preferably siddhasana/siddha yoni asana or padmasana.

Close the eyes and become aware of the whole body.

Keep the head and spine straight.

Relax the whole body and close the eyes.

Now shift the attention to the natural breathing process taking place within the body.

Become aware of every inhalation and exhalation.

Adopt nasagra mudra with the right hand, placing the index and middle fingers on the eyebrow centre, and place the left hand on the knee in chin or jnana mudra.

Inhale through both nostrils.
Close the right nostril with the thumb.
Inhale and exhale slowly through the left nostril 5 times.
The rate of inhlation/exhalation should be normal.
Be aware of each breath.
After 5 breaths release the pressure of the thumb on the right nostril and press the left nostril with the ring finger, blocking the flow of air.
Inhale and exhale through the right nostril 5 times, keeping the respiration rate normal.
Lower the hand and breathe 5 times through both nostrils together.
This is one round.
Practise 5 rounds for a few minutes.
After practising for 15 days go on to technique 2.

Technique 2: Alternate nostril breathing

In this technique the duration of inhalation/exhalation is controlled.
Close the right nostril and breathe in through the left nostril. At the same time count mentally , "1, Om; 2, Om; 3, Om", until the inhalation ends comfortably. This is the basic count.
Close the left nostril with the ring finger, relase the pressure of the thumb on the right nostril and while breathing out through the right nostril, simultaneously count, "1, Om; 2, Om; 3, Om". The time for inhalation and exhalation should be equal.
Inhale through the right nostril and exhale through the left nostril, keeping the same count.
This is one round.
Practise 10 rounds.

Ratio and timing: After a few days increase the length of inhalation/exhalation by one count. Continue increasing by one count, without straining, until the count of 24:24 is reached. Do not force the breath beyond its natural capacity. If there is any discomfort reduce the count.

After perfecting this ratio, it may be changed to 1:2. For example, inhale for a count of 4 and exhale for a count of 8, up to the count of 12:24.

When this technique can be performed with complete ease move on to technique 3.

Technique 3: with Antar Kumbhaka (inner retention)

In this technique antar kumbhaka or internal breath retention is introduced.

Inhale through the left nostril for a count of 5, close both nostrils and retain the air in the lungs for a count of 5.

The glottis may be slightly contracted to hold the air in the lungs.

Open the right nostril, inhale slightly and then exhale for a count of 5.

Inhale through the right nostril for a count of 5 and retain the breath for a count of 5 with both nostrils closed.

Open the left nostril, inhale slightly and then exhale for a count of 5.

This is one round.

Practise 10 rounds.

Ratio and timing: The maintenance of a strict ratio during inhalation, kumbhaka and exhalation is of the utmost importance. The ratio will change as the ability to hold the breath for longer periods of time develops. After mastering the ratio of 1:1:1, increase the ratio to 1:1:2. For example, inhale for a count of 5, perform internal kumbhaka for a count of 5 and exhale for a count of 10. After some weeks of practice, when this ratio has been mastered, increase the ratio to 1:2:2. Inhale for a count of 5, do internal kumbhaka for a count of 10 and exhale for a count of 10.

After mastering this ratio, gradually increase the count by adding one unit to the inhalation, 2 units to the retention and 2 units to the exhalation. The count of one round will be 6:12:12. When this has been perfected and there is no discomfort, increase the count to 7:14:14. Gradually increase the count over a period of one or two years to 24:48:48. Thereafter, gradually increase the ratio to 1:3:2, and then 1:4:2. Then move on to technique 4.

Technique 4: with Antar and Bahir Kumbhaka (internal and external retention)

In this technique bahir kumbhaka or outer breath retention is introduced.

Inhale through the left nostril, retain the breath inside as for technique 3, then exhale through the right nostril.

After exhalation, when the lungs are deflated as much as possible, close both nostrils and hold the breath out for the chosen count.

The glottis may be slightly contracted to hold the air out of the lungs.

Exhale slightly through the right nostril immediately before inhaling to release the lock on the lungs and the glottis.

Inhale slowly through the right nostril, retain the breath inside, then exhale through the left nostril.

Again hold the breath outside to the count, with both nostrils closed. This is one round. Practise 5 rounds.

Ratio and timing: The ratio should begin as 1:4:2:2 for inhalation, internal retention, exhalation and external retention. The duration of inhalation should be slowly increased from 5 to 6, then from 6 to 7 and so on, and the duration of exhalation and retention should be adjusted accordingly.

Advanced practice: Nadi shodhana may be practised in conjunction with jalandhara, moola and uddiyana bandhas. First practise jalandhara bandha with internal breath retention only. Once perfected, combine jalandhara bandha with external breath retention. Then introduce moola bandha with jalandhara during internal, then external retention. When this has been mastered, apply uddiyana bandha on external retention only.

Duration: 5 to 10 rounds or 10 to 15 minutes daily.

Benefits: Nadi shodhana ensures physical health and mental vitality. It clears pranic blockages and balances ida and pingala nadis causing sushumna nadi to flow, which leads to deep states of meditation and spiritual awakening.

Practice note: Many sadhakas use a mantra such as *Om Namah Shivaya* or Gayatri repeated a certain number of times to count the duration of breath. This combines the benefits of japa with those of pranayama, and also makes the practice easier. Nadi shodhana is most effective if it is followed by a concentrated type of meditation practice such as antar trataka or chidakasha dharana.

Ujjayi Pranayama (the psychic breath)

Practise the simple form of khechari mudra.

Contract the glottis in the throat.

When breathing under these circumstances a very soft snoring sound should automatically come from the throat region. It is like the sound of a sleeping baby.

One should feel that one is breathing through the throat and not the nose.

This practice can be done for a long time and during almost all meditation techniques, the exception being meditation practices that require audible mantra repetition.

Benefits: This is a very simple pranayama practice, but one which has powerful and subtle effects on the pranic body. It is very useful for practising during meditation, for it brings about great calmness of mind. When ujjayi pranayama is practised a slight pressure is exerted on the carotid sinuses in the throat which eventually lowers the blood pressure. This in turn reduces the tension and thought processes in the mind. In this way ujjayi pranayama is conducive to meditation practices.

Practice note: Ujjayi pranayama is generally practised in conjunction with khechari mudra, which helps to minimize the tendency for the throat to become sore.

Bhastrika Pranayama (bellows breath)

Technique 1: Basic method

Sit in a steady meditation pose with the hands in jnana or chin mudra.

Close the eyes and relax completely.

Be sure that the spine is perfectly erect and the head is level and centred.

Take a deep breath in and breathe out forcefully through the nose.

Immediately breathe in and out with the same force.

Count 10 breaths. This is one round.

Practise up to 10 rounds.

Practice note: Gradually increase the speed, keeping the breath rhythmical. Inhalation and exhalation must be equal.

Technique 2: Left, right and both nostrils

Sit in any comfortable meditation asana.

Perform nasagra mudra (see page 122), closing the right nostril with the right thumb.

Breathe in slowly through the left nostril.

Then begin rapid exhalations and inhalations as in technique 1.

Count up to 20 breaths.

The last exhalation should be slightly more forced and prolonged.

Close the left nostril, open the right and breathe in deeply and slowly through the right.

Begin rapid exhalations and inhalations through the right nostril, counting up to twenty.

The last exhalation should be deeper and prolonged.

After breathing through the right nostril, release nasagra mudra and place the hand on the knee.

Repeat the same process breathing through both nostrils.

This is one round, consisting of left, right and both nostrils together.

Practise 5 rounds.

Technique 3: with Antar Kumbhaka

Commence bhastrika in the left nostril and continue for 30 breaths.

Then inhale deeply through the left nostril, close both nostrils and hold the breath for as long as is comfortable.

Exhale fully through the left nostril.

Close the left nostril and open the right. Practise 30 rapid breaths.

Then inhale fully through the right nostril, close both nostrils, and hold the breath for as long as possible.

Exhale through the right nostril, release nasagra mudra and practise 30 bhastrika breaths through both nostrils.

After the last exhalation, inhale again fully through both nostrils, hold the breath in kumbhaka for as long as is comfortable, then exhale again through both nostrils.

This is one complete round.

Perform up to 10 rounds.

Do not strain.

Technique 4: with Antar Kumbhaka and Jalandhara Bandha

Practise technique 3. Increase the number of breaths to 40.

Practise jalandhara bandha during antar kumbhaka.

Equalize the duration of kumbhaka through the left and right nostrils. Practise a maximum of 10 rounds.

Technique 5: with Antar Kumbhaka, Jalandhara and Moola Bandhas

Practise technique 4. Increase the number of breaths to 50.

Include moola bandha with jalandhara bandha.

Increase the duration of kumbhaka.

Practise up to 10 rounds.

Technique 6: with Bahir Kumbhaka and Maha Bandha

The number of breaths may be increased up to 100.

Bahir kumbhaka (external retention) is practised instead of antar kumbhaka (internal retention). Hold for as long as possible.

Maha bandha is performed during kumbhaka, i.e. jalandhara, uddiyana and moola bandhas together.
Practise 10 rounds.

Precautions: A feeling of faintness or perspiration indicates that the practice is being executed incorrectly. Avoid violent respiration, facial contortion and excessive shaking of the body, as these also indicate incorrect practice.
One should be relaxed during the entire technique.
Beginners should take to its practice cautiously, preferably under expert guidance.

Contra-indications: Bhastrika should not be practised by people with high blood pressure, vertigo, circulatory problems or any coronary or respiratory ailment.

Benefits: This is one of the important pranayamas for meditation, as it purifies and forges the mind and nervous system by a process of oxygenation.
Bhastrika makes the mind introverted and one-pointed, and so it is very usefully practised just before one sits for meditation.

Practice note: Bhastrika pranayama should be followed immediately by a meditation practice such as japa, chidakasha dharana or antar mouna.

Note: *The word* bhastrika *literally means 'the bellows', as used by a blacksmith to heat metal.*

Kapalbhati Pranayama (frontal brain cleansing breath)

Technique I: Basic method

Sit in a steady meditation pose with the hands in jnana or chin mudra.
Close the eyes and relax the whole body.
Perform a series of rapid respirations with the emphasis on exhalation; practise to the speed of about one breath per second, for 10 breaths.
The exhalation should be strong and forced, and the inhalation completely automatic, as if it is occurring of its own accord.

When this can be done comfortably, increase the number of breaths to 20.

Technique 2: with Antar Kumbhaka

Practise 20 breaths as for the basic method.

On completion of the last exhalation, breathe in fully, hold the breath inside for as long as comfortable, then exhale completely.

Practise 5 rounds.

Technique 3: with Antar Kumbhaka, Jalandhara and Moola Bandhas

Repeat technique 2, but during antar kumbhaka, practise jalandhara and moola bandhas. Do not strain.

Increase the number of breaths up to 30 per round, then to 50 per round.

Practise up to 10 rounds.

Technique 4: with Bahir Kumbhaka and Maha Bandha

Practise 50 breaths.

Then inhale slowly and deeply, exhale completely and practise maha bandha.

Keep your awareness in the region of chidakasha.

You can bounce your awareness off the front, side and back walls of chidakasha, and also off the floor and ceiling.

Retain this attitude for as long as is comfortably possible.

Then release maha bandha, exhale slightly and slowly inhale.

Take a few natural breaths if necessary, and then repeat.

At first practise only 2 rounds.

Practise up to 10 rounds.

Precautions: Kapalbhati should be learned only after one has mastered bhastrika pranayama. This is a very powerful technique. Be careful not to strain.

Contra-indications: Kapalbhati is not for people with high blood pressure, vertigo, coronary or respiratory ailments or any related type of disease.

Benefits: This is one of the best preparatory techniques for meditation. It completely voids the mind of all thoughts and visions, and makes the practitioner completely introverted spontaneously. It will increase the efficacy of any meditation practice performed after it and will greatly help the practitioner to ascend to subtle realms of awareness. This power is also its drawback, however, and so it should be learned and practised with great care.

Practice note: After the end of your daily practice of kapalbhati, practise chidakasha dharana for at least ten minutes.

Note: *The Sanskrit word* kapal *means 'cranium' or 'forehead' and* bhati *means 'light' or 'splendour' and also 'perception' or 'knowledge'. Hence kapalbhati is the practice which brings a state of light or clarity to the frontal region of the brain.*

Bhramari Pranayama (humming bee breath)

Sit in a meditation pose with the hands in jnana or chin mudra.

Inhale fully through both nostrils.

Retain the breath inside and perform jalandhara and moola bandhas.

Hold the retention and bandhas for a count of five.

Then release the bandhas and raise the two hands to the level of the ears.

Plug the ears with the index fingers, keeping the other fingers lightly clenched and the elbows extended straight out. Keep the mouth closed with the teeth apart.

Slowly exhale while producing a long, continuous humming sound like that of a bee.

Feel the vibrations; be conscious only of this sound in your head. After exhalation, lower the hands, inhale and repeat the practice.

Start by practising 5 rounds, and add one round daily.

Precautions: Bhramari pranayama should never be practised in the prone position, for this can place great tension on the glottis.

Benefits: Bhramari stimulates and awakens the awareness of the nada, the subtle sounds within the practitioner. It relieves cerebral tension, removes anger, anxiety and frustration and lowers the blood pressure.

Note: *The name* bhramari *literally means 'the bee'. This is the humming pranayama which is used primarily in the practice of nada yoga, the yoga of psychic sounds.*

For more information on these practices refer to *Asana Pranayama Mudra Bandha* and *Prana Pranayama Prana Vidya*, published by Bihar School of Yoga.

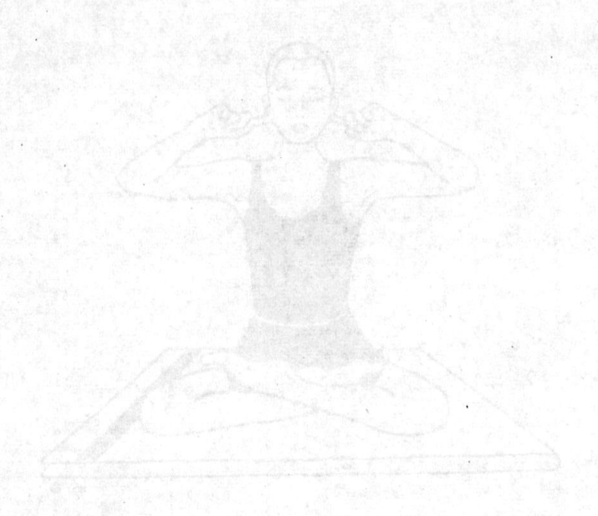

Practices for Meditation

13

Japa Yoga

Of all the systems of yoga used to induce pratyahara and intended to lead eventually to samadhi, japa yoga is the easiest and safest and can be practised by anyone at any time and under any conditions. The word *japa* itself means 'to rotate'. Japa yoga means union of the self with the highest existence through the rotation of consciousness.

A mantra is the first requirement for japa yoga. A mantra is a grouping of sound vibrations which have an effect on the mental and psychic consciousness of man. Tradition says it is best if it is given by a guru or in a dream. An important point is that the mind should be fully impressed by this mantra. When the mantra is spoken verbally or mentally, the sound vibrations create a certain form inside the human being. This is the inner or psychic symbol and it has a physical manifestation.

A mala or rosary is the second requirement for most types of japa. A mala is a string of small beads, usually 108 in number and separated from each other by a special kind of knot which is known as the *brahmagranthi* or knot of creation. At one point in the mala there is one extra bead, known as the *sumeru* or summit of the mala, which is offset from the continuity of the main loop of the mala. The significance of this sumeru bead is often lost to modern day practitioners of japa, but its importance cannot be overemphasized. The purpose of the sumeru is that while practising japa the mind often tends to become distracted from the mantra, either towards extraneous thoughts in the case of beginners, or unconscious and psychic phenomena in the case of more advanced practitioners. When this occurs, the rotation of the mala becomes spontaneous or automatic, continuing without awareness until the fingers reach the offset sumeru bead, which brings the awareness back to the japa in hand, so to speak.

In japa there is a continued rotation of consciousness centred on the mantra and the mind becomes concentrated and relaxed, which tends to bring all the physical and mental faculties of man to their most efficient working state. It should be pointed out, incidentally, that during the practice of japa the mind should not be forced to concentrate on the repetition of the mantra. The repetition of the mantra should seem to be a natural process emanating from within, and the mind should only be an unconcerned observer of this spontaneous process. When other thoughts enter the mind during the practice of japa, and they surely will, the awareness of the practitioner should watch these also as they come and go, feeling himself to be an unconcerned observer of them. He should not, however, let these thoughts distract him from the practice in hand and should continue his practice while watching these outside thoughts.

Types of japa

Japa is subdivided into four types, as follows:

1. *Baikhari* (audible): The beginner should practise his mantra in baikhari or audible japa, and by producing sound vibrations the brain will be gradually steadied and charged. After some weeks of this practice, the mind becomes quiet. By the practice of japa one can bring about a psychic condition in which the conceptualization of a psychic symbol becomes very easy. If you want to meditate on a particular object but find it difficult, practise baikhari or audible japa for about one hour and then sit for meditation.

2. *Upanshu* (whispering): Here the mantra is whispered in such a way that only the practitioner can hear it. There is a lip movement but almost no sound. This stage is more subtle than baikhari japa, and brings the mind to a point where it can go on the manasik japa. Upanshu japa is usually done by those people who want to practise the mantra for eight or ten hours a day for a specific purpose. According to mantra shastra, the science of mantra, a mantra can be used for correcting the errors of destiny. Whether it is true or not some people believe in it and there are certain mantras which are repeated especially for physical purposes.
3. *Manasik* (mental): Manasik japa should not be practised unless baikhari and upanshu have been mastered. Those who do not have a steady mind cannot make substantial progress without these preliminary practices. Manasik japa is both the most subtle and the most common form of japa. For persons who are ready for it, it is also the most powerful form. It is said by the sages and scriptures that the steady and devoted practice of manasik japa is enough to lead to enlightenment.
4. *Likhit* (written): This is usually prescribed for the aspirant who has successfully performed other practices of japa with a degree of progress in concentration. The practice of likhit japa is writing the mantra down in a note book hundreds of times in red, blue or green ink. The letters should be as small as possible and written with utmost care, concentration and a sense of beauty and proportion. The smaller the letters, the more the concentration. Likhit japa is always combined with manasik japa because the writing of a mantra requires simultaneous mental repetition of it.

If you have a mantra, a good way to practise it is to divide the practice and to do three parts in baikhari, two parts in upanshu and one part in manasik. The Hindu tradition says that once a person is initiated into a mantra he should continue it throughout his life. Japa yoga is a certain and sure path, though a long one. It enhances all other types of sadhana and gives the sadhaka unshakeable steadiness in his progress in spiritual life.

Japa anusthana

Anusthana means performance, observance or accomplishment of an act, the resolve to do a particular act with absolute discipline. Anusthana can pertain to japa and then it is called japa anusthana. Japa anusthana can be practised for two purposes: either for the purification of the self for spiritual progress through physical, mental and psychic discipline, or for the attainment of selfish purposes on the physical plane of consciousness.

Baikhari japa anusthanas are often practised in chorus by groups of aspirants. In some places in India one mantra is sung without a break for years together. In Rishikesh, since 1943, the maha mantra *Hare Rama, Hare Krishna* has been sung continuously for twenty-four hours daily, year after year. There have been no breaks at all, not even for one minute. Mantra chanting creates an atmosphere woven with powerful currents.

Japa anusthanas are very popular in India and are the best type of anusthana for people whose minds tend to wander. During the month of Shravan, Hindus all over the world follow a tradition of plucking leaves off the bilva tree for the purpose of writing mantras on these leaves. Each leaf has three petals and people usually write the mantra *Om Namah Shivaya* on these leaves with red powder paste. Then the leaves are offered to a deity. This kind of practice continues for a month during which they write all day.

Manasik japa anusthanas using the guru mantra are the most popular type of anusthana and this type is most effective for use by the spiritual aspirant. Before commencing this practice the aspirant should set a certain goal for himself, for example, to practise 10,800 mantras a day for ten days. He should keep track of the number of malas that he practises and not cease until he has attained his goal.

Sumirani japa is a type of japa that is practised on a twenty-seven bead mala, which is perfectly continuous and without a sumeru bead. A very important practice, it must be done as anusthana 24 hours a day for a set period, during which the mala should never leave the aspirant's hand. The aim in this type of anusthana is not to repeat the mantra. The mantra must come up automatically from within with the rotation of the twenty-seven bead mala. Even in sleep the mala should rotate.

Mantras

For a list of mantras used in various religions world-wide, refer to the appendix.

Rules and suggestions for japa

- Select any mantra or name of God, preferably one given by your guru. If you have no mantra, use *Om*, which is the universal mantra suitable for all. Repeat it from 108 to 1,080 times daily; that is, practise one to ten malas.
- Use a rudraksha or tulsi mala of 108 beads plus the sumeru for your guru mantra. For tantric mantras, a crystal mala can be used.
- Use only the middle finger and thumb of the right hand for rolling the beads; the index and little fingers should not touch the beads.
- Japa is best practised in a steady meditation asana such as padmasana or siddhasana/siddha yoni asana. The right hand with the mala can either rest on the right knee with the mala placed on the floor in front of the knee, or else the right hand can be held in front of the centre of the chest. In this case, the mala can be supported by a cloth bag hung on a strap from the shoulders and/or the right wrist can be supported by a cloth strap hung around the neck.
- The mala should not be visible to others. Keep it in a cloth or silk bag when it is not in use. A japa mala should not be worn.

- Do not cross the sumeru terminal bead while rolling the beads. Turn the mala around when you come to the sumeru.
- Do mental japa for some time. If the mind wanders while practising manasik japa, do baikhari for some time and then come back to mental japa again as soon as possible.
- Pronounce each letter of the mantra correctly and distinctly. Do not repeat it too fast or too slow. Increase the speed only when the mind starts to wander.
- Do not wish for any worldly objects while doing japa. Feel that your heart is being purified and the mind is becoming steady by the power of the mantra.
- Keep your guru mantra a secret; never disclose it to anyone.
- Carry on the current of japa mentally all the times, whatever work you may be engaged in.
- If possible the aspirant should face to the north or the east while practising.
- Japa is intended to bring the hidden, subconscious elements, fears and desires of the mind to the surface in the form of images and thoughts. When these come into your mind, watch them as an unaffected spectator, but do not lose track of your japa.

Japa repetition brings about chitta shuddhi or mental purification in which samskaras (past impressions) and vasanas (future desires) are naturally eliminated. This chitta shuddhi is very important in the preliminary stages of spiritual life because if the samskaras and vasanas are not removed early, they will become great obstructions later.

In yoga it is said that there are three great obstacles to meditation: impurity, ignorance and a distracted state of mind. These three obstacles can most easily be removed through japa practice, by constant and unbroken awareness of the mantra. In japa there should be no strain or tense concentration. Only by continuous and relaxed japa awareness does the mind detach itself automatically from the externalized state.

Our real nature is not our normal state of anxiety, excitement and tension. Our nature is samadhi, pure consciousness, calmness, tranquillity, equanimity. We can use the comparison of a mirror that is obscured by layers of grime and dust. Clean the mirror and its natural quality will be revealed, which is to reflect all objects. It is the restlessness of the mind which causes all unhappiness and complexes, but these are only impositions. Calm and purify the mind through your sadhana and experience your true self.

In meditation we are not trying to force the mind; we try to avoid effort at concentration. What we want is simply relaxed awareness. Not concentration as such, but we must try just to be aware; that is, we have one-pointed awareness though we do not fight with or try to suppress our thoughts. We remain only an impartial witness to them.

Sometimes the samskaras that come up will be so simple that you will wonder why they came up at all. This only means that your awareness of the mantra is superficial. When your mantra awareness is so deep that it occupies all of your awareness, then deeper and more important thoughts will surface. These will usually follow a few moments of thoughtlessness due to the one-pointedness of your consciousness. So you must relax yourself into japa and everything will happen automatically. Do not worry yourself about distractions. Everything will come in time just through japa and awareness of the mantra.

14

Mantra Siddhi Yoga

The following practices are actually preparation kriyas for kundalini yoga, since they awaken the practitioner's awareness of the chakras and enable him to locate their exact positions.

The common link between all of the following practices is that they are based firmly on the different basic types of japa which we discussed in the last section. The practices in this group additionally make up a special anusthana which can bring great benefits to the serious and relatively advanced practitioner with a week to a month to spend uninterruptedly on his sadhana. When done in this way, the sadhana is known as mantra siddhi yoga and is very useful in the tuning and stimulation of the psychic centres.

Technique 1: Manipura Shuddhi

Stage 1: Awareness of manipura

Sit in a meditation asana.

Centre your attention in manipura chakra. Be aware of your breath moving in and out of the manipura region.

Feel the breath expanding and contracting in the navel area. Do not concentrate, just be aware.

Practise this for 10 minutes.

Stage 2: Awareness of mantra

Keep the awareness of the natural breath in manipura chakra.

Mentally repeat *Om* when you inhale and when you exhale.
Practise for 10 minutes.

Technique 2: Anahata Shuddhi

Stage 1: Awareness of anahata

Sit in a meditation asana and become aware of anahata chakra.
Be aware of your breath moving in and out of the anahata region.
Continue for 10 minutes.

Stage 2: Awareness of mantra

Become aware of the chest expanding and contracting with the natural breath.
Mentally recite *Om* with every inhalation and exhalation.

Technique 3: Vishuddhi Shuddhi

Stage 1: Awareness of Om in the psychic breath

Sit in a meditation asana.
Become aware of the your psychic breath as it moves in and out of your body.
Your psychic breath will automatically travel upwards in your body with every inhalation and then downwards with every exhalation.
Be aware of this breath as it passes up and down through the throat and listen to the soft *Om* sound that it makes.
Continue for 5 minutes.

Stage 2: Awareness of mantra in frontal passage

Now with inhalation be aware of the breath and the mantra passing up from the navel area to the throat.
With exhalation the breath and the mantra will return to the navel area.

Stage 3: Vishuddhi to brumadhya awareness

Now be aware of the breath and the mantra ascending from vishuddhi to the unknown point in the base of the brain, which is located directly behind the top of your nose.

Then the breath and mantra will descend back to vishuddhi, before beginning their return journey upwards again to the unknown point.
Practise for 5 minutes.

Stage 4: Navel to brumadhya awareness

Now with inhalation watch the breath and the mantra rising from the navel area and passing through vishuddhi up to the unknown point in the base of the brain.
With exhalation they will pass back down to the navel area through vishuddhi.
Practise for 10 minutes.

Technique 4: Pingala Shuddhi and Ida Shuddhi

Sit in a meditation asana.
Mentally direct your breath through the right or pingala nostril.
Be aware of the breath passing through the right nostril, and synchronize the mantra *Om* with inhalation and exhalation.
Count the breaths, starting at 150 and counting down to zero.
Then repeat while breathing through the left or ida nostril.

Technique 5: Anuloma Viloma

Sit in a meditation asana.
Breathe in deep natural breaths.
Inhale through the left or ida nostril and exhale through the right or pingala nostril.
This alternation will occur through willpower alone. It is a psychic alternation.
Now inhale through the right nostril and exhale through the left.
Then again inhale through the left or ida nostril.
Continue alternating in this manner, simultaneously being aware of the *Om* sound of the breath.
Practise for 108 breaths.
A mala can be used in the right hand to count the breaths.

Technique 6: Prana Shuddhi

Sit in a meditation asana.
Breathe in deep natural breaths.
Inhale through both nostrils and be aware of the two streams of breath joining where the two nasal passages meet at the eyebrow centre, called trikuti.
The movement is V-shaped through the conical psychic passage (described in chapter 4).
Exhale in the same way from trikuti through the two nostrils; again the movement is V-shaped.
Now add awareness of the mantra *Om* to the breath.

Technique 7: Vak Shuddhi

Stage 1: Om chanting from manipura

Sit in a steady meditation asana throughout this practice.
Inhale deeply and naturally.
With a long exhalation chant *Om* audibly and quite deeply, chanting as low a note as possible.
The energy of the *Om* mantra will radiate upwards and outwards from manipura.
Continue this practice for 15 minutes.

Stage 2: Continuous Om chanting

Inhale deeply.
Retain the breath inside for one second.
Then, as you exhale, chant *Om* as many times in succession as is comfortable.
Establish a rhythm of chanting *Om Om Om Om*...
When you inhale repeat *Om* mentally so that there is no break in the natural flow of *Om*.
Practise for 15 minutes.

Technique 8: Trikuti Sandhanam

Feel the mantra *Om* emanating from trikuti with every pulsation.
Keep a constant, unbroken awareness of trikuti, the pulsating nadi located there, and the mantra.
Practise for 15 minutes.

Technique 9: Chakra Shuddhi

Prepare two malas, one with 11 beads and one with 21 beads. Two sumirani malas of 21 beads can be used by tying knots in them.

Sit in a steady meditation pose.

Hold the mala with 21 beads in the right hand and the 11 beaded mala in the left hand.

Centre your awareness on mooladhara chakra.

You must feel the mantra *Om* pulsating slowly and deeply there. The pulsations will feel as if the chakra is being struck from inside.

The mantra will pulsate at mooladhara 21 times. Each time it pulsates you will rotate one bead with your right hand.

After 21 pulsations, move your awareness to swadhisthana and pulsate the mantra there 21 times.

Continue upward in this manner through manipura, anahata, vishuddhi, ajna, bindu and sahasrara chakras.

After the 21st pulsation at sahasrara, rotate one bead on the mala in your left hand and return again to mooladhara.

Continue for 11 full rounds, by which time you will have reached the end of the mala in your left hand. This should take about 45 minutes.

15

Ajapa Japa

The constant repetition of a mantra is known as japa. Japa becomes ajapa (spontaneous) japa when the mantra automatically repeats itself without conscious effort. It is said that ajapa japa comes from the heart, whereas japa comes from the mouth.

Ajapa japa is a complete sadhana in itself which can take an aspirant from the most elementary level of body and environmental awareness to the highest stages of meditation. Its practice, if undertaken gradually and with full awareness, will eventually bring all the hidden desires, fears and complexes of the mind to the mental surface. When this occurs, little by little over a period of months, the practitioner should view these previously hidden samskaras and vasanas with the attitude of an unconcerned witness. Through this process, ajapa japa relieves the mind of all tensions, which in turn removes the root cause of most physical and mental ailments.

Ajapa japa exerts a direct influence on the nervous system's reticular activating nucleus, which is located in the midbrain. Ajapa japa can be practised in any meditation asana. It can also be practised while sitting in a chair or lying in shavasana, but this is not as beneficial. Try not to move your body once you have started your practice.

Any mantra can be used during the practice of ajapa, though traditionally the mantra *Soham* is utilized since it corresponds with the natural sounds of inhalation and exhalation. Many practitioners, however, have achieved great results in ajapa using their guru mantras, and we even know of aspirants who practise with the Gayatri mantra, repeating half the mantra with inhalation and half with exhalation.

Preliminary Ajapa Japa: Frontal passage rotation

During the preliminary ajapa japa techniques, the practitioner should try to feel the prana flowing in the frontal psychic passage between the navel and the throat. During inhalation feel the prana rising upwards from the navel to the throat, and during exhalation feel the prana descending from the throat to the navel. The practitioner will need to use a lot of imagination in the early stages. One way is to imagine the level of water rising and descending in a glass tube connected between the navel and throat, or to imagine the breath coming from the navel during inhalation and returning to the navel during exhalation.

Technique 1: Awareness of frontal passage and Soham

Sit in a comfortable meditation pose.
Close your eyes and practise jnana or chin mudra.
Make your spinal cord erect.
Relax yourself physically and mentally for a few minutes.
Forget all your problems and worries, at least for the duration of the practice. Feel calmness, serenity, peace.
Become conscious of the natural ingoing and outgoing breath.
Feel the breath moving in the frontal passage between the navel and the throat.
On inhalation it rises from the navel to the throat.
On exhalation it descends from the throat to the navel.
Be completely aware of the respiration.
Do not let one breath pass without your awareness.
Your respiration should be deep and relaxed.
Continue this practice for a few minutes.
Now, mentally synchronize the mantra *Soham* with the ingoing and outgoing breath.

So sounds during inhalation and the rising of the prana in the psychic passage.
Ham sounds during exhalation and the descending of the prana in the psychic passage.
Be totally aware of both the movement of prana and the mantra.
Continue in this way for the duration of the daily practice.
Practise this technique for a week or so, and then go on to technique 2.

Technique 2: Awareness of Hamso

Repeat the same procedure as in stage 1, but reverse the order of the mantras with the breath.
Each breath will now start with exhalation on the mantra *Ham*, followed by *So* on inhalation.
The mantra will now be *Hamso*.
After each *Hamso* there will be a slight pause.
Remember, be aware throughout.
Practise this daily for a week or so and then proceed to technique 3.

Technique 3: Rotation of Soham-Hamso

Sit in a comfortable meditation pose.
Close your eyes and practise jnana or chin mudra.
Relax yourself physically and mentally.
Breathe in and out from the navel to the throat.
Be completely aware of this process for a few minutes.
Then merge the mantra *So* with the ingoing breath and *Ham* with the outgoing breath.
In this stage your consciousness, which is identified with the two mantras, should be continuous, so the *So* merges with *Ham* and *Ham* merges with *So*.
Thus there is an endless circle, *Soham-Soham-Soham*.
Prolong the vibrations of *Ham* and join them with the ingoing vibrations of *So*.
Prolong the vibrations of *So* and join them with those of *Ham*.

Continuous repetition of *Soham* and *Hamso*, without any intermission.
Continue in this way for the duration of your practice.

Technique 4: Spontaneous alternation of Soham-Hamso

In this stage all the techniques of techniques 1, 2 and 3 are practised in a spontaneous alternation.
Sit in a comfortable meditation pose and be aware of your natural breath.
Relax yourself completely.
Feel the prana moving up the frontal passage from the navel to the throat with the mantra *So* on inhalation, and feel it descend from the throat to the navel with the mantra *Ham* on exhalation.
First be aware of the breath forming the cycle of *Soham*.
Practise this for a few minutes.
Now let your awareness shift to the continuation of *Hamso*.
After some time, you will find that the *So* and *Ham* have become connected at both ends.
Keep breathing with a continuous cycle of *Soham-Soham-Soham-Soham*.
After some time you may spontaneously feel a change take place to *Soham* or *Hamso*.
Let it follow its own course, spontaneously.
Be only a witness as your awareness shifts between the three mantras of its own accord.
Continue in this way for the duration of the practice.
Practise in this manner for some days before proceeding to technique 5.

Techniques 5, 6, 7 and 8: With ujjayi and khechari

These are exactly the same as techniques 1 to 4, except that they are practised with khechari mudra and ujjayi pranayama.
After you have fully mastered the stages of this technique go on to the intermediate practice of ajapa japa.

CLASS PRACTICE

Preliminary Ajapa Japa
Stage I: Preparation

Sit in padmasana, siddhasana, siddha yoni asana or sukhasana.
In this session we will take up the important subject of ajapa japa.
The word *japa* means repetition.
Ajapa japa means repetition without forced concentration, or spontaneous repetition.
There are different techniques used to keep the inner mind in touch with the mantra, whether it is the mantra *Om* or the mantra *Soham*.
We will use the mantra *Soham*.
Sah means He, the Supreme; *aham* means I, the individual soul. It is to remind yourself that *I am that*.
The mantra is also the inherent sound of the breath itself; *So* is the ingoing breath and *Ham* is the outgoing breath.
This practice forms the basis of kriya yoga and other parts of kundalini yoga.
The first stage needs attention.
Become aware of your breath and become aware that you have not been aware of your breath for some time.
You have not been aware of it all night.
Your centre of awareness is in the throat, the frontal counterpart to vishuddhi chakra, vishuddhi kshetram.
The breath should be normal but not nasal; it should be from the epiglottis as it is naturally at night when you are sleeping, almost like snoring.
There should be little sound; the breath is subtle.
Close your eyes and stop all physical movement.
Become aware of the whole body.
If you maintain awareness of the whole body it will become quiet.
Concentrate or become aware of the throat, the frontal counterpart to vishuddhi.

You can feel your breath, which is not gross enough to hear.
Let the breath adjust itself and move spontaneously.
Maintain awareness of your breath.
The throat must become part of your constant awareness.
The feeling of the breath in the throat is the object of attention.
You have one idea...'I know I am breathing in; I know I am breathing out.'
Each round of breathing should be the object of your awareness.
Do not try to go in.
If your mind wanders, let it but be aware of it.
Remember, 'I know I am breathing in; I know I am breathing out.'
The centre of awareness is vishuddhi.

Stage 2: Breathing in the frontal passage

Now to be more clear, instead of the suggestion, 'I am breathing in, I am breathing out,' suggest to yourself, 'I feel the breath ascending and descending, I know.'
Do not go in.
No suspension please.
Come out.
Do not fall forwards or sideways.
No blank mind, keep the mind moving externally.
Awareness of the ascending and descending breath and awareness of 'I know'.
You are aware that you are aware of the breath.
The second stage of this practice is awareness of the ascending and descending breath.
No shaking or jerking, do not lose track.
Super awareness of awareness.
Keep your body stiff mentally.
With an expanded mind as if you are fully awake.
You know you are aware.
In the depths of meditation and concentration there is awareness.

'Yes, I am sure I am not sleeping, I am in a state of wakefulness.'
Ascending and descending breath, between the navel, manipura kshetram, and the throat, vishuddhi kshetram.
Between these two points there is no loss of consciousness even for one second.
Awareness of the breath ascending and descending.
The sutra is awareness of the breath.
Awareness of ascension from the navel and descension from the throat.
The track and the way is the psychic way.
The path is for the psyche.
Keep awake, like a constant unfluctuating flame in a windless place.
Awareness of the psychic breath ascending and descending.
Practise and listen at the same time. This is important.

Stage 3: Awareness of Soham

This is the third stage.
Moving your psychic breath awareness between the navel and the throat.
The path is the psychic path.
You know you are aware of the ascending and descending movement.
Expanded inner consciousness.
You should be awake internally.
Descending...manipura...I know.
Ascending...vishuddhi...I know.
Awareness of awareness.
If you do it correctly for 5 minutes, the body is controlled by willpower, awareness is internalized, with alertness, as if you are counting coins, or driving a car through heavy traffic.
Be aware of the movements of your consciousness.
If you understand me, you are developing a deeper awareness of your personality.
You are a seer of awareness.
Become stiff like a statue, like a stone that does not move.

This idea of a psychic path between the navel and the throat must become very clear.
More than that, it is important to know that you are aware of it.
In this ascending and descending process you have to develop awareness of the sound *Soham*.
The ascending sound is *So*.
The descending breath awareness is *Ham*.
Do it...*Soham*.
If your mind is dissipated, know it.
Do not hide the truth.
You are practising awareness of the behaviour of your mind.
Know what you are doing.
No movement, you are like a statue.
Soham is a very powerful mantra which makes the mind quiet very quickly, but it also brings sleep.

Stage 4: Awareness of Hamso

Now reverse this awareness to *Hamso*.
From the throat to the navel be aware of *Ham*, and from the navel to the throat, *So*.
Continuous awareness of *Hamso*.
Practise each and every *Hamso* with total awareness, 'I know, I know.'
It is the total knowledge of *Hamso* which should remain protracted.
It is awareness of movement in the form of *Hamso* that is important.
Keep constant watch over your mind and consciousness.
Do not become absent-minded.
I know you are all at the point of running away from *Hamso* awareness.
Just as a bucket is firmly tied to a rope when it is dropped down a deep well, in the same way your grip on *Hamso* must be strong or the mind will slip.
The awareness of the central point *Hamso* should be very strong.

It does not matter what happens to your body; your mind must grip.
The more you control yourself and have a strong grip on the central point, the better the experience will be later on.
Ask yourself throughout, 'Am I aware of *Hamso*?
Is there expanded consciousness inside?
Wide and pleasant and quiet?
Am I internally awake?'

Stage 5: Awareness of Soham-Hamso

This is the next stage.
There is no rule or system here.
Awareness of *Soham* any number of times, then when you feel like it, change to *Hamso* for any number of times.
There is no rule here, but you must be aware of something.
Remain straight and stiff please.
You may practise alternately, but it is not compulsory.
Observe the vision in chidakasha carefully.
Be attentive or particular or alert and watch the vision, whether it is a blade of grass or a mango tree or a beautiful boat or an animal or just a vacuum, you must know whatever it is.
At the same time keep yourself continuously engaged with *Soham* or *Hamso*.
Do it in whatever way you like, you do not have to stick to one practice or method or system, but keep your mind engaged and relaxed.
This is one side of your awareness.
The other side is, 'Am I seeing anything in chidakasha?'
A bird or grass or a boat...you are also engaging your consciousness in a relaxed following of *So* and *Ham*.
You are trying to witness the scenes.
Trying to follow the mental pictures rather than the thoughts. You are converting the thoughts into pictures.
Keep the body stiff by willpower.
Move on with *So* and *Ham* but keep an eye on your visions.

If you pick up this practice very well, antar mouna and dhyana will be easy for you.
You are trying to develop the capacity to see mental forms.
So if you think of a burning fire or a rose, you can see it.
Maintain awareness of the mantra; keep doing something.
Keep an alert eye on the inner images...'What am I seeing? What did I see?'

Stage 6: Counting the breaths

Now start counting from one to twenty or thirty.
You must be aware of each and every number: 1, 2, 3, 4, 5 and so on.
Go on with the practice of ascending and descending breaths.
Another problem is one of maintaining constant alertness.
Now begin faultless, vigilant, conscious counting.
Careful counting, conscious counting of the process of ascending and descending breath.
Have control over the body.
Remember the body and the psychic path and also the counting.
If you have counted, you must know, 'I was counting.'
Do not let your mind be relaxed; better to be tense.
Now with the ascending and descending breath add *Soham*.
So is ascending and *Ham* is descending.
Awareness of the breath and awareness of *Soham* between the navel and the throat.
Remember the central point.
Upward moving consciousness *So* and downward moving *Ham*.
Now chant *Om* with me three times.
Please open your eyes and relax your body.

Hari Om Tat Sat

Intermediate Ajapa Japa: Spinal passage rotation

In these practices greater powers of imagination are required. Remember to be continually mindful of every activity that you do. This is most important because if you meditate and forget that you are meditating, you will never be successful in meditation. Therefore, always be aware of everything that you do. Be mindful that you are visualizing, breathing and so on, and if your mind wanders, then be aware that it is wandering. Similarly, if you concentrate, be aware that you are concentrating.

In this practice, instead of experiencing the flow of prana between the navel and the throat, you must try to feel the flow of prana in sushumna nadi. You must feel the prana moving through each of the chakras. The chakras are mooladhara, swadhisthana, manipura, anahata, vishuddhi and ajna.

Technique 1: Awareness of spinal passage

Sit in a comfortable meditation pose and close your eyes.
Relax yourself physically and mentally for a few minutes.
Practise khechari mudra and then become aware of the rhythmic and slow breathing in ujjayi pranayama.
Be totally aware.
During exhalation feel the prana moving continuously from ajna chakra to mooladhara chakra, passing through the other chakras in turn.
At first you will have to imagine the position of the chakras.
During inhalation feel the prana moving from mooladhara to ajna.
When you alternately reach ajna and mooladhara, hold the breath for a short time and concentrate on that chakra.
Continue in this way for about 5 minutes.
Then merge your mantra with your pranic movement.
As the prana rises, feel the vibrations of *So*.
As the prana descends, feel the vibrations of *Ham*.
Feel the vibrations moving through all the chakras in the spinal column.

Maintain awareness at ajna and mooladhara for a short time at the end of each ascent and descent.
Be continually aware of everything you do.
Continue in this way for the duration of your practice.
When you have perfected this technique, go on to the next.

Technique 2: Rotation of Soham

This is the same as technique1, except that there is a continuation between inhalation and exhalation, but not between exhalation and inhalation.
Thus the mantra will continue as *Soham, Soham, Soham* throughout the practice.
After some days, go on to technique 3.

Technique 3: Rotation of Hamso

In this stage there is a slight break between inhalation and exhalation, but exhalation and the following inhalation should be connected.
Thus the mantra becomes *Hamso, Hamso, Hamso*.
When this is mastered go on to technique 4.

Technique 4: Continuous rotation

Now inhalation, exhalation and inhalation are continuous, making the mantra *Soham-Soham-Soham*.
After some days go on to technique 5.

Technique 5: Spontaneous alternation of Soham-Hamso

In this stage the shifting from *Soham* to *Hamso* to *Soham-Hamso* will occur spontaneously.
When this is mastered, go on to the complete practice of ajapa japa.

Hari Om Tat Sat

Advanced Ajapa Japa

This is quite similar to intermediate ajapa japa and has five stages just like the preceding ones. The only difference is that the breath is longer and slower in this practice, and the psychic passage extends all the way from mooladhara to sahasrara chakra at the top of the head. In all other respects it should be practised in the same way as the five stages of intermediate ajapa japa.

CLASS PRACTICE

Advanced Ajapa Japa

Stage 1: Preparation

Sit in a meditation asana with the hands in jnana or chin mudra.
Close your eyes and stop all physical movement.
Body upright and straight; listen to the instructions for ajapa japa.
Khechari is the mother. Even as a baby lives in its mother's lap, so the yogi lives in khechari whenever he can.
Your association with khechari must begin and become an integral part of your being.
Now you must concentrate on the tongue, the tip and the palate.
In the beginning of the practice of khechari, remember that the physical body has its own limitations.
Even if you want to, you cannot practise khechari all day.
But as days and weeks go by, you can practise for a longer time.
Practise it with ujjayi pranayama in such a way that you feel the ascending and descending passage in the spinal column between mooladhara, at the bottom, and sahasrara, at the top.
The sound in ujjayi should be the kind of sound a person produces in deep sleep.
It should be continuous, not broken into waves, no fluctuations.

It is like the sound of steam escaping from a boiler.
From mooladhara ascending inhalation, from sahasrara descending exhalation, imagined in the spinal cord as a tiny and subtle passage or thread of illumination.
Start ujjayi with the mouth closed.

Stage 2: Breathing in the spinal passage

Become aware of ujjayi breathing in the spinal cord.
From sahasrara to mooladhara, from mooladhara to sahasrara.
Your own breath in this passage produces a sound as in deep sleep.
After some time it will become rarefied and subtle, but now you must consciously produce the sound.
From time to time you may release khechari, get out of your mother's lap, but get right back in.
The force of the breath should not be increased now or the throat will become too dry.
By maintaining khechari, after a while the secretions that maintain the irrigation of the throat will start to flow and dryness will be avoided.
The spinal column has within it the spinal cord, the great nerve sushumna.
When sushumna is asleep and dormant it is a simple nerve, but when it is awakened it is a path of illumination, full of currents.
The ujjayi breath consciousness has to pass through the spinal cord with the aid of your imagination.
You must distinctly try to feel the breath ascending to sahasrara and descending to mooladhara through the spinal cord.
That is what you have to accomplish now.

Stage 3: Awareness of Soham

In the same practice of ujjayi you have to add awareness of the mantra *Soham*.
So with the ascending inhalation, *Ham* with the descending exhalation.
Practise for only 5 minutes.

This is how you become aware of the music of the breath which is *Soham*.

The unbroken awareness of *Soham* is the form of ujjayi breathing in the spinal cord.

The awareness of *Soham* is a powerful form of consciousness.

Anytime of the day or night, whenever you are free, you can become aware of *Soham* in the spinal cord.

It will act with power on your consciousness.

The awareness of *Soham* should be constant, with or without khechari.

The yogi should try to maintain awareness of *Soham* all throughout the day and night in order to purify the deeper planes of consciousness.

At any time he should sit in the asana, close his eyes, stop all movements and switch to *Soham* awareness.

Stage 4: Awareness of Hamso

Thereafter he can reverse it to *Hamso* awareness.

It is like awareness of the mantra in japa, but it is *Soham* without the mala, with the breath instead of the mala, and in the spinal column instead of the hand.

If you are after this psychic awareness, a lot of work will be done on the inner plane.

Stage 5: Spontaneous alternation of Soham-Hamso

Soham...Hamso – sahasrara to mooladhara ascending and descending.

When you say *Ham* the whole body becomes relaxed; when you say *So* the consciousness goes to the top.

The *Ham* goes deep into mooladhara; sometimes the experience is very peculiar.

So goes up to the sky.

Practise at any time of the day; each time the experience will be different, morning, afternoon and evening.

It should be done for a minimum of 5 minutes and a maximum of half an hour.

Understand that it should be practised at different times: before and after lunch, dinner, bath; when you are too

hot or too cold; when you are fresh or tired; when you are bent or stretched; when you are ready or not ready.
It must be practised to develop the range of samskaras.
If a yogi is cautious and particular, he can get as many as 20 five minute periods in the day; that makes 100 minutes, almost two hours.
If you really practise *Soham* and *Hamso*, you are giving a chance for different types of samskaras and karmas to express themselves.
Please open your eyes and relax your body.
The practice of ajapa japa is now complete.

Hari Om Tat Sat

16

Yoga Nidra

Yoga nidra means psychic sleep. It is a state of sleepless sleep where one is on the borderline between sleep and wakefulness. It is a state of inner awareness and contact with the subconscious and higher consciousness. A speaker or narrator is needed in the initial stages of practice. For this reason it is a good idea, if possible, to put the directions on tape. Later on you will remember the instructions and you can practise alone.

Yoga nidra brings a state of deep relaxation and can be used as a preliminary to sleep. Most people do not know how to sleep. They fall asleep while thinking over some problem or while prey to some anxiety. In sleep their mind runs on and their body is tense. They wake up feeling lethargic and unrested and doze on for half an hour longer. One should learn the scientific way of sleeping, i.e. practise yoga nidra just before sleeping; it will relax the whole body and mind. The sleep will be deep, one will need fewer hours and one wakes up feeling fresh and energetic.

In yoga nidra the physical centres of the body become introverted. This is pratyahara. When the mind is fixed on a centre, blood and energy are drawn to it and this causes withdrawal of the senses at that centre. In the deep state of relaxation that results, tension is released, the mind becomes clear and thoughts are more powerful. In psychic sleep we contact our inner personality to change our attitude towards ourselves and others. It is a method of introspection. It has been used by yogis since time immemorial to bring them face to face with the inner self.

A resolve or sankalpa is made during the practice. It should be something of immense importance to you. Resolves are short sentences of moral significance to be embedded in the subconscious. In the state of yoga nidra passivity, this type of autosuggestion is very powerful. Such resolves can change your whole life. They will certainly come true if you repeat your resolve with enough conviction. By this method you can change old habits and cure certain mental illnesses. Sankalpas can have a spiritual objective like 'I shall become more aware.' Your sankalpa or resolve should be repeated several times during the practice and should be repeated in yoga nidra for days and days together. Reflect on your resolve or sankalpa immediately after yoga nidra, before opening the eyes.

In yoga nidra the mind should be totally taken up in following the instructions, which should be quick and require acute attentiveness. In normal practice, when you are not using yoga nidra as a means to sleep, you must remain minutely aware throughout. Above all, do not slumber. Do not try to understand or rationalize any of the words. Don't make efforts to remember them – that would exhaust your mind and send it to sleep.

Practise yoga nidra lying down with the head flat on the floor, in shavasana. The body should be straight and the head in line, legs slightly apart and arms close to the body, palms upwards. Lie completely still; the body must be totally relaxed with the clothes loose. There should be no physical movement once yoga nidra has begun. The stomach must not be full and the eyes must remain closed throughout.

Stages of yoga nidra

The following are approximately the stages of yoga nidra, though there can be variations of sequence and content.

1. A resolve or sankalpa is made.

2. Breath awareness.
3. Rotation of consciousness through the 76 parts of the body. The mind should move quickly from centre to centre. There are one to five rounds of this stage. The sequence of the parts of the body should not be changed, as the subconscious becomes used to the order.
4. Recollection or awakening of feelings of heaviness or lightness, heat or cold, pain or pleasure.
5. Conceptual awareness of the psychic centres and psychic symbols. When the right places are touched you may have visions and experiences. Rapid visualizations.
6. Repeat the resolve or the sankalpa. Awareness of unity with the supreme self, *Atman*.
7. Return to normal consciousness very gradually and slowly start to move the limbs. There should be no sudden jerks.

CLASS PRACTICES

I: Short practice

Preparation: Stop all physical movements and prepare for the practice of yoga nidra.

Resolve: Please make your resolve, and repeat it to yourself three times. (*pause*)

Relaxation: Now relax your body but remain alert.

Relax every part of your physical body and maintain awareness of relaxation.

Relaxation should be complete and homogeneous.

Mind, body, senses, all aspects of your personality, your entire being, the body, the senses, the feelings, the emotions, the mind, the intellect, all should be in a state of relaxation as happens at night during deep sleep.

Remain conscious and prepare yourself for carrying out further instructions.

Concentrate on the whole body and maintain constant, unbroken, unceasing awareness, homogeneous awareness of your whole body.

Body/floor contact: Concentrate on the body which is now resting on the floor and direct your attention to those parts where the different limbs of the body touch the floor.

Concentrate on the point where the right heel touches the floor.

Go on shifting your consciousness from point to point where the different limbs of the body touch the ground. Right heel, left heel, right calf muscle, left calf muscle, right hamstring, left hamstring, right buttock, left buttock, right shoulderblade, left shoulderblade, right hand, left hand, right elbow, left elbow, the back of the head, the back of the head.

Now concentrate on the meeting points only, where the body and the ground touch each other. Go on, without any break or intervention with the exercise. Feel those meeting points clearly and distinctly and continue with the practice.

Continue...continue...continue.

Maintain homogeneous awareness of the meeting points between the limbs of the body and the floor.

Continue...continue.

Maintain complete and homogeneous awareness of the meeting points and intensify your efforts.

All the rays of your awareness should be focused on the common points between the different limbs of your body and the floor.

Intensify your practice and make sure you can clearly feel the meeting points.

Continue. That is the line of gravity.

Next concentrate on the part where the two eyelids meet. Concentrate only on the meeting point where the eyelids touch the two eyes. Intensify your awareness and feel clearly the meeting points.

Now shift the centre of gravity of your consciousness from the eyelids to the meeting points of the lower and upper lips.

Concentrate on the sharp points where the two lips meet.
Concentrate.
Intensify awareness and feel those meeting points clearly.

Breathing: Become aware of your breathing.
Start to practise psychic nadi shodhana. With the count of 1,2, 3, 4, alternate nostrils; with 5, both nostrils; 6, 7, 8, 9, alternate nostrils; 10, both nostrils, and so on up to 30.
1, 1, 2, 2, 3, 3, 4, 4, 5, 5, 6, 6, 7, 7, 8, 8, 9, 9, 10, 10, 11, 11, 12, 12, 13, 13, 14, 14, 15, 15, 16, 16, 17, 17, 18, 18, 19, 19, 20, 20, 21, 21, 22, 22, 23, 23, 24, 24, 25, 25, 26, 27, 27, 28, 28, 29, 29, 30, 30.
Continue with intense awareness for about two minutes.
(*Pause*)

Resolve: Again repeat your resolve three times.

Finish: Now visualize your face as you see it in a mirror.
See your whole body lying on the floor.
Watch yourself for a few seconds.
Slowly open your eyes and sit up.
The practice of yoga nidra is complete.

Hari Om Tat Sat

2: Long practice

Preparation: Now psychic relaxation begins.
Kindly close your eyes and make yourself physically comfortable.
You can readjust your physical position for some time if you like.
Do not open your eyes until the whole practice is over.
Try to follow all the instructions mentally and not physically.
Make yourself free from all intellectual analysis and intellectual understanding.
You have to follow the instructions automatically.
There will be physical relaxation, mental and psychic in all.
You have to keep awake throughout. Do not sleep.

When relaxation becomes deep, sleep does come but you should try to keep yourself completely awake, from time to time thinking 'I am awake, I am awake, I am awake.'

From time to time during the relaxation you will have to keep yourself completely awake and check up on the condition of your consciousness.

Sometimes during the practice you may be able to understand or you may not; it does not matter. Just follow the voice.

When you begin the practice of psychic sleep every day, you should give yourself at least 7 to 10 minutes to make yourself physically calm and steady.

Do not begin your practice all of a sudden, but develop the consciousness in your mind in this way:

'Now I am going to practise psychic sleep. In this practice of psychic sleep I shall remain awake all throughout.'

And develop in your mind the experience which you have had at night when you go to bed completely relaxed and repeat to yourself mentally:

'My mind is free, my body is free. I am preparing for relaxation. I am listening to the instructions.'

This way every day you have to prepare yourself for about 10 minutes for the psychic relaxation.

If thoughts come from time to time and disturb you, it does not matter.

Now develop the awareness of your physical body right from the top to the toes and say in your mind *Ommm*.

Complete awareness of the whole body.

Complete awareness of the whole body.

Complete awareness of the whole body.

Complete awareness of the whole body.

Resolve: At this moment now you have to make a resolve.

You have to decide upon a resolve.

You have to discover a resolve.

You have to fix a resolve for yourself.

Do not be in a hurry to make a resolution for yourself, but try to discover one for yourself.

The resolve will have to be very simple.
Simple resolve, simple resolve, simple resolve.
Try to find out one for yourself.
Try to find out one for yourself.
The resolve that you make during the practice of psychic sleep will come true.
The mind becomes receptive to resolves when intellectual awareness becomes absent and simple awareness expresses itself.
Then the resolve becomes effective.
The resolve that you have to discover for yourself should not be lengthy, should not be ambiguous, should be very clear, direct and short.
Even as you prepare the earth's soil and sow the seed, in the same manner you have now to sow a resolve.
It is not necessary that you have to make a resolve today, but you have to find one for yourself.
The easiest one and a practical one.
Once you have found out a resolve for yourself, repeat it every day until it has come to fruition. During this practice the resolve has to be repeated twice, once at the beginning of psychic sleep and once at the end.
The resolve that you make during psychic sleep is bound to happen in your life.
It is bound to fructify without any doubt.
If you can convince your mind, you can do anything.
When the intellectual personality recedes, and is eliminated, the subconscious personality expresses itself, and the resolve that you made comes to pass and happens.
After you have made your resolve you should again switch to the awareness of the physical body, and the whole body right from the top to the toes, in the form:
'I am, I am', or 'my body, my body'.
Think of the whole body at one time, in one glance, in a thought.
Think of the whole body in one thought.
Develop whole body awareness at one moment.

'I am my body, I am my body.' This way you think, mentally, and go on developing awareness of the whole body.

And then again think 'I am listening to the instructions, I am not sleeping, I am not drowsy, I am not conscious of external sounds, but I am relaxed and I can sleep at any moment and I have to be awake.'

The first practice in psychic sleep begins.

Rotation of consciousness: Rotation of consciousness through different parts of the body.

Repeat the name of the particular part in your mind and try to develop awareness of that part of the body just for a moment, not for a very long time.

For instance, if I say 'right hand thumb', you have to say in your mind 'right hand thumb' without moving it, and then go on to the next.

I will lead your consciousness to different parts of the body and the speed will be somewhat greater.

Keep yourself alert, do not concentrate too intensely, just develop the awareness and try to move your mind as quickly as possible and as quickly as you are instructed by me.

If at any time you are unable to keep up with the speed it does not matter, go ahead to the next.

In the first round I will be slow, then I will gain speed.

Please understand that you will have to say the name of the particular organ mentally.

Right side: Say mentally: right hand thumb, second finger, third, fourth, fifth, palm, wrist, elbow, shoulder, armpit, waist, thigh, knee, calf muscle, ankle, heel, sole, right toes, one, two, three, four, five.

Left side: To the left. Left thumb, second finger, third, fourth, fifth, palm, wrist, elbow, shoulder, armpit, waist, thigh, knee, calf muscle, ankle, heel, sole, left toes, one, two, three, four, five.

Right side reverse: Go to the right toes, take your mind to the right toes. Start from the bottom: right toes, one, two, three, four, five, sole, heel, ankle, calf muscle, knee, thigh, waist, armpit, shoulder, elbow, wrist, palm, right thumb, second finger, third, fourth, fifth.

Left side reverse: Go to the left toes, go to the left toes. Left toes, one, two, three, four, five, sole, heel, ankle, calf muscle, knee, thigh, waist, armpit, shoulder, elbow, wrist, palm, left thumb, second finger, third, fourth, fifth.

Right side: Right again, from up to down. Right hand thumb, second finger, third, fourth, fifth, palm, wrist, elbow, shoulder, armpit, waist, thigh, knee, calf muscle, ankle, heel, sole, right toes, one, two, three, four, five, sole, heel, ankle, calf muscle, knee, thigh, waist, armpit, shoulder, elbow, wrist, right hand thumb, second finger, third, fourth, fifth.

Left side: Go to the left from the top. Left hand thumb, second finger, third, fourth, fifth, palm, wrist, elbow, shoulder, armpit, waist, thigh, knee, calf muscle, ankle, heel, sole, left toes, one, two, three, four, five, sole, heel, ankle, calf muscle, knee, thigh, waist, armpit, shoulder, elbow, wrist, palm, left thumb, second finger, third, fourth, fifth.

Whole back: Go to the back side, go to the back side. Take your mind to the back of the head which is touching the ground; the back side of the head, the back side of the head which is touching the ground. Right shoulderblade, left shoulderblade, spinal cord, right hip, left hip, right buttock, left buttock, right side underneath the thigh, left side underneath the thigh, right calf muscle, left calf muscle, right ankle, left ankle, right heel, left heel.

Reverse: Right ankle, left ankle, right calf muscle, left calf muscle, right side underneath the thigh, left side underneath the thigh, right buttock, left buttock, right hip, left hip, spinal cord, right shoulderblade, left shoulderblade, behind the head. Right shoulderblade, left shoulderblade, spinal cord, right hip, left hip, right buttock, left buttock, right side underneath the thigh, left side underneath the thigh, right calf muscle, left calf muscle, right ankle, left ankle, right heel, left heel, right ankle, left ankle, right calf muscle, left calf muscle, right side underneath the thigh, left side underneath the thigh, right buttock, left buttock, right hip, left hip, spinal cord, right shoulderblade, left shoulderblade, behind the head.

Whole front: Go to the front at the top of your head, to the top of your head, the crown, the top of the head, the crown, the crown, the forehead, right eyebrow, left eyebrow, centre of the eyebrows, right eye, left eye, right nostril, left nostril, right cheek, left cheek, right ear, left ear, upper lip, lower lip, chin, throat, right side of chest, left side of chest, the whole chest, navel, upper abdomen, lower abdomen, right abdomen, left abdomen, right pelvis, left pelvis, right side of groin, left side of groin, right thigh, left thigh, right knee, left knee, right toes, left toes.

Reverse: Left toes, right toes, left knee, right knee, left thigh, right thigh, left side of groin, right side of groin, left pelvis, right pelvis, left abdomen, right abdomen, lower abdomen, upper abdomen, navel, the whole chest, left side of chest, right side of chest, throat, chin, lower lip, upper lip, left ear, right ear, left cheek, right cheek, left nostril, right nostril, left eye, right eye, centre of the eyebrows, left eyebrow, right eyebrow, the forehead, the crown, the top of the head, the top of the head, the front at the top of the head, your eyebrow centre, eyebrow centre, the eyebrow centre.

'I am not sleeping, I am awake; I am not sleeping, I am awake; I am not sleeping, I am awake.'

Inner parts: Now the inner parts of the body. Take your mind to your tongue, teeth, palate, tongue, teeth, palate. Inside the nose with the breath. Inside the brain, large brain, inner nasal orifice which opens into the throat, the throat through which the wind passes, the right lung, the left lung.

Feel it with the breath, feel the lungs by filling the lungs, right lung, left lung.

The heart, feel the heart by concentrating on the heartbeat, that is the easiest.

Take your mind and go to the beat in the heart, go on mentally, the heart.

Now go to the alimentary canal, the canal which carries food from the mouth to the stomach, the alimentary canal, the food carrying canal, it is something like a spiral, the food goes down through this canal into the stomach. Try to feel it with the breath.

Stomach, liver, the liver, the stomach, kidneys, kidneys, kidneys, the whole abdomen internally.

Start from the top again. The brain, the brain, the brain, the nasal orifice, tongue, teeth, palate, right eardrum, left eardrum, the throat, the alimentary canal, right lung, left lung, heart, stomach, liver, kidneys, the whole of the abdomen internally.

Again from the top. Try to think, try to think, try to think internally. The brain, internal nasal orifice, right eardrum, left eardrum, tongue, teeth, palate, throat, alimentary canal, right lung, left lung, heart, stomach, liver, kidneys, abdomen internally, abdomen internally.

Major parts: Now the major parts of your body. The right leg, the left leg, both legs together. Right arm, left arm, both together. The whole of your back, the whole of your front, the head, the whole body. Visualize the whole body, say 'whole body' and visualize the whole body. Say 'whole body' and visualize the whole body. Intensify your awareness. The whole body, the whole body, the whole body, the whole body.

Spinal cord: Now take your mind into the spinal cord at the bottom, take your mind to the spinal cord at the bottom. Check whether you are sleeping or awake, dissipated or drowsy, and say 'I am awake'.

Go to the bottom of the spinal cord in the perineum, take your mind to the perineum. Say in your mind 'perineum' and think of it. A little higher in the bottom of the spinal cord, go to the part where the spinal cord terminates. Go behind the navel, just behind the navel in the spinal cord internally. Go up behind the heart in the spinal cord internally. Go up in the neck. At the top of the spinal cord in the smaller brain. Go up to the top of your head, the crown. Again backward movement. The crown, top of the head, back of the head, the neck, behind the heart, behind the navel, bottom of the cord, perineum. Again the perineum, perineum, bottom of the cord, bottom of the cord, behind the navel in the spinal cord, behind the navel, behind the heart, behind the heart, neck, neck, behind the head, behind the head, the top of the head, the top, the top, the crown, the crown, the top, the top, the top.

Behind the head, behind the neck, behind the heart, behind the heart, behind the navel, behind the navel, bottom of the cord, bottom of the cord, perineum, perineum.

'I am awake, I am awake, I am awake; I am conscious, I am conscious, I am conscious.'

Body/mirror awareness: Try to see the whole body as if you are seeing yourself in a mirror. As if a great mirror is hanging over you and you are trying to see you own body, you are trying to see your own reflection.

See your own body, you are trying to see your own reflection.

See your body, see your body as an object, your head, your arms, your chest, your legs, your clothes, everything as I'm seeing you, as I am seeing you, as I am seeing you. In the same manner you have to see yourself as an object; look at the mirror, look at yourself in the psychic mirror – 'My reflection, my body, my reflection, my body.'

Visualization: Now concentrate on all the different things that I will mention. Remain alert. I will name a lot of things and you will have to say the same things mentally and try to develop a vision of them one by one.

If you are able to develop the vision of them, it means that your relaxation for the time being is complete, and if you are not able to visualize, that means that you need a little more practice.

Blue lotus over a lake, blue lotus over a lake, blue lotus over a lake.
A burning candle, a burning candle, a burning candle.
Experience of drowsiness, experience of drowsiness.
Experience of heat, experience of heat.
Experience of heaviness, experience of heaviness, experience of heaviness.
An inverted red triangle, an inverted red triangle, an inverted red triangle. Flame of burning fire, flame of burning fire, flame of burning fire.
Experience of heat, experience of heat.
Snow capped mountains, snow capped mountains.
Stretches of landscape, stretches of landscape, stretches of landscape, stretches of landscape.
A star, a star in the sky, the small point of a star, a pink rose, a honey bee, a honey bee, a honey bee. A big bird flying in the air, flying bird, flying bird.
A boat sailing over a lake, sailing boat, sailing boat, sailing boat.
Starlit sky, starlit sky, starlit sky.
Experience of heaviness, experience of heaviness, experience of heaviness.
Your own breath, your own breath, your own breath.
Dark night, dark night.
Blue lotus over a lake, blue lotus over a lake.
Rain in showers, torrential rain, torrential rain.
Green leaf, green leaf.
Garden, garden, yellow flowers, yellow flowers, pink rose, pink rose, green grass, green grass, swimming pool, swimming pool, green grass, a big garden.
Inverted triangle, a tiger, a tiger, a tiger.
The whole body, the whole body, the whole body.
Try to see your whole body in the psychic mirror.
Relax all the efforts, draw your mind outside, make yourself extrovert, become aware of your surroundings.
I am practising yoga nidra, I was practising yoga nidra, I am lying quietly.

Resolve: Now again you will have to practise the resolve and repeat the resolve; make the resolve and repeat the resolve, one and the same resolve, do not change it, the same resolve. Your subconscious is exposed to resolves now.

Finish: Now keep the eyes closed and make physical movements of the body, and prepare yourself to get up. Keep the eyes closed, but make movements with the body. Prepare yourself to get up.
Now get up and open your eyes.

Hari Om Tat Sat

3: Complete practice

Preparation: Please get ready for yoga nidra.
Adjust your cover, your pillow, as best as you can and be sure that you will be able to practise yoga nidra for the whole period without any physical discomfort.
Adjust everything, your body position, pillow and the rest.
You can make suitable movements now, but once you have adjusted yourself finally, until yoga nidra is over, the body should not move. No movement then, no physical movement of any kind.
Become absolutely motionless, adjust yourself finally.
Concentrate on the physical body, concentrate on the physical body, concentrate on your physical being as a whole.
Be aware of the existence of the physical body, be aware of the existence of your physical body.
Develop awareness of the whole body from top to toe.
Develop awareness of your whole physical body from top to toe.
Your whole body, your whole body, your whole body should be the object of your awareness, should be the form of your awareness.
You are aware of the whole body, the physical being from top to toe, not merely awareness of legs or arms or trunk

or chest or head, but awareness of the whole body, awareness of the body as a whole, complete and constant awareness of the whole body.

Be aware that you are going to practise yoga nidra and say mentally, 'I am aware, I am going to practise yoga nidra; I am aware, I am going to practise yoga nidra; I am aware, I am going to practise yoga nidra; I am aware, I am going to practise yoga nidra.'

Go on thinking like this and be sure you are aware you are going to practise yoga nidra.

This should be the form of your awareness now.

Relaxation: Relax your body mentally, relax yourself mentally, relax your mind, your whole personality should be relaxed by breathing normally and concentrating on the normal breath in the nostrils on the basis of nadi shodhana.

Breathing through alternate nostrils, normal breathing through alternate nostrils.

With total awareness, with complete awareness within the nostrils.

Breathe in through the left nostril and breathe out through the right,

and again breathe in through the right and breathe out through the left.

Relax your breathing, normal breathing, breathe with concentration.

Go on practising psychic breathing.

This is how your whole personality will feel completely relaxed.

Not only the physical body, not merely the thinking process, but complete relaxation of body, senses, breathing, mind, awareness will take place through this practice.

Your mind, your consciousness, should go in and out with the help of the breath.

When you are able to relax yourself completely through this practice, you will find a change in your physical consciousness and also a great change in your mental awareness.

Any time if you breathe this way and if you concentrate on this normal breath through alternate nostrils, your whole personality will undergo a process of relaxation.
Please check yourself and be sure that you are fully awake, that you are listening to me and that you are not sleeping.

Resolve: Your sankalpa, the resolve, should be simple, short, in clear language, with frank expression, with faith.
Resolves made before and after yoga nidra are sure to become a truth and reality in your life.
Anything in life can fail but not the resolve made before and after yoga nidra.
The same resolve, in the same language, with the same understanding and with the same background, must be repeated day after day, at the beginning and end of yoga nidra.
Kindly remember to repeat the same resolve at the end of the process, before you open the eyes and come out of yoga nidra.
The resolve, the sankalpa is repeated three times in the beginning and three times at the end. Go on repeating, go on, go on repeating.

Rotation of consciousness: Yoga nidra begins now.
Rotation of consciousness in the physical centres.
The awareness is to jump from point to point as quickly as possible.
It is to rotate from point to point.
Of course you have to name it mentally.

Right side: Right hand thumb, tip, nail, the first joint and the root of the thumb.
Second finger, tip, nail, first joint, second joint and the root of the second finger.
Third finger, tip, nail, first joint, second joint and the root of the third finger.
Fourth finger, tip, nail, first joint, second joint and the root of the fourth finger.
Fifth finger, tip, nail, first joint, second joint and the root of the fifth finger.

Back of the hand, palm, mounts of the palm, Venus, Moon, Mercury, Sun, Saturn, Jupiter, Mars, middle of the palm.

Wrist, lower arm, inside of the lower arm, elbow, inside of the elbow, upper arm, inside of the upper arm, shoulder, armpit, left side of the chest, waist, hip, hamstrings, thigh, knee, back of the knee, calf muscle, shin.

Right foot, ankle, heel, middle of the sole, ball of the foot, instep of the foot, toes, big toe, tip, nail, first joint, root of the big toe.

Second toe, tip, nail, first joint, second joint and root of the second toe.

Third toe, tip, nail, first joint, second joint, root of the third toe.

Fourth toe, tip, nail, first joint, second joint, root of the fourth toe.

Fifth toe, tip, nail, first joint, second joint and root of the fifth toe.

Left side: Left hand thumb, tip, nail, the first joint and the root of the thumb.

Second finger, tip, nail, first joint, second joint and the root of the second finger.

Third finger, tip, nail, first joint, second joint and the root of the third finger.

Fourth finger, tip, nail, first joint, second joint and the root of the fourth finger.

Fifth finger, tip, nail, first joint, second joint and the root of the fifth finger.

Back of the hand, palm, mounts of the palm, Venus, Moon, Mercury, Sun, Saturn, Jupiter, Mars, middle of the palm.

Wrist, lower arm, inside of the lower arm, elbow, inside of the elbow, upper arm, inside of the upper arm, shoulder, armpit, left side of the chest, waist, hip, hamstring, thigh, knee, back of the knee, calf muscle, shin, left foot, ankle, heel, middle part of the sole, ball of the foot, instep of the foot.

Toes, big toe, tip, nail, first joint and root of the big toe.
Second toe, tip, nail, first joint, second joint and root of the second toe.
Third toe, tip, nail, first joint, second joint and root of the third toe.
Fourth toe, tip, nail, first joint, second joint and root of the fourth toe.
Fifth toe, tip, nail, first joint, second joint and root of the fifth toe.

Back: Right shoulderblade, left shoulderblade, right buttock, left buttock, right side of the back, left side of the back, spinal cord, neck, whole of the back together.

Front: Sahasrara, forehead, right eyebrow, left eyebrow, centre of the eyebrows, right temple, left temple, right eye, left eye, right eyelid, left eyelid, right cheek, left cheek, right ear, left ear, nose, nosetip, upper lip, lower lip, both lips together, tongue, chin, throat.
Right chest, left chest, both together, depression of the chest, heart, stomach, navel, abdomen, right leg, left leg, right arm, left arm, head, trunk.
Whole body, whole body, whole body, whole body, whole body, whole body, whole body.
Check your consciousness, be sure you are listening to me.
You are not asleep, you are awake.

Awareness of sensations

Heaviness: Awaken the feeling of heaviness, awaken the feeling of heaviness.
Become aware of the feeling of heaviness in the right hand thumb, second finger, third finger, fourth, fifth, palm, wrist, elbow, shoulder, armpit, waist, hip, hamstring, thigh, knee, calf, ankle, heel, sole, right toes, one, two, three, four, five.
Awaken the feeling of heaviness, awaken the feeling of heaviness.
Become aware of the feeling of heaviness in the left hand thumb, second finger, third finger, fourth, fifth, palm,

wrist, elbow, shoulder, armpit, waist, hip, hamstring, thigh, knee, calf, ankle, heel, sole, left toes, one, two, three, four, five.
Awaken the feeling of heaviness, awaken the feeling of heaviness.
Become aware of the feeling of heaviness in the right shoulderblade, left shoulderblade, right buttock, left buttock, right side of the back, left side of the back, spinal cord, the whole back.
Awaken the feeling of heaviness, awaken the feeling of heaviness.
Become aware of the feeling of heaviness in the right hand thumb, second finger, third, fourth, fifth, palm, wrist, elbow, shoulder, armpit, waist, hip, hamstring, thigh, knee, calf, ankle, heel, sole, right toes, one, two, three, four, five.
Left hand thumb, second finger, third finger, fourth, fifth, palm, wrist, elbow, shoulder, armpit, waist, hip, hamstring, thigh, knee, calf, ankle, heel, sole, left toes, one, two, three, four, five.
Awaken the feeling of heaviness, awaken the feeling of heaviness.
Become aware of heaviness in the right shoulderblade, left shoulderblade, right buttock, left buttock, right side of the back, left side of the back, spinal cord, the whole back.
Awaken the feeling of heaviness, awaken the feeling of heaviness.
Become aware of the feeling of heaviness in the right leg, left leg, both legs together, right arm, left arm, both arms together, head, trunk.
Awaken the feeling of heaviness, awaken the feeling of heaviness.
Become aware of the feeling of heaviness in the whole body, in the whole body, heaviness in the whole body, heaviness in the whole body, heaviness in the whole body, in the whole body, in the whole body, in the whole body.

Check your awareness and be sure that you are not sleeping.

Be sure that you are not sleeping, that you are listening to me, and that you are awake.

Lightness: Become aware of the feeling of lightness, become aware of the feeling of lightness, become aware of the feeling of lightness.

Awaken the feeling of lightness, awaken the feeling of lightness in the right hand thumb, second finger, third finger, fourth, fifth, palm, wrist, elbow, shoulder, armpit, waist, hip, hamstring, thigh, knee, calf, ankle, heel, sole, right toes, one, two, three, four, five. Awaken the feeling of lightness, awaken the feeling of lightness. Become aware of the feeling of lightness in the left hand thumb, second finger, third finger, fourth, fifth, palm, wrist, elbow, shoulder, armpit, waist, hip, hamstring, thigh, knee, calf, ankle, heel, sole, left toes, one, two, three, four, five.

Awaken the feeling of lightness, awaken the feeling of lightness.

Become aware of the feeling of lightness in the right shoulderblade, left shoulderblade, right buttock, left buttock, right side of back, left side of back, spinal cord, the whole back. Awaken the feeling of lightness, awaken the feeling of lightness.

Become aware of the feeling of lightness in right hand thumb, second finger, third finger, fourth, fifth, palm, wrist, elbow, shoulder, armpit, waist, hip, hamstring, thigh, knee, calf, ankle, heel, sole, right toes, one, two, three, four, five.

Left hand thumb, second finger, third finger, fourth, fifth, palm, wrist, elbow, shoulder, armpit, waist, hip, hamstring, thigh, knee, calf, ankle, heel, sole, left toes, one, two, three, four, five.

Awaken the feeling of lightness, awaken the feeling of lightness.

Become aware of lightness in the right shoulderblade, left shoulderblade, right buttock, left buttock, right side of the back, left side of the back, spinal cord, the whole back.

Awaken the feeling of lightness, awaken the feeling of lightness.

Become aware of the feeling of lightness in the right leg, left leg, both legs together, right arm, left arm, both arms together, head, trunk.

Awaken the feeling of lightness, awaken the feeling of lightness.

Become aware of the feeling of lightness in the whole body, in the whole body, lightness in the whole body, lightness in the whole body, lightness in the whole body, in the whole body, in the whole body, in the whole body.

Become aware that you are not sleeping, that you are listening to me, that you are awake; please check your consciousness.

Heat: Awaken the will and experience heat, imagine heat, recollect the experience of heat and superimpose the experience of heat in the right sole, right sole, left sole, left sole, right palm, right palm, left palm, left palm, lips, lips, right eye, right eye, left eye, left eye, right ear, right ear, left ear, left ear.

Become aware of the feeling of heat in the whole body, in the whole body, in the whole body.

Superimpose the experience of heat on the whole body, and this feeling should become real to you.

You must experience mentally what heat is, experience and awaken the feeling of heat in the right sole, right sole, left sole, left sole, right palm, right palm, left palm, left palm, lips, lips, right eye, right eye, left eye, left eye, right ear, right ear, left ear, left ear.

Feel the whole body hot, almost sweating, almost perspiring.

Awaken the will and experience the heat, the experience of, the sensation of heat in the whole body, in the whole body, in the whole body.

Be sure that you are awake, you are not sleeping and you are listening to me.

Cold: The experience of cold, awaken the experience of cold, awaken the experience of cold in the body, awaken the experience of cold in the body, awaken the experience of cold in the body.

Imagine you are walking on the cold floor during winter; how would your body feel?

That experience is to be awakened by you; feel the cold, feel the cold, feel the cold in the right sole, right sole, left sole, left sole, spinal cord, spinal cord, nose tip, nose tip, sahasrara, sahasrara.

Feel cold in the whole body as if the whole body is getting colder and colder.

Feel cold in the whole body as if the whole body is getting colder and colder, as if on a cold winter's night you sleep outside, without any covering over the body.

How cold would you feel?

Recollect the experience of cold and superimpose it on your body.

Say mentally 'I feel chilly, I feel cold.'

Then again try to awaken the feeling of cold in the right sole, right sole, left sole, left sole, spinal cord, spinal cord, nose tip, nose tip, sahasrara, sahasrara, whole body, cold in the whole body, cold in the whole body, cold in the whole body.

Feel that your whole body is experiencing cold, recollect the experience of cold and superimpose that feeling on your mind and body.

Pain: Recollect the feeling of pain, recollect any pain clearly, recollect any pain clearly.

Awaken your will and feel pain, awaken your will and feel pain, superimpose your mind there and feel that pain, remember the pain, feel that pain, feel the pain so intensely that you actually begin to experience it.

Quickly take your mind into that point and feel it, the feeling of pain, deepen your awareness, introvert your mind, assemble your mind and will and experience the pain.

The feeling of pain in any part of the body or the whole body is to be felt acutely.
Deepen your awareness and quickly introvert your mind.
Assemble the energy particles of will and experience the pain.

Pleasure: Then contemplate on the sensation of pleasure and experience the feeling of pleasure, any pleasure which you can recollect, which you can experience, which you can superimpose with much ease.
Maybe pleasure belonging to the sense of taste, pleasure belonging to the senses of hearing and seeing.
Contemplate on any pleasure, contemplate on any pleasure, so much so that the feeling and the experience of pleasure will become a truth and actuality to you.
Go deep in your awareness and direct your will to feel the pleasure, either experienced or wishing to experience.
It should be brought immediately before the mind and you should contemplate on it and become one with the experience of pleasure.
You should go deep, deepening your awareness by assembling the scattered energy particles of will and by directing the will to feel the pleasure.
Check up your awareness. Are you awake?
Are you sleeping? Are you listening to me?

Visualizations

Psychic centres: Discovery of the psychic centres in the physical body.
Mooladhara chakra is situated at the bottom between the excretory and urinary organs, or just below the uterus.
Above it is swadhisthana, at the lowest point of the spinal cord.
Above that is manipura in the spinal cord, situated just behind the navel.
Above that is anahata, situated in the spinal cord in line with the frontal depression in the chest.
Above that is vishuddhi in the neck where the cerebral structure begins.

Above that in the inferior brain is ajna chakra, the upper end of the spinal cord from where the superior brain begins.

Above that, on the top of the head at the point where the Hindu Brahmins have their tuft of hair is bindu.

And on the crown of the head is sahasrara.

Concentrate on them and touch the points.

Sahasrara, bindu, ajna, vishuddhi, anahata, manipura, swadhisthana, mooladhara.

Mooladhara, swadhisthana, manipura, anahata, vishuddhi, ajna, bindu, sahasrara.

Sahasrara, bindu, ajna, vishuddhi, anahata, manipura, swadhisthana, mooladhara.

Mooladhara, swadhisthana, manipura, anahata, vishuddhi, ajna, bindu, sahasrara.

Sahasrara, bindu, ajna, vishuddhi, anahata, manipura, swadhisthana, mooladhara.

Mooladhara, swadhisthana, manipura, anahata, vishuddhi, ajna, bindu, sahasrara.

Sahasrara, bindu, ajna, vishuddhi, anahata, manipura, swadhisthana, mooladhara.

Mooladhara, swadhisthana, manipura, anahata, vishuddhi, ajna, bindu, sahasrara.

Sahasrara, bindu, ajna, vishuddhi, anahata, manipura, swadhisthana, mooladhara.

Mooladhara, swadhisthana, manipura, anahata, vishuddhi, ajna bindu, sahasrara.

Sahasrara, bindu, ajna, vishuddhi, anahata, manipura, swadhisthana, mooladhara.

Psychic symbols: Concentrate on the psychic symbols of these centres. I will repeat the psychic symbols and you will have to find out the centre for yourself.

A red inverted triangle with a serpent, tail up, projecting a little outside the triangle, hood down projecting outside the triangle, pink in colour with three and a half coils, a flame emanating from the fangs.

Then next unconsciousness, the grey sleepy void.

Then next a bright yellow lotus giving off heat.
Then next a small flame of a solitary lamp.
Then next nectar drops and sensation of cold.
Then next drowsiness and intoxicated mood.
Then next an infinitely petalled lotus, very big, much bigger than many heads, infinitely petalled red lotus with an oval shaped shivalingam in the centre of it.
Repeating them again: inverted red triangle, serpent with three and a half coils, pink serpent, unconsciousness, bright yellow lotus, solitary flame of a lamp, nectar drops and cold, semiconscious state, crescent moon and moonlit night, very big and infinitely petalled red lotus with a shivalingam on it.

Rapid images: Now become aware of these images as I name them...
Shivalingam, standing Christ, a flickering lamp, a big mango tree, a tall palm tree, a car moving on the road, a burning fire, coloured clouds, yellow clouds, white clouds, blue clouds, clouds coming from the western side, clouds moving fast with the wind, a starry night, a starry night, a moonlit night, a moonlit night, a full moon, a dog standing, a cat lying, a horse racing, an antelope racing, an elephant moving, the sun rising, the sun setting, waves of the ocean, waves of the ocean, church bells ringing, over the church a cross, in the church a priest kneeling, a devotee praying, an aeroplane in flight, sandy beach, people relaxing on the hot sand, a red triangle, a golden spider web.

Different bodies: See yourself lying down without clothes, see yourself lying down without clothes, see your transparent body outside your physical body.
See the third smoky body. See the fourth luminous body.
Go deep into your brain, go deep into your brain.
A small golden egg, a golden egg, small size, luminous in character.
See a golden bird, the bank of a river, a sailing boat, sailors rowing a boat, crystal water, ripples on it, on a big

lake a blue lotus, on a big lake a red lotus, on a big lake a white lotus, on a big lake a yellow lotus, an old house, from the chimney smoke is rising, in the cold winter a fire is burning in the house, a crocodile, a big tiger, a fish swimming in the crystal water, an elephant, an antelope, a cobra, blue lotus on a lake.

Transparent body: Now the golden cord from your navel, the golden cord attached to the navel; at the other end of the golden cord your transparent body, your transparent body.

Try to see your transparent body from the physical body, and try to see this physical body from the transparent body.

See it again and again, see it again and again.

See the spinal cord, the spinal cord inside your backbone.

A creeping sensation in the spinal cord, moving upward.

Watch your body as I watch your body from anywhere outside.

See your physical body from top to toe, see your physical body from top to toe, the different parts.

All parts of your body, head, trunk, neck, right arm, left arm, right leg, left leg, the whole body, the whole body.

Try to see your whole body, as I see your whole body, as if you are seeing it from outside.

Then from the physical body look up at the end of the golden cord and see the transparent body without any distinction of eyes, nose, ears, with simple outlines, with simple outlines, transparent, beyond which the sky can be seen, try to see the transparent body.

Try to see the transparent body from this physical body.

Try to see this physical body from the transparent body, try to see this physical body from the transparent body, try to see this physical body from the transparent body.

As if you are seeing your physical body by being outside of it, as if you are trying to see your physical body by being outside of it, your head, your chest, abdomen, hands, legs and everything, the whole body.

Try to see the physical body as if you see it from the transparent body, try to see the physical body as if you see it from the transparent body, as if you are outside of it.
Then from the physical body look up at the end of the golden cord and see the transparent body without the distinction of eyes, nose, ears, etc., with simple outlines.
Transparent body beyond which the sky can be seen.
See yourself doing all the different asanas, in yogamudra, shashankasana, supta vajrasana, bhujangasana, shalabasana, dhanurasana, paschimottanasana, sarvangasana, halasana, matsyasana, sirshasana, shavasana, lotus pose, practising meditation on chidakasha.
See yourself in the lotus pose practising meditation on chidakasha, a yogi in meditation, a sannyasin in his coloured gown, a Buddha in lotus pose, standing Christ, kneeling Mary, an illuminated cross.
Go into your physical body, go into your physical body, find the life force, become aware of the life force.
Become aware of prana, prana the life force, experience it as heat.
Experience it as all round movement.

Aura: See your own aura, around your face, either from within the body or from outside the body.
Find your own aura, is it yellow, green, violet, white, deep yellow, burning yellow, golden yellow, pink, red, purple, brown, black?
Find out your own aura, look at yourself from a different angle.
Try to see the spinal cord and three nadis inside it, red, white and blue.
See which is where, which is red, which side, which is white, which side, which is blue, which side.
Go to bindu and try to discover a sound.
There is a sound, an infinite ocean, calm and quiet, dark green jungle with cobras, lions and goats living in love and peace, a cottage in front of which a rishi is sitting in samadhi.

Om: Experience *Om*, experience the chanting of *Om* everywhere, experience the chanting of *Om* everywhere.

Concentrate on the form of *Om*, concentrate on the form of *Om*, concentrate on the form of *Om*.

Hear the chanting of *Om*.

Become aware of a sacrificial fire, the smoke arising from the fire, the smell of incense, the fragrance of flowers.

Become aware of yourself, find out and question yourself, 'Am I aware of myself, am I asleep, am I attuned to Swamiji?'

Body: Look at your body, in parts and as a whole, see your right thumb, second finger, third finger, fourth finger, fifth finger, palm, wrist, elbow, shoulder, armpit, waist, hip, hamstring, thigh, knee, calf, ankle, heel, sole, right toes, one, two, three, four, five; see your left thumb, second finger, third finger, fourth finger, fifth finger, palm, wrist, elbow, shoulder, armpit, waist, hip, hamstring, thigh, knee, calf, ankle, heel, sole, left toes, one, two, three, four, five.

See your whole body from the top, see your body from the top, your face, your nose, your eyes, your eyebrows, your head, your teeth, your body, up and down, as clearly as I see it, try to see your body by being outside of it.

Senses: Now look to your senses, five karmendriyas and five jnanendriyas.

The karmendriyas or senses of action are the right hand, left hand, right foot, left foot, tongue which speaks, reproductory and excretory organs.

Now the jnanendriyas or the senses of knowledge, the right eye, left eye, right ear, left ear, nose, tongue which tastes, skin all over the body.

Mind: Now become aware of your mind, now become aware of your mind, the mind by which you know, become aware of the faculty of awareness, become aware of the faculty of awareness. Become aware of yourself.

Develop the awareness that you are practising yoga nidra, become aware that you are practising yoga nidra.

Prana: Look within yourself, look within yourself and become aware of the existence of prana in your body, in the form of heat and all round movement.

Golden egg: Again, look within and become aware of the existence of consciousness, through which you are practising yoga nidra; again look within and become aware of the existence of your consciousness, by which you know that you are practising yoga nidra.

Look within your body and become aware of the golden egg in the centre of your brain; look within your body and become aware of the golden egg in the centre of your brain, a golden egg, very small, very small, very small, and that is the seat of the highest consciousness in man. Golden egg, very very small in size, and that is the seat of the supreme consciousness, highest consciousness, the centre of the consciousness in man.

A golden egg, not big, but small, and that is the seat of supreme consciousness in man.

Try to become your own witness, try to become your own witness, try to become your own witness.

Say to yourself: 'I am not this body, I am not these senses, I am not this mind, I am not this prana, I am not these thoughts, I am not this awareness, I am not this awareness, I am not this body, I am not heaviness, I am not pain, I am not cold. I am not mind, I am not karma, This body, the senses, the mind, the awareness, the prana, the feeling, experiences and everything that is physical, mental, psychic, unconscious, I am not. Immortal Self I am.'

Again and again go into your brain, and find that golden egg within you, and try to see yourself in that.

And again and again try to go into your brain, look within into the golden egg and try to identify yourself with it.

Try to find that golden egg within you, and see yourself as that.

Again, 'Beyond the mind, body, senses, the karma, the nature, and everything that is physical, mental, psychic, unconscious, I am in the form of this golden egg.'

Become aware of your physical body, try to see your physical body by being outside of it.

Try to see your physical body as if you are seeing it from outside.

Go into your brain, go within, in the centre of your brain, and try to concentrate on and try to become aware of a golden egg, bright golden egg, the cosmic consciousness in you.

And try to locate the golden egg in the centre of yourself, try to become aware of it, and say to yourself, 'I am that'.

Resolve: Now repeat your resolve three times. (*Pause*)

Finish: Yoga nidra is now complete.

Hari Om Tat Sat

17

Antar Mouna

The Sanskrit word *mouna* means 'silence', and *antar* means 'inner'. Therefore, the English name of this practice is 'inner silence' and it is a great sadhana designed to make the aspirant aware of the inner silence as well as the inner noise which generally prevents one from knowing the silence.

In our daily life our minds are almost continually externalized. We see and hear only what is going on outside of us, and we have little understanding of the events taking place in our inner environment. The practice of antar mouna is designed to turn this around, so that for at least a short period we can see the workings of our mind and understand them. In reality antar mouna is one of the few 'permanent sadhanas' which can be practised spontaneously all the twenty-four hours of the day by anyone who is really determined to know oneself. By maintaining awareness of one's internal environment, thoughts, emotional reactions, etc., one can speed up one's personal evolution to the utmost degree. It will make one understand the workings of one's own rational and irrational mind, as well as giving one an understanding of what makes other people tick.

The technique for the meditational practice of antar mouna is the first step toward attaining this permanent state of inner understanding. Although it is to be practised for a maximum of one hour a day, its effects carry on after the practice is over and one will automatically start to know his own 'hidden side' and to see how he is reacting to life's situations in a clear and honest manner.

The practice of antar mouna is subdivided into a number of stages. The first stage of the technique is to be aware of all the outside sounds and occurrences that are going on around you. The second stage is to withdraw oneself from all outside stimuli and to be aware only of the workings of the mind: what it is thinking, how it is reacting and what images are coming from the subconscious. The third stage is the conscious creation of thoughts, which is followed in stage 4 by awareness and dissolution of spontaneous thoughts. Stage 5, the last practicable stage, is the suppression or removal of all thoughts, or the awareness of shoonya (the void), followed in stage 6 by the state of spontaneous meditation.

Antar mouna is a complete training system for the awareness process; it teaches one how to know the processes of the mind and ways in which one can bring them under control. It can be practised at any time by simply reflecting on the question, "What am I thinking? What is occurring now in my mental sphere?" When practised many times daily, this witnessing process becomes an automatic occurrence continuing by itself and showing you who you are, what you are doing here and where you are going. It can truly be said that in this practice through the awareness of inner noise you will come to know the voice of silence, the golden sound that sings of eternity.

CLASS PRACTICES

1: Complete practice (stages 1–5)

Stage 1: Awareness of external stimuli

The practice of antar mouna begins.

Please close your eyes and keep them closed throughout.

The asana is steady, the position is steady, the eyes are closed, the spinal cord is erect.

'I am prepared for inner silence' – this should be the mood of the mind.

Preliminary practice is not awareness of internal things, but awareness of external sensual experiences, different sounds, different sensations, different sensual experiences. Concentrate on the external sounds and sensations, not at all considering them to be disturbances in concentration. With absolute concentration, with total external awareness do this practice until you find a change of atmosphere in your mind.

Don't fight with your senses, do not struggle with your sense expressions and sense experiences but become aware, or become a spectator of them.

You should be aware.

You should also awaken the awareness of 'I am aware, I am hearing, I am aware that I am hearing Swamiji speaking.'

In this way the mind and the senses should be trained to become undisturbed by the sensual experiences.

Neither the sound nor the taste nor the touch or anything else should disturb you at any cost.

In spite of the fact that you hear the outer sounds or that you experience different sensations in your physical body, such as itching, laziness, scratching and so on, you should not be disturbed by them. This particular aspect of sadhana is known as pratyahara, the fifth step of raja yoga.

Pratyahara means withdrawal of the senses, as hinted by Sri Krishna in the second chapter of the Gita.

"Even as the tortoise withdraws its body within the framework of the shell, in the same manner the senses should be withdrawn."

Not by force but by a technique the senses should be withdrawn from the respective objects of the senses.

The senses should be calmed down by the *drashta* or *sakshi* attitude.

The senses should be calmed down by the attitude of 'I am witnessing the experience of hearing and I am aware of the sound, the music of birds.'

'I' is the third thing in this process.

First is the ears, second is the object of experience, the sound, thê music of the birds, and third is I, who is the spectator, who is the witness of this process of sense experiences.

Then in this way you should distinctly and deeply and intensely, with classification, develop this threefold awareness in the first stage of antar mouna.

The experiencer, the object of experience and the seer of both.

The subject and the object, the ears and the sound, the eyes and the form, the skin and the touch, the tongue and the taste, the nose and the smell.

This should be witnessed properly, without any sense of disturbance.

This is the introversion of your sense experiences, and this you should do at any time, not at all hating the outer experiences, but looking at them with *drashta bhava*, with the attitude of a witness.

You will find within a few moments there is an atmosphere of calm, tranquility and peace, and then you will be ready for meditation.

This is your homework for today.

Please practise it at home, at night, in the evening or in the daytime; in the car or in the rickshaw; wherever you are, amidst your friends or alone.

Do not wait for calmness and silence.

There will be noise, there will be disturbances, the body will shake but you must develop the dharma of a calm and silent witness.

Stage 2: Awareness of spontaneous thought process

The second stage of antar mouna consists of becoming aware of your thinking process.

You should become aware of thoughts, the spontaneous thought process, thoughts that come and go of their own accord.

You don't have to bring in a thought flow.

Let it come spontaneously and let it go of its own accord.

You must remain a silent witness of every thought that is going through your mind.
When you become aware of a particular thought you will have to say to your mind, 'Yes, I am thinking about this and that.'
If the mind supposedly becomes free of thought you should try to become aware of that state also.
There can come a stage of thoughtlessness even in the case of a beginner.
You are looking at the process of your thoughts and you are bound to be sure of the thoughts that are passing through.
You should remain alert all throughout, and the form of this is not to check the thoughts but to know the thoughts.
If sometimes you become absentminded and then you revive your consciousness, say to yourself,
'Well, I became absentminded for some time and during those moments I was thinking of this and that.'
But please try to be aware of all thoughts that are spontaneously coming up, that are manifesting on your conscious plane.
They may be good thoughts, or they may be bad thoughts, but those thoughts do not come from anywhere outside.
They are expressions of your inner personality, they are expressions of yourself.
In the first kriya, in the first practice, the sense experiences came from outside.
Here, in this kriya the thoughts are manifestations or expressions of your inner self.
So therefore when you are able to see your own thoughts, you are able to know the content of your personality.
If bad thoughts do not come to your conscious mind continually, it means that either you have become a liberated sage, or only that the suppression is still there and the suppression is too tight, the suppressions of the subconscious mind are not released.
Therefore, remember that you are an aspirant.

Remember you are a practitioner of dharana.
Remember you are a practitioner of pratyahara.
Bad thoughts and good thoughts will come.
They should come and you must bring them up.
If they come, please look at them indifferently, with absolute detachment, as a witness or as a spectator.
This is the second stage of antar mouna.
It is the practice of pratyahara in raja yoga.
The first step in raja yoga is yama, then niyama, then asana, then pranayama, and then comes pratyahara.
Pratyahara means return, pratyahara means retreat, pratyahara means withdrawal.
Please listen with absolute attention.
When bad thoughts come to your mind, do not stop them; immediately become alert, become aware that you are thinking of murder, of revenge, of robbery and so on.
If bad thoughts come to you and you set them aside, if you do not want to observe them, if you suppress them, they will come to you with greater force next time.

Stage 3: Creation and disposal of thoughts at will

Bring to mind any thought which you want to think.
Don't let it come spontaneously, but bring it in by your will.
Think it over for some time and then – dash it off.
Do not allow spontaneous thoughts to express and to manifest at all, but create a thought voluntarily at will.
Maintain it for some time, brood over the thought, and then suddenly, with a jerk, dash it off!
If a spontaneous thought wants to express itself, however good or bad or interesting or inspiring the thought may be, do not allow it to manifest but say, 'No! I don't want you now.'
Then again think another thought, maintain it and brood over it for some time and then with a sudden jerk, dash it off.
Then go on to the third; create a thought, maintain it for some time, and when you have thought over it for some

time dash it off and go on to any other thought, of course at will.
It is not difficult to get rid of good thoughts, but evil thoughts are very stubborn.
Once bad thoughts come to your mind, at any time of the day, it becomes very difficult to get rid of them, and therefore the mental training should proceed this way:
You create a bad thought at will, brood over it for a minute or so and then with a jerk dash it off.
If you practise it for some time, for a month or so, your mind will definitely develop a habit of dashing off, throwing off, or disposing of the bad thoughts that come up from the depths of your subconscious.
This very important exercise in antar mouna is unknown to many people.
It is definitely a great achievement if an aspirant, or anybody for that matter, is able to shake off, or dispose of bad thoughts as and when they come in the mind.
It is definitely a very great achievement.
To awaken good thoughts is not a very great achievement for a spiritual beginner, but it is a great achievement when you are able to dispose of the evil thoughts when they come up to the surface of the mind.

Stage 4: Awareness and disposal of spontaneous thoughts

Now in the fourth stage of inner silence spontaneous thoughts are to be awakened; the thoughts are to be allowed spontaneity.
Spontaneity of thoughts.
You don't bring thoughts at will, as you did in stage 3.
Just allow thoughts to come, and think about them for some time.
But when the point of disposal comes, when the point of disposing of the thought comes, you should dispose of the thought at will.
It is not that a particular thought goes away spontaneously.
Its arrival is spontaneous, but its departure should depend upon your own will.

This is the fourth stage.

In this fourth exercise I am not asking you to allow bad thoughts only.

Good and bad both from your subconscious mind should be allowed to come up spontaneously.

Inner silence is the fifth stage of raja yoga.

It is known as pratyahara.

When you have perfected this inner silence, then dharana begins.

It is impossible for anyone to meditate if he cannot withdraw his senses from the sense objects.

Nobody can meditate, nobody should meditate without perfecting the practice of pratyahara.

When pratyahara is perfect, dharana begins, and when dharana is perfect, only then can we think of meditation.

And the moment that meditation dawns, samadhi is at the very threshold of life.

Stage 5: Awareness of the inner space

This is the fifth step in antar mouna.

Now look within.

Awareness of the inner space, awareness of the inner space, awareness of the inner space.

Be aware of chidakasha.

Be aware of the inner space, be aware of the colourless and formless inner space of your psyche, and then be aware of thoughts.

If you think any thought, if a thought comes into your mind, dash it off, dispose of it, immediately, without brooding over it.

Keep yourself absolutely alert, alert in the sense that if any thought comes into your mind you immediately dispose of it.

You do not brood over the thought, you do not recognize it at all.

A thought comes up and you immediately push it down and out.

This is the stage where thoughtlessness is practised.

Any thought that comes into your chidakasha, any thought that manifests from within, and it will manifest, has to be dashed off.

If in place of thoughts, forms and visions come into your conscious plane, then you will have to employ a different method, and that is the method of dissolving the form into formlessness.

Sometimes you look into your inner space and the space is devoid of colour and form.

But in certain cases the forms, like dreams or like visions, not of course ideas and imaginations, but clear-cut forms come up on the surface of that consciousness.

Supposing that it is a bird or a woman or a tree or a landscape, you should immediately try to disperse it, as if a drop of water is spilled over a canvas where you have made a picture.

And immediately within a moment you find that the whole picture, that the whole work of art is dissolved.

Therefore, there are two different sadhanas in this stage.

One is that you become aware of the inner space.

You become aware of the inner space, and if any idea comes in the form of thought and imagination, you just dispose of it.

Try to maintain a state of thoughtlessness.

Try to maintain a state of thoughtlessness by remaining aware of one thought that 'I shall have no thought.'

This is the real state of inner silence in which every thought that tries to manifest on the inner surface of consciousness is immediately disposed of, is not allowed to manifest, is not allowed to manifest.

The forms and the visions that flow on the surface of consciousness are to be correctly and very properly dissolved in the formless chidakasha that is within your psychic self, that is your own psychic personality.

'I do not want any thought, I do not want any thought, I do not want to think any thought.'

Only one thought, only one thought should be allowed

to remain in your consciousness, and that single thought is that 'I shall have no thoughts.'

The first stage of inner silence, broadly speaking, is to remain aware of sense experiences with absolute indifference and with an attitude of a witness.

Stage 2 is the spontaneous incoming and outgoing of thought processes.

Stage 3 is thinking at will, brooding at will and disposing at will of your thoughts.

Stage 4 , incoming of spontaneous thoughts, disposal of thoughts at will.

Stage 5, no thinking process; every thought that emanates from your consciousness is to be immediately disposed of. You should not allow your mind to think any thought, and if the mind tries to do so, stop it.

This is the complete practice of inner silence.

Please open your eyes and relax your body.

Hari Om Tat Sat

2: Short practice (stage 2)

Sit or lie down comfortably.

Don't create any mental inhibition, don't withdraw your mind.

Don't hate any experience, don't love any experience, don't react to any experience.

Don't react to any desirable experience, thought or feeling.

Let the sense capacities flow in freedom.

Don't withdraw the mind from disturbances, but follow the disturbances of thought, sound or any kind of disturbance.

Thoughts are stimulated and spontaneous from the depth of your mind.

Thoughts without stimuli, or thoughts with stimuli from outside sounds.

Listen to any disturbing sound and follow it with awareness and concentration.

Follow every thought as a witness, as if you are looking from one corner of your brain.
'I am thinking...I am listening...I am having this sensation.'
Keep on listening, seeing, witnessing the process of your concentration.
You will find thoughts coming up, unstimulated, unagitated, from the very depth of your past.
Meaningless, insignificant thoughts, in the form of a glimpse or in the twinkling of an eye.
Unless you are a careful witness, it will not be possible for you to follow the swift speed of your consciousness.
You will follow the free flow of your consciousness.
Spontaneous, desirable, undesirable.
Sometimes there is a mental block and no thoughts come.
It means that consciousness is not manifesting itself.
The mind goes on thinking.
Even now you are thinking, although you do not see it.
There is a veil put over the thought process.
Tear it off and find thought after thought.
They belong to past, present, different associations, like lightning.
When a thought comes, see it and register it in your mind.
Many thoughts you don't want to remember, you want to escape from.
This is natural.
To escape from the thought is our psychological nature.
Memory or past; everything is suppressed.
If the veil is removed it can manifest itself, and when it works in freedom there is joy and happiness.
If the past expresses itself while you are practising detached witnessing, you become free from agony and other reactions.
Most important is to see yourself.
One – allow freedom.
Two – see yourself.
The whole process of manifesting, of course.

Don't oppose any thought, don't hesitate, don't suffer from any thought of guilt.
Free thinking but vigilant seeing.
You are not the thought, but you are the witness of the thought. Absolute detachment.
Don't associate yourself with any thought, keep yourself separate, as a seer of thoughts, as a beholder of experiences.
You are not the thought, you are not the energy of your consciousness, you do not hate any thought, you do not love any thought, you do not like any thought, and you do not dislike any thought, but allow them to manifest.
You do not see yourself thinking.
It is difficult to see yourself thinking.
It is easy to think unconsciously; it is difficult to think consciously.
The thinking process is spontaneous.
Sometimes the process is stimulated by external influences.
Spontaneous thoughts come from the very depth of your personality.
Withdraw the curtain of inhibition, then the thoughts come spontaneously.
But if they don't come spontaneously, then we shall stimulate the thinking process.
When the consciousness manifests itself freely, when the curtains of the inhibitions are fully or partially withdrawn, then first the horrible thoughts will come.
Good thoughts will come later.
If they come in the beginning, they come on account of your social behaviour or environment, because you have been taught to be good, merciful, etc., but this is not a true manifestation of your consciousness.
That is the negative face of your consciousness, your personality, your past; it has to come out and if not in thoughts, then it comes out in actions.
Don't be shy or tense; remain a witness of the whole process.

Don't identify yourself with any thoughts, remain a witness, apart.
It may be the feeling of sleep, of drowsiness, any thought from outside, or the thought of this sound.
Always say, 'I am a witness of what I hear, of thoughts passing in my mind, feelings of whatever, or the thought of the practice.'
Be a witness of any thought, of any silly thought.
Constant awareness of anything happening in and outside you, in your consciousness or in your subconsciousness.
In you the witnessing consciousness, in you the ever alert consciousness of witnessing thoughts.
The more you come to that inner consciousness, the more you become that beholding.
If you are able to awaken the inner consciousness in the form of a witness, then nothing in your mind will go unnoticed.
Even the flickering of your eye, or scratching of the body, or the slightest thought, everything will be noticed by you.
If you will be able to keep your inner consciousness alert, then no phenomena concerning you will go unnoticed.
No thought, no feeling; consciousness, unconsciousness and subconsciousness will be unfolded to you; your whole consciousness will be unfolded to you.
The most important things are to keep the inner consciousness constant, and that you yourself should manifest thoughts, feelings, senses and processes.
The inner consciousness must be constantly vigilant, should watch peace, agitation, disturbance, desirable and undesirable thoughts.
You must behold all feelings, all thoughts, all dimensions of consciousness.
Anything your mind can comprehend, your inner consciousness must be a constant beholder of that.
And if the thoughts stop in a mental block – nothing comes, then you must behold that nothing is coming.

Any painful situation which might come up, witness it. Register constantly what you see, hear, know, feel. 'I know, I feel, I hear, I see', and so on.
This will be a truly wonderful experience of self-purification, self-witnessing and self-analysis, free mind and alert consciousness.
Go on thinking and beholding, open the door of your thoughts, open your subconscious mind, go on seeing it. Now withdraw your mind from freedom because the practice of antar mouna is over.

Hari Om Tat Sat

18

Inner Visualization

What is concentration? It is one-pointedness of mind, the ability to hold the awareness of the mind on one object without wavering. Its perfection leads to meditation. In the state of concentration, the mind is not aware of the environment or other peripheral things that surround the object of concentration.

Why is concentration so powerful? This can be best illustrated by comparing the mind of an average person to a light bulb. The rays of light from the bulb go in all directions; the energy spreads. If one stands five feet away from the bulb one sees the light but does not feel the heat, even though there is great heat in the centre of the bulb at the filament. In the same way, the average mind has great power in a potential form but it is dissipated in all directions. The mind thinks of different things one after the other, without dwelling in depth on any one subject. The average mind does not utilize its power. Science has produced something that was once only described in science fiction novels, the laser. It is a method where all the rays of light from a source are lined up with each other so that they go in the same direction and in unison with each other. They vibrate in harmony with each other. The original source of light need not be any greater than a light bulb, yet if we stood three meters from a laser beam source, the beam would burn a hole straight through our body. This is concentrated light.

In exactly the same manner, concentrated thought, although unlikely to burn a hole in anyone, also has greater power; it has the power of heightened perception, the ability to see more of the underlying truths behind phenomena. It has the power to do 'impossible' amounts of work. A concentrated mind can do anything. Many people who have found it to be true by developing their concentration have said this. Also, a concentrated mind is automatically a relaxed mind. The reader has probably experienced this himself. Whenever one becomes deeply engrossed in something, perhaps an interesting book, one comes to a state of relaxation and calmness of mind when one completes the activity.

Concentration in relation to meditation is absolutely necessary, for it prevents the mind wandering aimlessly in all directions. Concentration is also vital for everything that we do in life; without concentration we can achieve nothing. One only needs to look around to see the truth of this statement–a person with a concentrated mind can do all kinds of work with great efficiency. Not only this, but work done with a concentrated mind becomes more enjoyable. A person who is unable to concentrate, who thinks of others while he does the work in hand, makes mistakes, takes an unnecessary length of time to complete the task, if he does at all, and on top of this is likely to be unhappy while in his state of mental fog. He will be continuously thinking how the time is going slowly, thinking about meal time, or mulling over his problems. So concentration is essential in day to day life as well as in meditation.

In many respects we can liken the mind of the average person to a kitten. The kitten will chase a ball of wool for a few seconds, discard it and then start to chase its own tail. After doing this for a short time, it will run into the next room for no apparent reason and then continue its uninhibited play. Our mind, under normal circumstances, behaves in exactly the same erratic manner. It is only by practice and the realization of the need to change ourselves that we can become more concentrated.

Concentration in any form allows us to see more clearly or perceive something of the underlying reality behind everything. Our mind is continually caught in a web of constantly changing events; it jumps from one happening to the next without really seeing any of them. When we concentrate on one thing, the mind is kept confined to a limited field of interest and this helps to break the tangle with other objects, which prevents us seeing any one object in its true light. Simultaneously, the mind itself becomes calmer and so is more able to allow the illuminating consciousness to shine through. The individual is more able to comprehend the deeper significance behind life's phenomena.

Let us now discuss various practices for developing concentration.

Pure visualization (dharana)

This is the most common type of meditational practice, which is done by millions of people all over the world and is a most important part of all religious systems. Generally known as concentration, this practice is done in many different ways. The object to be visualized can be seen to be located in any of many different centres throughout the body, such as chidakasha, hridayakasha, daharakasha (the space at mooladhara), in any of the chakras, or as a full sized form outside of and in front of the body.

The concentration can also be done on the different parts of the practitioner's own body, the physical processes of the body, the stillness of the body, or the relaxation or tension of the body. The breath is also used as the object of concentration by many practitioners, in such techniques as manipura and anahata shuddhi given in the section on mantra siddhi yoga.

The system of yoga teaches that almost any object can be used as the basis for concentration. The only important factor is that the object must have some meaning to the practitioner, and that he should use the same object day after day in his practices. The object should come to his attention spontaneously, and for most aspirants it will come to symbolize the totality of existence in a single, meaningful form known as the ishta devata.

Objects of concentration

To some people an object for use in meditation comes by itself in the form of a vision or a dream. This is the best. Other people, however, have difficulty in locating a suitable form for themselves, and in order to assist these people in locating their own psychic symbols we are including the following list. It should be noted that the following are only examples; in fact there is almost an infinite number of suitable objects, scenes, scents, sounds and symbols which can be used for visualization.

Our advice to the aspirant searching for his symbol is that he should go through this list quickly; perhaps one of the listed items will strike him as being suitable, and perhaps not. Even if he does not find a suitable symbol in this list, however, we are sure that the many ideas which we have included will set off his own memory or imagination, and it will assist the correct symbol to come into his mind spontaneously, most likely at a time of complete relaxation.

Gods, saints, people and parts of the body: Vishnu, Brahma, Shiva, the trimurti, Rama, Radha, the beautiful Sita, Saraswati playing music, Parvati, Arjuna in his chariot, Sarada, the Garuda bird with wings outstretched, Kunti, Ganesha, Hanuman up to tricks, Lakshmi, Durga seated on a tiger, Kali with the necklace of skulls, Varuna, Vayu, Indra and Mahakali, Jehovah, Zarathustra, standing Christ, kneeling Joseph, seated Mary, the Buddha seated on a lotus, Abraham, Lao-tze, Confucius, Moses standing on the mountain, Milarepa, Naropa, the Pope, Saint Ambrose, Saint Theresa, Swami Sivananda, all other deities and saints, guru, your father, mother, husband, wife, son, daughter, relative, friend, see a single eye, a hand in a mudra, the lotus feet of a master, the tip of the nose, a head, a chin, the eyebrow centre.

Sacred objects: the shivalingam, Shiva's trident, shaligram, the everburning jyoti (lamp), the cross in its many shapes, a mala, an altar, magnificent cathedral window with the sun streaming through, the Eucharist, the chalice, a prayer wheel turning noisily, a candelabra holding a lighted candle, a crystal ball, a priest in coloured robes, a prayer rug, a statue of a happy Buddha, statues of patron saints, tantric statuary, the Venus de Milo, the archangel in the Louvre, Michelangelo's Madonna and Child, David and Medici, the statue of winged Perseus and the dreaded Medusa, the kundalini, the squared circle, the noble and perfect Grecian columns, the ring of skulls, the symbol of the crescent moon and the conch shell.

Features and phenomena: a church, a chapel, a soaring gothic cathedral, a Tibetan chorten, the Nile pyramids, a towering mosque, a monastery, an ashram, a temple in gold and red, a mansion, a winged pagoda and a sun drenched villa, a massive mountain, rolling hills, green and gentle valleys, a desert, a thirst quenching oasis, rugged cliffs, sloping sandhills, a long white beach, a green dripping cool jungle, a forest grove, a quiet wood, paddy fields drying in the sun, a plantation of gently waving trees, an orchard, a flower garden, a vegetable garden, clouds in the sky, the rolling thunder darkened sky, rain, fog, storm, hail, a twisting turning tornado, an earthquake, the restless murmuring sea rolling on the seashore, the gentle patter of falling raindrops, a Japanese garden, a lotus pond, a shady glade, sun streaming through the trees, view from a mountain top, a headland reaching out into the sea, a boat in sail, a deep dark well, waves rippling on a lake, a stream rushing over small rocks, a spring gushing out of the earth, a pool of water.

Living things: an elephant, an antelope, a lion surveying his realm, a tiger poised and waiting, a monkey, a white cow grazing, a shy deer listening, a soaring eagle, a swooping swallow, a swan gliding gently on the water, a flamingo, a lyre bird, a red breasted robin, a butterfly gently poised on a leaf, a peacock proudly displaying his feathers, angel fish, a sea horse, a star fish in beautiful colour, an octopus waving its arms gently in the sea, a beautiful sea anemone like a plant in the breeze, a crocodile basking in the sun, a coiled serpent, a yellow lotus, a tulip, a blood red rose newly opened, a tiny violet, a large yellow sunflower full blown to the sun, daffodils, white lilies tinkling in the breeze, a foxglove, bluebells, a fragile orchid with dew on its petals, leaves, bonsai trees, a verdant damp grassy lawn, a peepul tree, damp moss.

The material universe: the material elements: earth, fire, air, water and ether; the physical elements: tamas, rajas and sattwa; the constellations: Aquarius, Pisces, Virgo, Libra, Gemini, Capricorn, Sagittarius, Scorpio, Leo, Taurus, Cancer and Aries; the fire of the precious ruby, onyx, agate, the star reflected in sapphire, the sunlight captured by the diamond, jasper, topaz, the secrets hidden in the crystal, amethyst, the gleam of the opal, the coolness of jade, the garnet and the pale lustre of the pearl, the beryl; pewter, iron, the crystallized sunlight of gold, tin, brass, the moonglow of silver and the dull fireglow in copper; the circling planets of Earth, Mars, Venus, ringed Saturn, Jupiter, Neptune, tiny Mercury, mysterious Uranus and lonely Pluto.

Colours and shapes: the colour red, blue like the sky on a clear day, the green of lush grass, yellow, indigo, orange like a sannyasin's dhoti, white, black, the pink of an evening sky, purple like the royal colour, the light of the sun on a hot day, the pale moon by night, the colour in the sky at sunrise, at sunset, gentle rays of the sun reaching through trees, a fire glowing in the dark, a candle still and bright, lightning, a bright star glowing in the night sky, a circle, bindu – the point, an inverted triangle, a star with many points, a hexagon, a rectangle, a rose petal shaped like a human heart, a clover leaf pattern, the shape of a leaf from a tree, a small golden egg, the leaf of a peepul tree, batik prints and the shapes printed on cloth, any of the yantras, the Sanskrit beeja mantras, a chakra, the ida, pingala and sushumna nadis intercrossing at the chakras, radiant with prana.

Trataka

This is discussed later in this book. It is a most powerful practice for developing concentration in which the mind is directed towards some external or internal object. It is also an excellent method of developing inner visualization – in other words, the ability to see and maintain a clear image of any object in front of the closed eyes.

General advice

The reader should not become despondent if he finds these practices difficult; he will not be unusual in this respect. Most of us are so used to thinking in terms of words that we lose our ability to visualize. It is to break down this limitation in our lives that these techniques are partly intended. Another thing is that many of us walk through life as if in a daydream. We see objects that surround us, yet at the same time we do not really see them. We look at a tree for example, yet the fact that we are looking at the tree or the details of the tree doesn't really register in our brain. It is only during times when the object we are looking at has deep meaning for us that we really register its shape, characteristics, etc.

Concentration should not involve any strain in any way. This seems contradictory to many people, for they automatically associate concentration with some form of strong effort. They perhaps have a mental picture of a man grunting and grinding his teeth, biting his nails or frowning when they think of someone who is in deep concentration. These physical manifestations are actually signs of some kind of mental conflict and, of course, strain. They do not indicate the intensity of concentration.

Deep meditation, which is the prime reason for developing the powers of concentration in this book, can only spontaneously occur if there is deep concentration together with a totally relaxed mind. Don't fight the mind. Meditation, which is freedom and ecstasy, cannot take root in a tense and manipulated mind; so train the mind, coax the mind, but do not battle it.

When you do these exercises, don't expect to be able to do them at first attempt; if you can then you are fortunate. For most people it is necessary to stimulate the unconscious activities and to train them to formulate the images. This takes time, but eventually, perhaps after a few days or weeks, depending on the intensity with which you do the exercises, the unconscious will almost automatically produce the image at your request. Therefore be patient and you will surely succeed.

Simple visualizations

Technique 1: Association of ideas

Choose a pleasant object, such as a dog or a beautiful picture.

Concentrate on the object; we will for the sake of argument assume it is a dog.

Don't keep your mind totally absorbed on the dog but try to relate it to relevant objects and ideas which are connected with the dog. Always, however, keep the dog as your central theme; don't let your mind wander off onto a completely irrelevant line of thought.

Think of the shape of the dog. Think of the different types of dogs. Bring your mind back to your central object – the dog. Think of the food the dog eats. Think of the close relationship that exists between a dog and man. Return to the central object and so on, bringing in as many related topics as possible. Don't let your mind think of anything that is unrelated.

Duration: Try to do this practice for ten minutes every day.

Benefits: This method is an excellent way of developing the power to control ideas and thoughts at will. It is an invaluable method of training the mind to follow a fixed path of association instead of jumping from one subject to a totally unrelated topic. It is useful for training the mind for meditation, as well as everyday activity.

Practice note: Different objects can be chosen when you have exhausted the field of exploration of one object.

Technique 2: Recall by visualization

Remember your walk to a friend's house. Try to visualize, with the eyes closed, as many details of the journey as you are able.

What were the houses like? Try to see each house. Try to see the parked cars and the people you passed or met. Try to visualize and relive every detail.

Alternatively, while you are in a room, slowly and carefully look around, then close the eyes and try to visualize every object.

While reading a book, close the eyes and try to see a clear picture of the environment the book is trying to describe.

Count from 1 to 20 and try to imagine each number as a picture in front of your closed eyes as you mentally repeat it.

Duration: Try to do this practice for ten minutes every day.

Benefits: This technique is useful for developing a deeper awareness of your surroundings, and for improving memory. It develops the powers of concentration, recollection and inner visualization.

Practice note: It can be done in any surroundings, in a train, bus, or in almost any situation where the mind is unoccupied with the affairs of the world. The possibilities are almost infinite; the following are suggestions.

A class transcription of a technique following this system, known as the visualization test, is given at the end of this chapter.

Technique 3: Contraction and expansion of scenery

Look at a picture of a beautiful scene which has a prominent object in the centre; a real scene, of course, can be utilized for the same purpose. Study the scene for some time until you think you are fully aware of its basic details.

Close your eyes and visualize the same scene internally. Try to see a clear inner picture. Then progressively erase the background from the scene. For example, remove the sky, then remove the trees in the background, then progressively remove what surrounds the central theme of the scene. Eventually you should only picture the central object or theme: perhaps a cow, or a man. Keep your awareness on this object for a short time.

Then start progressively to build up the picture in the same, but reversed, order in which you broke it down previously. Eventually you should see the whole scene again.

Benefits: This technique is useful for developing visualization and memory.

Technique 4: Object visualization at will

Close your eyes. Look at the blank space in front of your closed eyes.

Think of any object and try to picture it as an image. After a short time, say half a minute, think of another object and again try to imagine a picture of it.

Carry on in this way for as long as you have time.

You can choose any object – perhaps a swan, a candle, a tree, a pen and so on.

Duration: This simple practice can be done at any time in the day.

Benefits: Again it develops powers of inner visualization.

Technique 5: Contraction and expansion of viewpoint

Choose a hollow object such as a cupboard, match box, pencil box and so on.

First, imagine that you are inside the chosen object, you have reduced in size so that you exist at the central point of the enclosed space.

See the inside of the object from this viewpoint. What do you see? Try to visualize the objects that you would see from this point of view.

Carry on this practice for a few minutes. Then expand your viewpoint so that you are much larger than the hollow object.

See the object from different angles – from underneath, from the top, from each side and so on. Then again contract your viewpoint so that you once more exist at the centre of the enclosed space.

Repeat this expansion and contraction a few times.

When and if this practice is perfected with one object, choose another hollow object.

Benefits: This develops the powers of imagination and of visualization.

CLASS PRACTICE

Visualization Test (Psychic writing)

Stage 1: Preparation

Sit in a comfortable meditation posture.

Close your eyes.

Stop all movements and wait for the instructions.

Become aware of chidakasha, the dark space in front of the closed eyes.

Stage 2: Psychic writing in chidakasha

Visualize the blackboard. On the blackboard do psychic writing very clearly with a piece of chalk.

Follow my instructions very carefully.

You must be able to see what you write in the colour chalk that I tell you to use.

Numbers: Please remain alert and visualize the board. Hold the chalk and as I count, start writing the numbers 1, 2, 3, 4, 5, 6, 7, 8, 9, 10.

You have to write, not visualize, you have to do all the actions as you would on the blackboard.

Wipe out that line with the duster.

Take the chalk again and write 11, 12, 13, 14, 15, 16, 17, 18, 19, 20.

Wipe out that line with the duster and get ready to write another line.

Words: First write at the top N–O S–L–E–E–P–I–N–G, no sleeping.

On the next line write again with the chalk.
I A–M N–O–T S–L–E–E–P–I–N–G, I am not sleeping.
Write it very carefully, letter by letter.
Wipe out the two lines.

Numbers: Again get ready to write the numbers 21, 22, 23, 24, 25, 26, 27, 28, 29, 30.
Wipe out that line with the help of the duster and look at the blackboard.

Lines: Remember that you are writing with a piece of chalk on the blackboard.
You are in front of the blackboard, and you start to draw a wavy line from one side of the blackboard to the other.
The wavy line keeps on moving from side to side, from one side to the other.
When you have finished one line go on to the next and the next. Go on drawing the wavy lines with the chalk on the blackboard.

Numbers: Wipe out what you have drawn, and on the blackboard with the chalk write the numbers again clearly, 41, 42, 43, 44, 45, 46, 47, 48, 49, 50.
Wipe out the line with the duster.
Now take a pink chalk and write on the blackboard 51–.
A dash is a long sign, it is a double hyphen, 52–53–54–55–56–57–58–59–60.
Wipe out that line with the duster and take the pink chalk.

Words: With the pink chalk write on the blackboard something very important, N–O S–L–E–E–P–I–N–G, no sleeping.
Write another line with the pink chalk, I–, capital I, space, am– A–M, space, not–, N–O–T, space, sleeping– S–L–E–E–P–I–N–G, full stop.
Read the writing in pink chalk again, *I am not sleeping*.
Wipe out these two lines with the duster.

Numbers: Look at the blackboard on which you are writing.
On the blackboard you are going to write with a pink chalk 61–62–63–64–65–66–67–68–69–70.
Wipe out that line with the duster.

Zeroes: Get ready to write again with a yellow chalk, O–O–O go on writing O–O–O–O–O–O change the line, O–yellow chalk, O–O–O–O–O–O–O–O–O change the line, O–O–O–O–change the line, make the mind steady, see the blackboard.

Take the yellow chalk O–O–O–O–O–O–O–O–O–O–O.

Take the duster and wipe out all the zeroes.

Triangles: Take the yellow chalk again and on the blackboard draw a small geometrical triangle, draw a triangle, another triangle, another triangle, another triangle, another triangle, another triangle, another triangle, change the line, another triangle, a yellow colour, another triangle, another triangle.

Wipe out all the lines with the duster and take the white chalk again.

Crosses: With the white chalk draw a cross, the arithmetic sign of multiplication, the cross of multiplication, draw another cross with the white chalk, another cross, draw another cross, draw another cross, draw another cross, change the line, another cross, draw another cross, draw another cross, draw another cross, draw another cross.

Wipe out these two lines with the duster.

Numbers: Take the white chalk. Be ready to write on the blackboard in front of you. Remember the blackboard, remember the chalk. You are writing on the blackboard with the white chalk the numbers 90, 89, 88, 87, 86, 85, 84, 83, 82, 81.

Change the line, 80, 79, 78, 77, 76, 75, 74, 73, 72, 71.

Wipe out that line with the duster.

Straight lines: Take the white chalk and draw straight lines on the blackboard from one side to the other, one line underneath the other.

Go on drawing the lines, line after line, with the white chalk, from one side to the other.

When one line is finished, draw another.

Keep on drawing straight lines with the white chalk.

Wipe out the lines with the duster.

Wavy lines: Take the white chalk and draw wavy lines. Wipe out the lines with the duster.

Zeroes: Take the pink chalk and write on the blackboard O, O, O, O, O, O, O, O, O, O.

Sevens: On another line with the pink chalk write 7, 7, 7, 7, 7, 7, 7.

Points: Change the line and write one point, another point, another point, another point, another point, another point, another point, another point, another point. Change the line.

Stars: With the pink chalk draw a star, a star with corners, draw another star, another star, another star, another star, another star, another star.

Wipe out the line with a duster.

Name: With the pink chalk write your name on the blackboard. Write your name letter by letter on the blackboard.

Om: Wipe out the line with the duster and with the pink chalk write the symbol of *Om*, another *Om*, quickly, another *Om*, another *Om*, another *Om*, another *Om*, change the line, another *Om*, steady the body and mind, another *Om*, you are writing another *Om*, another *Om*, another *Om*, another *Om*, another *Om*.

Wipe out the lines with the duster.

Triangles: Take the yellow chalk and draw a very big triangle, the base of the triangle is as wide as the base of the blackboard and the top of the triangle is the upper part of the blackboard.

Now draw an inverted triangle, the base of which is the upper part of the blackboard. You can see that the two triangles intersect each other, the upper portion of each triangle is dividing the base of the other triangle in the centre.

Wipe out these triangles with the duster.

Put aside the yellow chalk.

Take the white chalk and draw a triangle, the base of the triangle is the base of the blackboard. Draw an inverted triangle with the base at the top. These two triangles intersect each other, the top of each triangle is at the base of the other triangle.

Wipe out the lines with the duster.

Perpendicular lines: Take the white chalk and draw perpendicular lines on the blackboard, as straight as possible.

Draw perpendicular lines from the top of the blackboard to the bottom of the blackboard.

When one line is over, draw another line; the distance from one line to another is almost one inch.

Keep on drawing.

Wipe out the perpendicular lines with the duster.

Name: With the white chalk write your name on the blackboard in any language, in any alphabet. Write your name letter by letter.

Om: With the white chalk write the symbol, *Om, Om, Om, Om, Om, Om, Om, Om.*

Zeroes: On another line write with white chalk, O, O, O, O, O, O, O. Change the line, O, O, O, O, O, change the line, O, O, O, O, O, O, O.

Wipe out the lines with the duster.

Steady your mind and body and look at the blackboard.

Numbers: Take a white chalk and write again, 1, 2, 3, 4 5, 6, 7, 8, 9, 10. Change the line and write 11, go deep and write clearly 12, 13, 14, 15, 16, 17, 18, 19, 20. Change the line and write 21, 22, 23, 24, 25, 26, 27, 28, 29, 30.

Wipe out the lines with the duster.

Name: Look at the blackboard. Put down the white chalk and take up the yellow chalk. With the yellow chalk write your name on the blackboard.

Om: On another line write the symbol *Om*, the symbol *Om*, the symbol *Om*, the symbol *Om*. Wipe out these lines with the duster.

Circles: Take the pink chalk and draw a small circle. Go on drawing it so that the circle becomes broader and broader until the whole blackboard is covered. Start from the small circle inside and go on clearly drawing the circles with the pink chalk, covering the whole of the blackboard so that it becomes a very big affair. Wipe out the circles.

Triangles: Now take the white chalk and draw a number of small triangles on the blackboard. Draw some inverted triangles also. Wipe out the triangles with the duster.

Numbers: Take the green chalk and write on the blackboard the numbers from one on, with commas in between.

Carry on the exercise independently.

The chalk is green, the blackboard is black, write from number one on clearly, say the numbers from one clearly to yourself, with commas in between, changing the line at the proper place.

Continue writing the numbers with green chalk on the blackboard, with commas in between, changing the line at the proper place.

Wipe out the lines and now take up the white chalk.

Triangles: Draw a triangle with white chalk, wipe out the triangle with the duster.

Take a pink chalk and with the pink chalk draw a triangle on the blackboard, thick lines.

Wipe out the triangle with the duster, take the yellow chalk, yellow chalk, and draw a triangle on the blackboard with the yellow chalk, thick lines.

Wipe out the triangles with the duster.

Take a blue chalk and draw a triangle on the blackboard.

Wipe out the triangle with the duster and take a green chalk, a green chalk and draw a triangle with deep lines on the blackboard with the green chalk, thick lines.

Wipe out the triangle with the duster, wipe out the triangle with the duster, take a deep red chalk and draw a triangle with the deep red chalk.

Wipe out the triangle with the duster and take a violet chalk, draw a triangle on the blackboard with the violet chalk, a triangle with thick lines.

Wipe out the triangle with the duster. Take a geru chalk and draw a triangle with thick lines on the blackboard.

Wipe out the triangle with the duster.

Dashes: On the blackboard draw a small dash.

What is a dash? Two hyphens make a dash.

One dash with white chalk, another dash with white chalk, a third dash with white chalk.

Then, start a new line.

Take a pink chalk, *dash, dash, dash*, take the yellow chalk and draw *dash, dash, dash*, take the green chalk and draw *dash, dash, dash*, take the red chalk and draw *dash, dash, dash*, take the blue chalk and draw *dash, dash, dash*, take the geru chalk and draw *dash, dash, dash*, take the violet chalk and draw *dash, dash, dash*.

Try to see it again from the top. First line white *dashes*, second line pink *dashes*, third line yellow *dashes*, green *dashes*, red *dashes*, blue *dashes*, geru *dashes*, violet *dashes*.

Again go to the top and just see the first line, *dashes* in white, see the second line which you have drawn in pink, the third one in yellow, the fourth green, the fifth red, the sixth blue, the seventh geru, the eighth violet.

Straight lines: Wipe out all the lines with the duster and quickly take a white chalk. Draw a straight line.

Take a pink chalk and draw a straight pink line. Take a yellow chalk and draw a straight yellow line. Take a green chalk and draw a straight green line. Take the red chalk and draw a straight red line, the line is thick. Take a blue chalk and draw a straight blue line. Take a violet chalk and draw a straight violet line.

Look at the blackboard. Wipe out all those lines with the duster.

Zeroes: With the white chalk write O, O, continue writing O, O with the white chalk, change the line when necessary, go on writing O, O, O, O, with the white chalk, changing the line at the proper place.

Stage 3: Ending the practice

Now wipe out all the lines with the duster. Relax all efforts at visualization. Become aware of your surroundings and your body.

The practice is over.

19

Chidakasha Dharana

Chidakasha dharana is really a type of pure visualization technique as described in the preceding chapter; however, it is also a special kind of meditational practice in itself. Chidakasha literally means 'the space of consciousness'. It is the viewing screen of ajna chakra, the jet black room where psychic phenomena manifest for the benefit of the physical mind. It is the link between the conscious, the subconscious and the superconscious, and is the point where the object of meditation is most easily perceived.

The chidakasha is visualized as a black room with four walls, a floor and a ceiling. In the floor of chidakasha near the centre of the rear wall is a small hole leading downwards. This is the sushumna nadi, extending downwards through the lower chakras. In the front wall is a screen on which visions will appear if you are able to relax the tensions and complexes which now inhibit them.

Chidakasha dharana is a meditation technique which can unlock the gates to the secret realms of awareness, the stage of mind and states of consciousness which are now beyond our mortal sight. To him who perfects this kriya comes light and wisdom, untainted by the aberrations and limitations of our physical eyes.

CLASS PRACTICES

1: Seated in a meditation posture

Stage 1: Body awareness

Sit in a comfortable meditation posture.

Make sure that your spinal cord and head are erect, the hands interlocked or placed on the knees in chin or jnana mudra.

Be sure that you can sit motionless for some time without feeling any strain in the physical body.

Try to be aware of the different sounds taking place around you – the ticking of the clock, the noise of the moving fan, my voice reaching you in the form of instructions, the singing of the birds and the rhythmic sound of melodious music.

Become aware of your physical being, the body, total awareness of the body.

Maintain a perpetual flow of awareness of the physical body.

Be sure that you are aware of the physical body, not of any part in particular, but awareness of the body as a whole.

The more aware you are of your physical body, the steadier the mind becomes.

Stage 2: Breath awareness

Then switch to your breathing process but at the same time maintain awareness of the body.

A perpetual flow of awareness of the physical being should continue. In addition to that become aware of the breathing process, the natural, effortless breathing process, by looking within and becoming aware of your breath, the physical breath.

You don't have to breathe; the breathing process is natural and automatic, sometimes deep, sometimes long, sometimes coarse, sometimes short, and the breathing goes on.

Awareness of breathing as well as maintaining awareness of the physical body.

Stage 3: The space of chidakasha

Suddenly switch to the essence of your being, the space of chidakasha that is in you, space that permeates every atom of your physical and mental being, space that is not within and that is not without but that is everywhere.
It is not the space in front of your forehead,
it is not the space over your head,
it is not the space behind your head,
it is not the space of the heart,
it is not the space of the abdomen or navel,
it is not the space of the lower part of the body,
but it is the total space which includes the physical being in toto.
When you are aware of chidakasha you are aware of the space which is in the body, throughout the body, permeating the whole body, including the whole body, not a particular point in the body.

Stage 4: Perception of colours

Become aware of chidakasha, the totality of your formless existence, the space in which your body exists.
It is black in colour, it is formless.
Try to maintain awareness of the colour of chidakasha.
What is the form of the chidakasha colour?
Is it black, light black or any other colour?
It changes from moment to moment.
The colour of chidakasha changes from colour to colour.
If you observe minutely the colours that are passing.
you will find that the colour is changing very, very swiftly.
Sometimes it is difficult to keep pace with the moving colours and vibrations of the colours.
Sometimes they are distinct and sometimes they are not distinct.
You can't understand them, you can't see them, you can't read them.
These colours are not the same every day.
At this moment, tomorrow, the colour of your space, the colour within will not be the same as it is now.

Try to be aware of the quickly changing colours, overwhelming colours, overpowering colours, passing through your chidakasha.
Chidakasha is a formless existence that supports your physical being, but it has colour.
If you look at it attentively, if you remain aware of chidakasha, you will find colour vibrations moving very fast.
These colours are symbolic expressions of the life force within you.
Try to be aware of these colours.
Chidakasha is the formless existence, the formless essence, the formless reality of your physical being.
It is not the chidakasha which you see in front of your forehead,
it is not the chidakasha which you see at the top of your head,
it is not the chidakasha behind your head,
it is not the chidakasha in the region of your heart or navel, or your back,
it is not the chidakasha in the lower part of the body.
It includes the chidakasha of every centre, total chidakasha.
You should intensify your awareness.
Then be aware of the colour and say – 'I am investigating, watching and recording the colour.'
If you can read the colour, say it mentally – red, blue, violet, etc.
If you can't understand, say, 'I can't understand.'
Sometimes the colours are so complex that it is not possible to understand them, but whether you understand or not, you should be aware of the colours.
Try to maintain an unbroken and unceasing flow of awareness of this chidakasha.
Do not let not your mental awareness break in between.
Constant, unceasing, unbroken and spontaneous awareness of the total chidakasha, which includes all the aspects so far unknown.

In this formless space your physical body exists.
Chidakasha is not the body, but the body is in chidakasha.
While practising chidakasha dharana you may come across shades of light, a flash of light, a host of light, any vision or anything or any thought or any object.
But with all that you must maintain awareness of the whole chidakasha.
If your mind goes to the chidakasha in front of the forehead, tell your mind, 'I want to be aware of the total chidakasha.'
Firstly you must understand chidakasha, and when you are able to read the colours, then you should bring your awareness to the centre of the eyebrows and become aware of a cave, a circular cave, a circular opening within.
You are aware that it is a cave but you are not able to get into it.

Stage 5: Repetition of Stages 1–4

Repeat the practice again.
Become aware of your physical body, intensify your awareness of your physical body, awaken the body awareness until you are completely aware of the existence of your body as a whole.
Then switch to the normal breathing process.
Watch it with unbroken awareness, continuous unbroken awareness of the breathing process.
At the same time there should be total awareness of the body as well.
You must practise this breath awareness with absolute attention, with absolute care and vigilance.
Then, with a jerk, become aware of chidakasha – the space within, the space without, the space without form, the space which is undefined.
You are within that space.
Become aware of the colours. If you are not able to record the quickly flowing colours, it does not matter.
But be aware that colours are coming and going with terrific speed from moment to moment.

See the colours change in every part of the body. Watch them with care and vigilance.
Perception of colour, witnessing the colours, pursuing the colours, noting down the colours, reading them with care. That is your main duty now in chidakasha.
When I say chidakasha I do not mean the dark area of the inner firmament in front of the forehead, or above the head, or behind the head, or on the back or in the front or below.
I mean the totality of all forms of awareness of chidakasha.
If you are able to understand chidakasha, you are able to understand the essence of your body.
If you are able to feel it, you are able to feel the psychic principle in man.
Go to bhrumadhya. Carve a cave with a circular opening and glance at it from a distance.
You see it is dark.
You go near the opening and peep inside. It is very dark, nothing can be seen, nothing can be understood.
If by chance you went into it, you could not see even yourself, and that is the deeper aspect of chidakasha.

Stage 6: Ending the practice

Now chant *Om* seven times.
While producing this *Om* please convert the sound waves into subtle psychic waves by becoming aware of the entire personality in chidakasha, devoid of physical awareness.
Do not lose awareness of the dark area, the formless chidakasha.
In between there appears to be flickering, a fraction of awareness of my existence, the body.
Imagine it in this way – all around, all within and everywhere, the inner space.
The body seems to be the form of awareness.
You should do this now while you practise *Omkar – Ommm... Ommm... Ommm... Ommm... Ommm... Ommm... Ommm...*
Gradually take your mind outside.
Become aware of your physical body.

Then expand your awareness outside, become aware of the sounds, the movements of the persons sitting around you and my instructions.
Be sure that you have become extrovert, that you are aware of outer things.
Are you aware of the music, the fans, my voice, the others around you, yourself sitting in your meditation posture?
You have been practising chidakasha awareness.
Now relax your body and open your eyes.

Hari Om Tat Sat

2: Lying in shavasana

Stage 1: Preparation

Lie down on the floor with your head facing the front.
Close your eyes and try to maintain complete physical immobility.
Adjust your body so that you do not have to make any movement for about thirty minutes.
The first important point in practising meditation is to adjust yourself so that you are not disturbed by the outer surroundings.
Once you have made yourself comfortable, then try to become quiet physically.
Throughout the meditation practice, be sure that you are not sleeping, and you are awake throughout.

Stage 2: Physical immobility

Concentrate on your physical body.
Awareness of the body as a whole from top to the toe.
Do not concentrate on a particular part, but on the whole body from top to toe.
The whole body is lying on the floor.
You are aware of the whole body in the form of homogeneous awareness.
It is not only awareness of the head, or arms, or feet, or back, or your fingers, but it is a homogeneous awareness which includes the whole body at one glimpse.

When you concentrate on your whole body you have to go on suggesting to yourself, 'The whole body, the whole body, the whole body', and at the same time you are aware that you are lying on the floor.
Concentration on the physical body, and also concentration on physical immobility, side by side.
If by chance you happen to make any physical movement you should become aware of that movement, it should not be an unconscious movement.
Try your level best not to move the body even slightly. This is the first lesson in inner yoga.
It is immaterial if you are unable to concentrate your mind, but it is of the utmost importance that you are aware of the whole body, and that the body does not make even the slightest movement.
When you concentrate on the whole body and you keep your body motionless, there comes an experience called levitation.
The experience should be as though the body is becoming detached from the floor; of course it really doesn't move but there is an astral feeling.
You do not have to concentrate your mind on anything, you just have to be aware of the body.
This is the most important and basic part of meditation.
Whether you practise your meditation with a religious spirit or in the lotus pose or in vajrasana or while lying down, does not matter much, but the most common rule is not to move the body at all.
Everbody has an unconscious habit of moving the body without knowing it, but that should be controlled by a conscious motivation.
The unconscious movement of the body, the unconscious movement of fingers and toes, the unconscious movement of head and eyes, should all be controlled by conscious awareness.
When you are able to concentrate on the whole body, then you experience the whole body as if it were a statue.

When you control your physical movements, you control a portion of your brain and a portion of your mind.
You want to make a movement, but then you become conscious of this and you say to yourself, 'No movement.'
When you concentrate on the whole body and when you remain conscious of each and every physical movement that is about to take place in the body, then the body becomes like a statue and the consciousness changes.
When you concentrate on the whole body, consciously controlling each and every physical and nervous movement, a relaxed attitude happens in the brain.
Now there should be no movement whatsoever, you have to force your body not to move.
Become conscious of one fact, 'Am I immobile or am I moving?'
Do not not make even the slightest movement of the eyes, nose, lips, toes or anywhere else.
Control the impulse.
It is easy only if you remain conscious throughout.
This is the most important basic practice in yoga.
Before you try to control the mind, you must have the strength to control the body.
Before you try to concentrate on subtle things, you should be able to concentrate on the gross body.
It should become easy because you know your own body, you can feel your own body, you can develop awareness of the whole body.
Therefore, it should be easy for you to concentrate upon your own body which is gross, visible and subject to experience.

Stage 3: Breath awareness

Now, subtler than the body is the breath.
Concentrate on the natural breath that is flowing in your nostrils.
When you concentrate on your breath say to yourself, 'I am breathing in, I am breathing out.'
Concentrate on your own natural breath.

The breath is effortless.
It is the natural breath.
When you breathe in, know you are breathing in.
When you breathe out, know you are breathing out.
Do not breathe unconsciously.
Maintain constant awareness of the process of breathing.
Every time you breathe in and out be aware that you are breathing in and out, 'I am aware that I am breathing in and out.'
Unbroken and unceasing awareness of the breathing process.
The breath is natural and it is flowing in your nostrils.
It enters through both nostrils and it becomes one in the eyebrow centre.
The breath forms a triangle and the top of the triangle is the eyebrow centre.
The breath goes in through the nostrils and goes out through the nostrils in the form of a triangle.
Practise awareness of the passage of breath through the nostrils to the eyebrow centre.
Constant and unbroken awareness of the breath that is being formed in the shape of a triangle.
Concentrate on the breath.
Bring yourself closer to the breath.

Stage 4: Mantra awareness

With this breath feel the mantra *Om* with the ingoing breath and with the outgoing breath.
Feel *Om* with inhalation and with exhalation.
Be aware that you are breathing in and out through the nostrils up to the eyebrow centre, and become aware of the mantra at the same time.
Continue with this practice for two minutes.
Breath and *Om* together.
Bring yourself closer to breath and mantra.
Total awareness. No sleeping.
Work the breath and the mantra together in the form of a triangle.

Stage 5: The inner space

Withdraw your mind and concentrate on the forehead from inside as though you are looking at the inner side of a wall.

The whole brain, the whole skull is like a room. The forehead is like the front wall and you are trying to see the inner side of the front wall.

Concentrate on the inner side of the forehead.

When you concentrate on the inner wall of the forehead you become aware of the inner space or the inner sky which is known as chidakasha.

Awareness of this inner space should be completely relaxed.

This brain, this skull is like a house, like a room, and the forehead is the front wall.

The right temple is the right wall.

The left temple is the left wall.

The back of the head is the back wall.

The top of the head is the top of the room.

Now try to see the inner walls of this room.

Concentrate on the inner side of the front wall.

Now take your mind to the right side and try to see the inner side of the right wall.

Shift your mind to the left side and try to see the inner portion of the left wall.

Shift your mind to the back and try to become aware of the inner side of the back wall.

Shift your mind to the top and try to see the ceiling.

Become aware of the space from inside as though you are sitting in a room and trying to see the walls of the room from the centre of the room.

See the front, front, front, right, right, right, left, left, left, behind, behind, behind, top, top, top, front, front, front, right, right, right, left, left, left, behind, behind, behind.

See the top from inside, top, top, top, front, front, front, right, right, right, left, left, left, behind, behind, behind, top, top, top.

Stage 6: Ending the practice

Now become aware of the whole space which is surrounded by the four walls and the ceiling.

Be aware of the homogeneous space which is inside.

See this space, and feel yourself inside it.

Develop awareness of the physical body. Be aware of your breathing. Be aware of your surroundings.

Chidakasha dharana is now complete.

Hari Om Tat Sat

20

Trataka and Antar Trataka

The word *trataka* means 'to gaze steadily', and the practice of trataka develops the concentration. The power of the mind is great, but through desires and energy-wasting pastimes, this energy of mind is dissipated in all directions. If we can apply this widely spread mental power to one purpose, either spiritual or worldly, we cannot fail to succeed. We are subjected to a continual bombardment of sensory data and we are unaware of the multitudes of thoughts that are passing through our mind. It is only when we relax and partially cut off the sense awareness that we become conscious of all this mental activity.

In order to concentrate on an object, either internal or external, the mind must be kept under control so that it is not distracted. One way of doing this is by choosing something as the object of concentration which will make the mind experience peace and steadiness. For this purpose the mantra *Om*, a flower, a picture of your guru, a deity, or the flame of a candle can be chosen. The candle flame is the most convenient and practical object for beginners.

Trataka consists of two stages – bahir trataka and antar trataka. In bahir or external trataka the concentration is on an outer object because this is easier for the untrained mind, since the mind likes to attach itself to outside objects. When we close our eyes to concentrate on an inner symbol or point, the mind immediately gets bored and wavers. In antar trataka, or inner visualization, the mind is trained to introvert. When operating through the medium of the senses the mind loses energy, but when concentration is on an inner object, withdrawn from the senses, it gains energy.

The practice of trataka has many beneficial effects. Daily practice helps to develop concentration power and memory. It also helps to strengthen the eye muscles and so improves the eyesight. Trataka opens up a storehouse of energy. In India, trataka is used as the most important exercise to achieve occult powers. Although they do not realize it, Christians have for centuries practised trataka on icons, holy pictures and religious symbols.

Trataka develops the power of concentration, as the conscious energy is directed towards one point, one focus of attention. The practice automatically leads to meditation. Even beginners will have experiences after a short period of practice. Trataka should be practised in the steadiest possible posture. Although it can be done sitting in a chair or in sukhasana, it is far better to practise it in rock steady siddhasana, siddha yoni asana or padmasana.

In both external and internal trataka, the eyes should not blink or move in any way. At first this is a little difficult, but with practice it becomes very easy; the important thing is relaxation of the eyes. This is essential to obtain a clear inner image. The mind should be kept only on the object or image, nothing else. If the mind starts to think of other things, gently bring it back to the object of concentration.

Objects of concentration

Any object can be used for concentration; the following are a few suggestions: a candle flame, a black dot, your psychic symbol or ishta devata, the tip of the nose, the eyebrow centre, a shivalingam, sky or water, the moon, a star, a crystal ball, your own shadow, darkness, emptiness, a mirror, a yantra or mandala.

In the method described in this book, we will use a candle flame for trataka. This is particularly powerful, for it acts like a magnet for the eyes and mind. It also leaves a very clear after-image when one practises inner trataka, because of its brightness. In the method described here, external trataka is practised first. This is then discontinued and inner trataka practised utilizing the after-image of the object concentrated on during external trataka.

The object, in this case the candle, should be placed so that it is at arm's length from the eyes and at eye level. It should be placed directly in front of the body when in the sitting position. If you have eye defects, position the object so that you do not see double. The after-image will have a tendency to move up and down or sideways. Try to hold it steady in one place, preferably at the eyebrow centre.

Trataka on a candle flame

Stage 1: Preparation

Place the lighted candle an arm's length away at eye level.
Hold your back, neck and head in a comfortable and erect position. Close your eyes.
Be aware of your whole body.
Adjust yourself so that you have no need to move throughout the entire practice.
Feel the steadiness of the whole body.
Do this for two or three minutes.
Chant *Om* seven times, and feel the vibrations surging through your whole body and brain.

Stage 2: Outer gazing

Open your eyes and gaze at the top of the wick.
Your eyes should be wide open but without strain.
Try to consciously relax the eye muscles.
Do not close the eyes and try not to blink.
If, however, you feel discomfort, blink the eyes and continue the practice. Do not move the pupils.
Keep your mind on the wick of the candle.
If your mind wanders, gently bring it back.
Do this for three minutes or as long as you are able comfortably, then close your eyes.

Stage 3: Inner trataka

Visualize the after-image of the candle flame at the eyebrow centre; try to keep the image steady.
Keep your mind only on the image.
If experiences arise, try to remain a witness.
Do this for as long as the image is clear.

Stage 4: Repetition of stages 2 and 3

Again open your eyes and gaze at the top of the wick.
All your awareness should be focused on the top of the wick.
Continue this practice for three minutes or as long as is comfortable, then again close your eyes and concentrate on the after-image.
Do this for as long as the image is sharp and clear.
Repeat this procedure for between ten and thirty minutes according to how much time you have, then chant *Om* seven times.

Stage 5: Ending the practice

Keep the eyes closed for a short time and merely watch the activities,or lack of activities of the mind.
Be a witness to any experiences that are occurring.
Then open your eyes and blow out the candle.

CLASS PRACTICE

Trataka on a candle flame

Stage 1: Preparation

Adjust your position so that you are one arm's length away from the candle flame.
Ideally, the flame should be at eye level.
If it is lower, it will create strain when you are practising, if it is too high it will also create strain.
The correct level is exactly at eye level.
Close your eyes and make sure that you are comfortable.
Chant *Om* three times – breathe in *Ommm...Ommm... Ommm...*
Keep your eyes closed.

Stage 2: Body awareness

Become aware of your body.

Create a mental picture of your body, or feel your body, but be aware of your whole body.

Feel that your body is growing from the ground like a tree.

Your whole body is firm like a tree growing from the ground.

Your legs are the roots, and the rest of your body is the trunk.

Feel the firmness of your body.

Your whole body is fixed in the ground, it is part of the ground.

There is no difference between your body and the ground.

Your body is growing from the ground.

Try to experience this.

Be aware of your whole body, and its firmness on the ground.

Your whole body is fixed firmly in the ground.

Total awareness of your body.

Be aware of your right foot, your left foot. Either you can feel it, or you can create a mental picture of it or both. Your right knee – total awareness. Your left knee. Your right thigh, your left thigh. Your right buttock, your left buttock. Your whole back – be aware. Your abdomen. Your chest. Your right arm – total awareness. Your left arm. Your head. Your whole body.

Be aware of your whole body – nothing else.

Now open your eyes.

Stage 3: Outer gazing

Look directly into the middle of the flame at the top of the wick.

Try not to blink your eyes. The less you try the easier it is, so don't use too much effort.

Allow your eyes to relax.

Fix your eyes at the top of the wick in the middle of the flame.

Focus your whole attention at the top of the wick.
There is nothing else but the top of the wick.
If you must blink your eyes, then do so – don't strain, but as much as possible look at the top of the wick without flickering or blinking your eyes.
Your whole vision should be focused on the top of the wick. (*Long pause*)
Try to pierce the top of the wick with your vision.
Total concentration. (*Long pause*)
Fix your vision on the top of the wick.
There is nothing else, only the top of the wick.
Your vision is almost pulled to the top of the wick, like a magnet attracts iron filings.
Feel as though your vision, your attention, is being pulled to the top of the wick.

Stage 4: Inner trataka

Now close your eyes.
Watch the after-image of the candle if you can see it.
If you can see it, watch it, as a witness.
If you cannot see it, don't worry, merely watch whatever happens in front of your closed eyes.
You must only be a witness; don't involve yourself with what is happening in front of your closed eyes.
See it as happening outside yourself, as something separate from yourself. Be aware. (*Long pause*)
Whatever happens in front of your closed eyes, let it happen. Don't suppress it. (*Long pause*)

Stage 5: Repetition of stages 3 and 4

Now open your eyes and look into the candle.
Again concentrate on the top of the wick, in the middle of the flame.
Allow your eyes to relax, but try not to blink or flicker your eyes.
Try to fix, to rivet your attention on the top of the wick in the middle of the flame.
Feel the magnetic attraction of the top of the wick. (*Long pause*)

There is nothing else but the top of the wick.
Be totally absorbed in watching the wick in the centre of the flame.
Try to pierce the top of the wick with your vision.
Now close your eyes.
Again, watch the after-image if you can see it.
If you can't see it, then watch the space in front of your closed eyes.
Watch anything that might occur there.
You must be a witness, an observer.
Don't become emotionally involved in what happens there.
Only watch, nothing more. (*Long pause*)
If you can still see a clear image of the candle, then focus your attention on the wick, if you are able to.
If you see visions or pretty pictures, watch them as though you were watching television, but don't interfere with the program.
Only watch. (*Long pause*)
Now open your eyes for the last round.
Again focus your whole attention on the top of the wick.
Look into the centre of the flame, into the middle of the flame, into the very core of the flame.
Try not to blink or to flicker your eyes.
The less you try, the easier it becomes.
When you try too hard, it is difficult.
When you relax more, and do not try so hard, it becomes easier. So try, but not too hard.
Focus your attention on the top of the wick, on nothing else. (*Long pause*)
Look into the heart of the flame, at the wick.
Now close your eyes.
The procedure is the same.
Watch the after-image of the candle if you can see it.
Otherwise watch the black space, and see what happens.
Be a witness.
Whatever happens, be a witness, nothing more.
Don't interfere, only observe. (*Long pause*)

Stage 6: Ending the practice

Now chant *Om* five times. Feel the vibrations of *Om* throughout your whole body, your whole brain, the whole room, everywhere. Feel that you are a transmitting station of *Om*, and also feel that you are a receiving station.

Feel the vibrations of *Om* pulsating, vibrating, reverberating, everywhere.

Breathe in, *Ommm...Ommm...Ommm...Ommm...Ommm...*

Keep your eyes closed for one minute and be aware of your feelings, of your state of mind, of the sounds outside, but sit quietly for one minute. (*Pause*)

Hari Om Tat Sat

Antar Trataka

Now we come to the fully psychic practice where we become aware not of an outer object, but of an inner object or point. For this practice you need peace of mind and steadiness of the body.

Technique

Stage 1: Body steadiness

First you must practise kaya sthairyam, total physical steadiness.

Sit with the spine straight, head erect and eyes closed.

Then mentally relax every muscle and joint in your body and extend your awareness to the whole body.

Your body should become as motionless as a statue.

Gradually the weight of the body will decrease and there will be a development of psychic stiffening in the body.

Kaya sthairyam is a powerful tool for pacifying the mind.

Stage 2: Psychic breath awareness

Then become aware of the psychic breath; watch it, feel it going in and out.

There should be no points of tension in your body.

Relax them, and you will find that the speed of the breath will slow down until it is hardly moving and all you will feel is the subtle breath drifting through the throat area.

Now chant *Om* seven times, loud, long and clear, with fading *mmmm*.

Stage 3: Inner visualization

Bring your awareness into the centre of the eyebrows, called bhrumadhya.

Take your awareness there slowly and quietly, step by step, no tense efforts.

Concentrate your awareness in the eyebrow centre.

If it seems difficult, lick your fourth finger and make a dot with your finger between the centre of the eyebrows.

Leave your finger there for a few seconds, then remove it.

Hold your awareness at the eyebrow centre, and if possible try to see a small star.

If you can't see it, then try to imagine it.

Perhaps it will appear for a moment and then vanish, this does not matter.

Keep on watching it.

Imagine a star in the sky, a single small star in an endless sky; it suddenly winks.

After long practice, this inner star becomes a natural occurrence and is a development of your spiritual imagination.

If you can see the star in bhrumadhya, it means you have developed a new kind of vision.

There is another point. In bhrumadhya you will become conscious of an eye. This is the third eye.

Develop awareness of the third eye; it is the symbol of cosmic consciousness in man.

Incessant, concentrated awareness and sensation of bhrumadhya, the eyebrow centre.

This is antar trataka, in which you try to focus on the inner point.

Hari Om Tat Sat

CLASS PRACTICE

Antar trataka

Stage 1: Preparation

Adjust you sitting position and forget everything else.
Do not make any physical movement hereafter.
Ommm (chanted together).
When you chant *Om* allow the vibrations to permeate the whole of your being so that you are completely saturated.
Ommm...Ommm (again chanted together twice).
When you chant *Om* you should feel that the sound *Om* is not coming out of your mouth, but that the sound vibrations of *Om* are permeating and becoming all pervading in your whole being as if the vibrations are consumed by yourself.
Ommm...Ommm...Ommm...Ommm...Ommm...(chanted together).
Become aware of your physical body.
No more physical movement.
Concentrate on your physical body, so that you can achieve steadiness.

Stage 2: Awareness of eyebrow centre

Become aware of chidakasha.
Concentrate on the centre between the two eyebrows, either from inside or outside.
If you are not able to feel that point, then apply a little saliva with one of your fingers and then concentrate on the pressure point.

Stage 3: Inner visualization

Star: Visualize or imagine a tiny star.
Sometimes during the rainy season the whole sky is covered with clouds, but at a particular point you see a star shining all alone.
That is the kind of star you have to visualize or imagine.
You can even visualize the seed star which you saw after the practice of trataka. Try to visualize or imagine a star.
If this is not possible, then try this little womb of light.
Either visualize or imagine this little internal dot.

Candle flame: Practise internal trataka.
Mentally place the small table in front of you.
Imagine it in all its details.
Place the candle on it.
The candle is white.
Encompass the flame and the upper ignited point of the wick.
Visualize everybody else in this hall practising trataka.
You are also practising trataka. The desk is in front of you.
Visualize or imagine it in detail.
Place the candle on it and see the flame of the candle, the ignited point of the wick at the top.
See the flame, the golden flame.
The flame flickers.
Become aware also of the candles of the others who are practising trataka.
Practise internal trataka.
Visualize the desk, the candle, the ignited point of the wick, and the flame, a tiny star in the centre between the two eyebrows.
Awareness of internal trataka.

Shivalingam: Concentrate on the centre between the two eyebrows.
Develop the vision of a shivalingam, an oval shaped stone, oval, a white flat form which is the symbol of your astral consciousness.
Develop the vision of the shivalingam, the symbol of your astral consciousness.

Human eye: Concentrate on the centre between the two eyebrows and locate the pressure point.
Develop the vision of the human eye.
The living human eye, the open eye.
Visualize the eye with all its details.
The bright human eye.

Third eye: Concentrate on the centre between the two eyebrows, a little behind the eyebrow centre.

Imagine a small gland, pink in colour.
The fleshy body resembles an eye which is closed, not open.
Make a psychic effort to open the third eye, just behind the eyebrow centre.
It resembles an eye, but it is closed.
It is like a small piece of garlic.
A psychic effort has to be made to create an opening.
Concentrate on the third eye behind the eyebrow centre.
Create a mental psychic activity, as if you are trying your level best to open the eye.
Do whatever you can but do not think too much.
Go ahead with your opening efforts.
Concentrate on the centre between the two eyebrows.
Find the tiny star there.
Superimpose the idea or the vision of a tiny star there.
Develop the vision of a human eye, an open eye.
A little deeper in the centre between the two eyebrows is the third eye.
Develop the vision of the third eye in the form of a fleshy body resembling the eye, and try to make an effort to open it.

Crystal ball: Concentrate on the centre between the two eyebrows.
Develop the vision of a crystal ball in front of you, as if you are practising trataka on the crystal ball.
Try to look into the depths of the crystal ball.
Develop the vision of the symbol of your choice.
Develop the vision of your ishta devata.
This is important.
Continue.
Develop the vision of internal trataka.

Candle flame: Remember when you were practising trataka at 4 o'clock in the morning, yourself and all the others in this hall.
How did you arrange the desk?
How did you place the candle?

Was it lit?
Remember the flame of the candle, gold in colour, the ignited point on top which you did trataka on.
Develop a homogeneous vision of internal trataka.
So many candle lights are burning in this hall. In front of you are many, many candles and you look at them.
See the candle and the wick and the flame in detail.
Again develop the vision of internal trataka.
Remember this morning at 4 o'clock when you came and established yourself in your sitting position with a table in front of you.
The candle was placed on it.
It was kindled point by point from person to person.
After a while the whole hall had many, many candles and many, many practitioners of trataka.
Every candle was standing on a desk, the bright point of the wick and the flame, golden in colour, in front of you.
To your side, right and left, and behind, were many, many candles, and many people sitting in absolutely steady positions, practising trataka with eyes open, and then with eyes closed.
When the eyes were closed they saw a tiny star.
Develop this vision.
Candle and flame, candle and flame.
Concentrate on the centre between the two eyebrows and develop the vision of a crystal ball in front of you.
Look into its depths.
Concentrate on your ishta devata in it.
This is important.

The seer: Concentrate on the whole of your being which represents 'I'.
Not only the body, not only your thoughts, but the whole 'I' in the form of awareness of yourself.
Concentrate on that 'I' which has remained unchanged throughout the years, and will remain unchanged in years to come.
'I' the seer of this body.

'I' the seer of the thoughts.
'I' the witness of everything, inside and outside.
The homogeneous conception of 'I'.
Do it in your own way according to your evolution.
When you develop the homogeneous awareness of 'I', everything becomes one with it.
Nothing is different from it.
Everything is included in it.
The homogeneous conception of 'I'.
Develop self-awareness, 'I am' in everything.
Include every awareness in this 'I' awareness.
Become aware of your whole self. Become aware of your whole self. Become aware of your *whole* self.
Become aware of the awareness of everything in you.
Ommm...Ommm...Ommm...Ommm... (chanted together).
Do not relax.
Ask yourself, 'Who am I?'
Repeat the same question exactly with feeling, with awareness and with meaning. 'Who am I?'
'I' is the awareness by which everything is known, including myself.
I know 'I am'.
I do not only exist but I know that I exist.
The 'I' knows the body.
I know I have a body, I experience it.
I experience my own body. I see it. I feel it. I know it.
I remember having this body for many years and I am aware that I have a body.
I do not only think but at the same time I know that I think.
I am aware of the thinking process.
I am the seer of all my thoughts.
I am aware of the past.
I am aware of my whole being.
I am the seer of myself.
Now become practically aware of this awareness in you, through which you know you are.

Do it in your own way according to your evolution.
Concentrate on awareness.
Concentrate on the process of awareness.
Ommm...Ommm...Ommm... (chanted together).
Do not relax.
No movement at any cost.
Imagine yourself as a seer.
Concentrate on yourself as the seer, and concentrate on yourself as the seer of your body.
'Yes, I am aware of the body. I see the body.'
Continue to develop this dual awareness of the seer and the seen.
Seer as an abstract something and the seen as the material physical body.
Go on seeing the body.
Turn within and try to become aware of the seeing, a faculty which was aware of the body.
Again turn within and try to see the next seer who is seeing you as a witness of the body, who is aware of the whole process of seeing the body.
Repeat this again, yourself, within a minute. Do it quickly.
Body awareness. See the seer. And see its seer.
Now do it again yourself. Be quick.
Ommm...Ommm...Ommm.

Hari Om Tat Sat

21
Nada Yoga

The etymological meaning of *nada* is 'flow of consciousness'; the usual meaning of the word is 'sound'. There are four stages of tonal manifestations of sound by which the technique of nada yoga develops.

1. *Para nada* or transcendental sound. This is a sound of such great vibrational frequency that it has gone beyond vibration and is of infinite wavelength. The *Upanishads*, call it *Om* and say its nature is jyoti, or light. Ultimately, *Om* is silence. In meditation, light and silence are the same. *Om* is anahata, or unstruck sound, differentiating it from normal sounds and giving it an uncaused or spontaneous origin, and *Om* is anahada, without any boundaries or quality, indicating non-tone. It is the inner silence, the root sound or possibility of sound. For the Pythagoreans, this sound stood for the nought or the junction of chi. Para is the last stage before samadhi.
2. *Pashyanti* or mental sound. Visualization of a sound or melody that haunts you; music heard in a dream. It is a sound nearer to your mind than your ear.
3. *Madhyama* or in between sound. A sound with lower frequencies than the two preceding but higher frequencies than baikhari. A whispering sound with almost no audible effect.
4. *Baikhari* or sound produced by striking two objects. Speech and music are of this category.

The world system of the nada yogis – the belief that the universe is a projection of sound vibrations alone – was formulated from actual experience. In the Indian pantheon the last transcendental sound of para is on the same level as the cosmic source, i.e. para or Brahman. Muslim saints have said the world evolved from sound and form, and even the Christian *Bible* says, "In the beginning was the word (sound) and the word was with God and the word was God."

The development of musical systems in the past was in strict accordance with the logic of nada yoga sadhanas. Different waves of nada are attractive to different stages of conscious awareness. Certain vibrations of nada are disagreeable and others are agreeable at a particular time of day or to different people. These nada vibration in music are known as raga or musical notes. The morning music of India, with short vibrations, appeals to some but not to all. The ragas appropriate for the evening or midnight music tend to be more popular. The music must be listened to for several hours for the effect to be felt.

Nada yoga divides existence into five spheres: the physical, pranic, mental, supramental and ananda or atmic. The nada of each sphere is a symbol enabling the mind to pass into deeper layers of consciousness. The nada of the physical body are the sounds of vibrations of the heart, lungs, brain, blood circulation and the process of metabolism. When the physical plane is transcended, the subtle sounds of the movements of pranic consciousness are heard. Nada yogis follow the chain of ever subtler sounds to a point-like centre in their innermost being. For bhaktas, this centre is in anahata chakra; for yogis, it is in ajna (the third eye); for vedantins, it is in sahasrara. Nada yogis find the nada, or continuous, inaudible and spontaneous sound, in bindu.

Nada yoga is allegorized in the *Bhagavata*. "Lord Krishna left his place at midnight and went into a jungle. It was a full moon night of the first month of winter. He began to play the flute. The echo of the flute spread in the calm and undisturbed atmosphere. Music rose from the wild jungle and it was heard by the gopis (cowherd girls). When they heard the sound of the flute, they immediately left their houses and their husbands and forgot all their duties and past life. They ran without consideration to the place where the nada from the flute was emanating. They started dancing about the flute bearer. After some time it so happened that each one found herself dancing with the original Krishna."

Krishna represents the higher consciousness and his flute playing is the nada sadhana. The senses (gopis) forget the outer reality (their husbands) and withdraw from their sense organs to dance around the divine nada or the flute-like sound. The flute sounds belong to the pashyanti state – actual sounds are not heard but the frequencies, which are compared with the sounds of flutes and bells, are sensed.

Some describe the ultimate sound as *Om*, others say it is like the unceasing sound of honey bees. According to nada yoga, it comes from the sphere beyond anandamaya kosha, or the third dimension of consciousness, which is a body full of bliss – a point where the individual realizes his highest consciousness in nada and sees the whole universe in the form of sound.

The practice of nada yoga

This technique is the method of penetrating the deeper layers of mind utilizing sound as a medium. This science of yoga, as well as various philosophies and religions, regard the manifested universe as having sound as its basis. Science also agrees that everything in the universe is nothing but the continual interplay of vibrations, of vibrational energy; sound is no more than a particular form of vibration. Yoga believes that even the different layers of mind and body, gross and subtle, are nothing but the manifestation of an uncountable number of different sound vibrations in a multitude of permutations and combinations. We can say that the mind and body are the solidification of sound.

This practice tries to take the practitioner through progressively subtle manifestations of sound, to hear the full spectrum of gross and subtle sounds. It is an excellent practice for inducing pratyahara (dissociation of the mind from the surroundings and senses). It can induce states of meditation. Just as music can create subtle states of mind, nada tries to do the same thing.

Beginners should practise at a time when the surroundings are very quiet; this is to prevent external sounds interfering with perception of the internal sounds. Late at night or very early in the morning are recommended. As one becomes able to detect the subtle sounds without difficulty, then nada yoga can be practised at any time, any place, and even without closing the ears. To gain noticeable experiences, it is essential to practise every day. Try to assign fifteen minutes or more to this technique in the beginning. After attaining experiences, the time can be extended to suit yourself.

Preliminary practice in nada yoga

Stage 1: Preparation

Sit in nadanusandhana asana.
The back and head must be straight.
Close the ears with the thumbs.
Relax the whole body and mind.
Now you are totally at peace.
Now you are only interested in the meditational practice itself.

Stage 2: Humming sound

Inhale deeply and while exhaling produce a humming sound.
Keep the teeth separated slightly and the mouth closed.
It should be like the sound of a bee.
Feel it vibrate throughout your whole head, starting from the throat pit.
Do this for about thirty seconds.
Continue repeating this humming sound for up to five minutes.
Keep your mind totally on the sound vibrations.

Stage 3: Perception of subtle inner sound

Now, stop the humming sounds.

Try to hear subtle sound manifestations, try to pick up any sound.

Go on listening.

You will find that one sound becomes clearer and clearer; feel its intensity and purity.

Keep your mind totally on this sound; listen very carefully.

If your hearing is sufficiently sensitive you may find that you can hear another sound in the background of the present predominant sound.

It may be very faint but it is perceivable.

Leave the first sound.

Concentrate on the new sound emerging behind it.

Transcend the first sound; try to experience the fullness of the new or second sound.

Carry on in this way.

Again with practice and if you have developed your sensitivity, you may be able to hear another sound start to emerge.

It will be faintly perceptible behind the louder second sound.

Direct your awareness to this new sound.

Let this new sound occupy your whole attention.

Continue in this way.

Perceive a sound, then disregard it when you perceive a more subtle sound.

The more subtle the sound you perceive, the deeper you will delve into the depths of the mind.

With practice, this technique can take you directly to meditation.

If you cannot detect any subtle sound at your first attempt, don't despair; with only a little practice you will surely make progress.

You will develop the knack of transcending first the external sound and then the progressively more subtle sounds.

The sounds to be heard will be discovered by the practitioner, but they can include sounds that resemble those of a bell, a lute, a bird and so on.

This is a powerful yet simple method of revealing the experiences of your innermost being.

Stage 4: Ending the practice

Now slowly externalize your awareness.

Become aware of your body and your surroundings.

The practice is complete.

CLASS PRACTICE

Stage 1: Preparation

Sit in a comfortable meditation posture, head and spine straight, eyes closed.

Now, with eyes closed, practise ujjayi breathing in the spinal cord.

Forget everything, breathe in and out in ujjayi in the spinal cord. Go on practising ujjayi with ever increasing concentration.

Stage 2: Bhramari pranayama

In this stage plug your ears, either with your index fingers or thumbs, whichever you can do for some time.

Inhale in the form of ujjayi from the bottom to the top of the spinal cord, and then exhale with a humming sound – *hummmm*.

When you are producing this sound, in the background rhythmically chant *Om Om Om* mentally.

The ears should remain closed throughout, but if you are tired place your hands on your knees for some time, and keep practising even with the ears open.

Breathe in through the spinal cord in the form of ujjayi, breathe out with the ears closed, synchronizing the sound vibration with the mental vibration of *Om Om Om* or your own mantra.

The sound of *Om Om Om* should be done mentally and rhythmically.

If you have your own mantra, then you can use that instead of *Om*.

Stage 3: Perception of subtle inner sound

Now stop producing the humming sound.
Keep your eyes closed.
Begin to listen very carefully to any sound that comes to you spontaneously, internally. (*Long pause*)
After some time, you may begin to hear a second sound in the background of the first sound.
It may be the sound of a bee, or a motor or the sea.
But whatever this second sound is, tune yourself to it.
Disregard the first sound that you heard and hear only this second new sound. (*Long pause*)
Again a new sound will come.
It may be the first sound that you heard, returning.
Or it may be a completely new sound.
But whatever it is, go on listening only to the new sound that is appearing.
Continue in this way for five minutes.
Each time a new sound comes, tune into it. (*Very long pause*)

Stage 4: Awareness of chidakasha

Lower your hands to the knees.
No movement in the body, eyes closed.
This method of nada yoga reduces nervous excitement and then you can meditate on any form, on anything.
The meditation is to be done on the inner wall of the forehead.
Draw the image or the form which you want to meditate upon on the inner wall of the forehead, as if the inner wall of the forehead is a blackboard.
Draw the image mentally, concentrate only on one image.
Practise for three minutes, without stress or strain, only deep concentration.

Stage 5: Ending the practice

Now get ready to end the practice.
Bring your awareness back to the physical dimension.

Bring your awareness to the slow, steady flow of the natural breath.
Become aware of the whole physical body seated on the floor.
Be aware of any sensations in the physical body.
Listen to the sounds in the external environment.
The practice is complete.

Hari Om Tat Sat

22

Abstract Meditations

One can meditate on anything, there is no limit. The following are only a few ideas which illustrate methods of meditation. Before trying any of them carefully read its contents. Try to grasp its deeper message and then try to experience its meaning. The reader should experiment for himself to find meditations that are in tune with his particular natural and inner feelings. Take various parts from different meditational techniques and combine them together, add your own ideas, and find a system that is especially suitable for yourself.

The Life Stream (Rabindranath Tagore)

The same stream of life
that runs through my veins night and day,
runs through the word and dances in rhythmic measures.
It is the same life that shouts in joy through the dust of the earth in numberless blades of grass,
and breaks into tumultuous waves of leaves and flowers.
It is the same life that is rocked in the ocean cradle of birth and of death, in ebb and flow.
My limbs are made glorious by the touch of this world of life.
And my pride is from the life throb of the ages
dancing in my blood this moment.

The Essence of Existence

I am contented, I smile.
Because the sounds, the colours, the feelings,
that I hear with my ears,
that I see with my eyes,
that I experience with my heart,
will exist even when
my ears, my eyes, my heart, are no more.

Commune with Nature

Watch the moon,
the glowing, peaceful, soft moon;
feel its multitude of light particles
pierce and caress your skin.
Walk in the hills, in the mountains, in the countryside;
tune in with nature.
Be quiet and know that you are part of everything.
Leave your worldly games and worries behind.
Relax, tune in, close your eyes,
feel the harmony in yourself and nature.
Feel the infinite power surrounding you.
Let yourself merge,
let your worries blend
into that which encompasses you.
This is the source of life.
This is life.
This is existence.
You are existence.
You and That are one.

Perfect Oneness (William Blake)

To see a world in a grain of sand
and heaven in a wildflower,
hold infinity in the palm of your hand
and eternity in an hour.

The Pulsating Throb of Life

Be aware of your beating heart;
experience its powerful pumping action
pulsating throughout all the arteries and veins of the body.
Know that it is this that nourishes
every cell in your body with the life force.
Yet this heart is not unique.
It exists in the same form in every human being
whether black, white, yellow, red, Indian, British, Mongolian.
Your heart is identical with
the heart of every other human being.
The life force that throbs through your body is the same
as that which throbs through every other human body.
Now think of the animal.
Each has a heart,
though perhaps of a slightly different type.
The very same life force that throbs through your body
also throbs through their bodies.
Your life and all other forms of life
are manifestations of the one life force
that vibrates throughout the whole universe.

The Sea of Bliss

Everything is divine energy,
infinite, shimmering, vibrant, flowing.
The whole body is vibrating in harmony with the universe.
The whole universe is vibrating in tune with the body.
Bathe in this sea of infinite energy,
light energy, bioenergy, electricity, sound.
Float in silence, in peace, in timelessness.
All is energy.

Categories (*Chuang Tse*)

Suppose here is a statement.
We do not know whether
it belongs to one category or another.
But if we put the different categories in one,
then the differences of category cease to exist.
For example, if there was a beginning,
then there was a time before that beginning;
and a time before the time
which was before the time of that beginning.
If there is existence,
then there must have been non-existence.
And if there was a time when nothing existed,
then there must have been a time
when even nothing did not exist.
All of a sudden nothing came into existence.
Can one say then
really whether it belongs to the category of existence
or of non-existence?
Even the very words I have just written,
I cannot say whether they are something or not.

Who Am I?

Ask yourself the question, 'Who am I?'
Am I the physical body?
No, I cannot be,
for this is in a state of continual change;
last year my body was different to what it now is.
When I was a child,
my body was different to what it now is.
My body is in a continual state of flux, of change,
it cannot be my inner nature.
Am I my mind?
No, my inner nature cannot be the mind,
for it is in a continual state of change;
one moment it is happy, other times it is unhappy,
It is continually fluctuating in mood.

How can the mind be my true nature?
Am I a Hindu, a Christian, an Englishman, an Indian?
No, these are only minor forms of identity;
they don't represent my inner nature.
Continue asking yourself this type of question.
Then, 'Who am I?'
I am the witness
behind the phenomena of the universe.
I am existence, unchangeable existence.
I am consciousness, pure consciousness.
I am indestructible being.
My nature is *is-ness*.
I am.

Divine Symphony (Inayat Khan)

When I open my eyes to the outer world,
I feel myself as a drop in the sea;
But when I close my eyes and look within,
I see the whole universe as a bubble
raised in the ocean of my heart.

Fullness (*Ishavasya Upanishad*)

That is full, this is full.
From full, the full is taken;
the full has come.
If you take out fullness from the full,
the full alone remains.

23

Miscellaneous Meditations

The following techniques are really compound practices which utilize many of the different methods of meditation joined together into one homogenous technique. They are excellent and powerful practices which are very useful in bringing about pratyahara, by utilizing a progression of different kriyas which lead the mind through different phases of awareness.

The reader should note how the different systems are joined together in these and many of the other class transcriptions given in this book, so that he may formulate his own compound practices to suit his own mental and psychic make-up.

Mantra yoga
Stage 1: Preparation

Sit in a comfortable meditation pose.
Place the hands on the knees in chin or jnana mudra.
Make your spinal cord erect and upright.
Keep your eyes closed throughout the practice of mantra yoga.
Try your best not to make any unnecessary movements to the body.
Don't worry if the mind moves, or runs riot.
The system of meditation, the system of relaxation that we will practise today has mantra or japa as its basis.

In this practice you will have to visualize mentally a particular sound.
That sound will be the basis of movement in your mental plane.
The sound, the word, the mantra will become the centre of your consciousness.
The centre is in between the two eyebrows.
The method is simple and not at all complicated, but it needs perseverance and practice.
Suppose you choose the sound *Ram,* for example, then you have to create it mentally and rhythmically between the eyebrows.
The rhythm should be neither too slow nor too fast, and this rhythmic movement should be carried on for at least twenty minutes.
After that you can stop the movement in the eyebrow centre and develop awareness of a room instead of a sound.
If the sound is *Ram,* you will have to feel the mental vibration in the middle of the eyebrows as *Ram Ram Ram,* non-stop, unceasing for twenty minutes or more.
Different kinds of thoughts will come and try to intervene.
You should not worry about their intervention.
Do not react to the disturbances that are created by your thoughts.
Within the period of twenty minutes, sometimes disturbing thoughts will reign supreme.
Then again awareness of the rhythmic movement of the mantra will come to the forefront.
Again thoughts will intervene.
The whole process will take place in this way.
If disturbing thoughts intervene, you should not worry at all.
You should not react at all, but keep on with the rhythmic movement of the sound.
Therefore, as an example, first we will have rhythmic chanting so that it becomes clear to you.

Stage 2: Mantra chanting

We will now take up the sound *Om* for our chanting.

I will set the rhythm in motion and you will all follow me in the same way.

The chanting is only to give you an example of how to practise it mentally.

Just as you practise on the outer plane, so you will have to practise on the mental plane.

The difference is that here, for example, we try to create a sound and chant mantras, whereas in real practice there is no chanting, there is only mental perception and mental experience.

When you practise for about twenty minutes, then the consciousness is withdrawn to a great extent.

You then take the symbol or the form on which you are trying to meditate.

Now, when I chant rhythmically the mantra *Om Om Om*, you will follow me.

Begin chanting mentally and rhythmically.

Those who have their own mantra may use it.

Those who do not have a mantra may use *Om*.

Now follow me in rhythmic chanting of the mantra.

(Om Om Om is chanted rhythmically fifty times)

Gradually take your mind to the centre of the two eyebrows and start chanting the mantra mentally.

Rhythmic chanting of the mantra, ceaselessly. Do not worry about the mental vagaries.

Centre your awareness in between the two eyebrows.

We will practise for five minutes only, therefore, do it with concentration.

(*Five minutes practice*)

Stage 3: Ending the practice

Chant *Om* with me three times. *Ommm Ommm Ommm.*

Now relax your mind and let it become extroverted. Relax the position of your body and open your eyes.

Hari Om Tat Sat

Unmani Kriya

Stage 1: Preparation

Sit in a steady position, with the spinal cord upright and straight.

Place your hands on the knees.

First we will practise kapalbhati pranayama, which I will demonstrate.

(*Demonstration of kapalbhati pranayama*)

You will need to perform one hundred expulsions.

Adjust your exhalations so that you are able to continue for one hundred rounds without any difficulty.

If you feel any discomfort during the practice, you may discontinue it.

When you have finished the hundredth round, exhale and perform jalandhara bandha by pressing the hands on the knees, raising the shoulders and locking the chin against the chest.

Then perform uddiyana bandha by contracting the abdomen, and do moola bandha by contracting the perineum or cervix.

Then release moola bandha, uddiyana bandha and jalandhara bandha and breathe in.

When you have finished one hundred rounds of kapalbhati with the three bandhas, you may change your position if necessary, but do not open your eyes.

(*The class practises one hundred respirations and maha bandha*)

Stage 2: Ujjayi and Om chanting

Now practise ujjayi pranayama in the spinal passage, starting from the bottom of the tailbone up through the spinal cord from mooladhara to ajna chakra.

Inhale up the spine from mooladhara to ajna.

Then as you exhale hum *Om* from ajna down to mooladhara.

When you are humming *Om* from ajna down to mooladhara, the duration of the *O* is short and the duration of the *mmm* is long.

The chant is *Ommm* not *Oooom*.

The sound *O* starts at ajna, and the *mmm* continues right down to mooladhara.
From mooladhara to ajna is breath consciousness.
From ajna to mooladhara is *Om* consciousness.
Practise this *Om* consciousness thirteen times.
(*Om is chanted thirteen times by the class*)

Stage 3: Breath awareness

When you have finished the thirteen rounds continue with ujjayi breathing.
You may change your position if necessary, but do not open your eyes.
Once you have settled into the posture continue your breathing from mooladhara to ajna and from ajna back down to mooladhara.
Carefully count forty-nine rounds of ujjayi breathing.
Go on counting carefully and feel the breath in the spinal cord.
This practice is known as breath awareness.

Stage 4: Soham awareness

When you have finished the forty-nine rounds of breath awareness add the mantra *Soham* to the breath.
Perform fifty-nine rounds.
Inhale from mooladhara to ajna with *So* and exhale from ajna down to mooladhara with *Ham*.
Count carefully.
After practising *Soham* awareness for fifty-nine rounds, go to chidakasha and concentrate on the inner side of the forehead.

Stage 5: Ending the practice

Chant *Om* with me three times.
Ommm...Ommm...Ommm (*chanted together*).
Relax your body.
Change your position.
Open your eyes.

Hari Om Tat Sat

Unconscious meditation

Stage 1: Preparation

Sit quietly with the spinal cord straight.

Before starting meditation you should sit down quietly for five to ten minutes.

The first rule in meditation is not to start the moment you sit down for meditation.

Wait for a few minutes to allow the body or the physical condition to become steady and calm, and watch your thoughts.

During this period readjust your position and make yourself comfortable, but keep the eyes closed.

Stage 2: Awareness of thoughts

Ask yourself, 'What am I thinking?'

See your thoughts, do not stop your thoughts, do not suppress any thoughts, let a thought come and watch it.

Make a special effort to find out what you are thinking.

Ask yourself, 'What am I thinking now?'

Watch every thought, do not become a thinker but become a seer.

Do not lose yourself in the thoughts, but remain detached from the thinking process.

Do not identify yourself with your thoughts, but remain an impartial spectator of your thoughts.

Do not hate a thought, do not love it, do not run after it, do not suppress it, do not avoid it, let it come.

Go on watching every thought with great diligence, and if there are no thoughts, watch that condition also.

If there is mental disturbance do not suppress it, but try to see it as an impartial spectator.

Whether thoughts are of happiness or of pain, see them impartially.

Expose each and every thought before your consciousness.

If there is no thought, then be aware of that.

When there is anxiety, then see it.

If there is restlessness, try to be a spectator.

If there is peace, see it.

Do not identify yourself with peace, do not identify yourself with restlessness, do not identify yourself with pain and anxiety.
Be aloof, and say 'I am not the thinker, I am the seer of my thoughts; I am not a hearer, I am the seer of the hearing.'
Become aware that you are listening to my instructions.
If you hear any disturbing sound from outside, do not react, but witness it.
Concentrate on the disturbing sound and overcome it, then concentrate on the disturbing thoughts and overcome them, concentrate on bad thoughts and overcome them. Concentrate on every item of thought and thus overcome it.
Do not suppress any thought.
If no thoughts come, be aware of this and say, 'There is no thought, there is a blank.'
Do not react to any thoughts, do not react to any external disturbance or to any external experience.
Try to see your own thought process as you see something on the television screen.
Remain aware throughout.
'I am not the thinker, I am the seer.'

Stage 3: Om chanting in the spinal passage

Now comes the chanting of *Om*.
With ujjayi, inhale up the spinal cord from the bottom to the top and while chanting *Om* loudly, descend to the bottom. Inhale with the ascending breath and exhale with the descending breath and the chanting of *Om*.
Inhale up through the spinal cord and chant *Om*.
Practise this eight times.

Stage 4: Breath awareness in the spinal passage

Now practise ujjayi in the spinal cord.
Rotate your awareness up and down the spinal cord with inhalation and exhalation.
Try to feel that the breath is circulating in the spinal cord, right from the bottom to the top.

Continue with awareness.
Try to make the sound as imperceptible as possible to others.
Breathe in and out in such a way that only you can hear it distinctly.
Prolong the breath, deepen the breath, make it thin and long.
The duration of the breath and the distance of the spinal cord from the bottom to the top should be synchronized.
The breath should be absolutely perceptible to you.
You should be able to listen to this magic breath, the breath of life.
The energy will go up and down the spinal cord through your willpower.
Go up and down with the breath.
Make your consciousness ascend and descend in the spinal cord using the breath as the basis.
The breath should be perceptible to you, it should be relaxing, it should be prolonged, it should be felt within the spinal cord.
It is a thin current, it is a very thin and long flow of sound going up and down in the spinal cord.
Practise it right from the bottom to the top and right from the top to the bottom.
The consciousness goes up and down, the spinal cord is the path, the breath is the basis.
The breath should become pure and very fine and almost imperceptible to others.
But remain conscious of the breath throughout.
There should be constant awareness of 'I am breathing up and I am breathing down.'
Think throughout that the spinal cord is the path, the bottom is the beginning, the top is the end.
Inhale from the bottom to the top, exhale from the top to the bottom. The more imperceptible the breath, the better will be the feeling.
'I am breathing, I am breathing.'

Continue in this way.
Deepen the concentration for three more minutes.
Withdraw your mind from all sides into the spinal cord.

Stage 5: Mantra awareness in the spinal passage

Now synchronize your mantra with inhalation and exhalation.
If you do not have a mantra use *Soham, So* with inhalation and *Ham* with exhalation.
The spinal cord is the path, the breath is the basis, and the mantra is to be realized.
Concentrate on the process of breathing, concentrate on the mantra.
Intense concentration for two minutes.

Stage 6: The inner space

Withdraw your mind from the spinal cord and elsewhere and take it to the inner side of your forehead.
Try to see the inner wall of the forehead from inside, as if the inner side of the forehead is the front wall of a room.
See the internal wall of the forehead from inside. Take your mind to the crown as if the crown were the ceiling of a house.
From inside concentrate on the crown, this is the ceiling of a room.
See the internal walls of the house. Go to the top of the head from inside.
See the ceiling from the inside, see the inner side of the top from inside.
Take your mind to the back.
Try to see the back of the head from the inside, the inner wall of the smaller brain.
Now again see the inner wall of the forehead,
the ceiling of the crown, the internal wall behind,
the internal wall of the right temple,
the internal wall of the left temple,
the internal wall of the forehead,
the ceiling of the crown, the ceiling of the top,
the internal wall of the back,

the internal wall of the right temple,
the internal wall of the left temple.
And see the floor.
Then again, the front, the crown, the ceiling, the right wall, the left wall, as though you are in a room.
Now see all the walls of the room.
See carefully the front wall, the ceiling of the crown, the ceiling of the top, the back wall, the right wall, the left wall, the floor, front, crown, top, behind right, right, behind left, left, ground.
Again see the front, crown, ceiling, back wall, right wall, left wall, the floor at the posterior side.
At the back of the ground floor, try to see an opening downward which goes into the spinal cord. This is a small passage through which the awareness goes down into the spinal cord.
This is a room with a floor. On the back side is a small opening downward.
Repeat this again.
You are in the room, see the front, the top, the ceiling, the back side, the right wall, the left wall, the ground, the opening at the back side.

Stage 7: Ending the practice

Become aware of the external environment.
Do not open your eyes, but change the position of your body and relax.
Relax yourself completely, but do not sleep.
In this practice, first there was preparation for meditation, then awareness of thoughts, then chanting of *Om*, then concentration on the breath in the spinal cord, then practice of mantra in the spinal cord, then concentration on the inner space.
Now you can open your eyes.

Hari Om Tat Sat

The psychic screen

Stage 1: Preparation

Lie down in shavasana, legs slightly apart and arms close to the body, palms upwards.

Close your eyes.

This is a practice in relaxation not a practice in concentration.

This practice is quite easy, but it is very valuable and significant.

Do not open your eyes during the practice and try not to make any physical movements.

Stage 2: Awareness of external stimuli

In this practice you will try to become aware of sense experiences.

Do not concentrate your mind, but allow your mind to move in the direction it wants to.

Make your mind completely extrovert and become aware of things that are external and not mental.

Do not withdraw the mind inside, but let it move in any direction it likes and is attracted to.

Do not be tense.

Completely relax yourself as you do at night when you go to bed after completing all your jobs of the day.

The mind is attracted by external sounds.

The mind is attracted by external touch.

The mind is attracted by external surroundings, so let it wander.

You may hear the sound of a car, a radio, a bird, a dog or anything for that matter.

In this particular practice you have to let your mind move in external sense experience.

You must be like the microphone of a recorder which records and registers every sound that comes within a particular range.

Or like radar which receives impressions from outside.

Bear in mind that you are not practising concentration and control of the mind.

Relax your mind.
Have the same mental condition as when you go to bed after completing your day's work.
Become aware of externals.
How do you do it?
Should you try to be aware of external things?
This point is very important.
Please bear in mind that there are two kinds of awareness.
One is called voluntary awareness, and the other is involuntary awareness.
If your mind is thinking that many people are lying in this room and that I am giving a particular practice and that the tape recorder is doing its job, this is called voluntary awareness which you are trying to develop in yourself.
But if your awareness is drawn by a particular sound, if your awareness is drawn by a particular experience, then it is involuntary awareness.
Now in this particular practice, what you have to do is keep yourself completely empty.
If you hear a sound from outside, then accept that.
Or if you become aware of the people in this room, accept that.
Or if you become aware of any other sensation, accept it.
Please do this for three minutes by yourself.
Do not worry about anything, let your mind receive what it wants to.
Maybe even what I am saying.
Maybe any other sound that is able to attract your attention.
Now practise this awareness for three minutes.
Keep on moving in the external world.
Try to become aware of every sound and of every event that is taking place in the external world and not the internal world.
Remain a witness of the external world.
Do not go in.

Avoid sleep.
Let your mind run outside and become aware of all that is taking place in the external world.
This is practice number one.

Stage 3: Awareness of thoughts

In practice number two you allow yourself to think, but you try to remain a detached unaffected witness of all the thoughts of your mind.
Whether it is a good thought or a bad thought doesn't matter.
What matters is that you are thinking and feeling.
Ask yourself, 'What am I thinking?'
Become aware of your thinking process.
Do not control any thought.
Allow your mind to develop any thought, good, bad or both.
Do not be affected by any thought, neither the positive nor the negative effect.
Allow your mind to think anything it likes, do not stand in the way.
But you should be aware of what thoughts are coming into your mind.
'What am I thinking?'
From moment to moment remind yourself, 'What am I thinking?
What am I thinking?'
If it is not possible for you to see your thinking process, what you should do is allow thoughts to come for some time, and after they have come for a while, then suddenly you should try to become aware of what you are thinking.
Practise this for three minutes.
Do not worry about any mental disturbances.
Do not worry about any thoughts.
Do not worry if your mind goes in and out.
Do not control the mind, but only see your thoughts.
Remain watchful.
'What am I thinking? What am I thinking?'

Stage 4: Chidakasha awareness

Concentrate on chidakasha.

Concentrate on chidakasha which is the inner part of the forehead.

If you try to see the inner wall of the forehead you will see chidakasha.

Now this chidakasha is the screen, and on this you will try to see what kind of thoughts are coming into your mind.

Keep on seeing chidakasha and you will find different figures and symbols coming on the background of chidakasha.

On the background of chidakasha keep on seeing any symbol, or diagram, or flower, or thought, or vision that comes.

It does not matter if the thoughts are visualized or a symbol, but keep on looking into the chidakasha.

If you keep on looking, chidakasha will have different symbols, known and unknown points.

Always remain in chidakasha, and keep on seeing anything that comes and also if nothing comes.

There should be no tension, it should be a relaxed state of chidakasha.

'What comes in chidakasha? What do I see in chidakasha?'

Maybe when you are looking in chidakasha suddenly the thought of a book, or the thought of a friend, or a spiritual thought, or a worldly thought, or vision of a garden, or the thought of a flower, or a diagram, or anything can come up of its own accord.

Please keep on looking at chidakasha.

Develop constant awareness of all that you see.

If you do not see anything, do not lose awareness.

You are a witness of all that is taking place in chidakasha.

Maybe visions and diagrams, or maybe nothing.

Maybe just midnight.

This process of perception should be a conscious process and not an unconscious one, not like a dream.

It could be a diagram, like triangles, or flowers, birds, gardens, houses, people, animals, rivers, midnight, darkness, starlight, or a full moon night, or the daylight, anything.

It could be anything.

Just remain aware of this.

Take care that you do not sleep.

That is very important.

You are looking at chidakasha.

This is the relaxed way of looking at chidakasha.

In chidakasha whether you see anything or don't see anything, remain a witness of both and let things develop on their own.

Keep awake and keep looking at chidakasha.

Stage 5: Ending the practice

Make your mind extrovert and slowly become aware of your external surroundings.

Now open your eyes and relax your position.

Hari Om Tat Sat

24

Prana Vidya

This practice is known as *prana vidya,* or 'the knowledge of prana'. It is the yogic technique of psychic energy control and healing, which has gained great fame around the world under many titles. In the technique of prana vidya, prana passes on its route with inhalation in ujjayi pranayama, and khechari mudra is also useful if it can be performed comfortably. The body position can be any one which is comfortable – sitting, lying on the side, stomach or back, but the spine should be reasonably straight.

There are two basic stages, each of which has many variations. The first stage is the bringing of prana to ajna chakra, which acts as the storehouse. The prana can come from manipura or can be breathed in from outside the body through the skin. Whichever is practised, however, the prana always flows toward ajna with inhalation in this first stage.

The second stage is the sending of prana from ajna. The prana in this stage can be distributed to the entire body, to an ailing part, or to the hand for transfer to the body of another person. In this stage, however, the prana always flows from ajna toward its destination with inhalation.

These two stages are distinct, and the practitioner must be able to distinguish between them as he practises. The transfer from one stage to the other is imperceptible, and the practice will continuously alternate between the two, but the distinction should be kept clear throughout the practice.

Prana vidya uses the psychic passage of pingala, as described in the chapter 'Yoga's Psychic Physiology'. It should never be practised using the opposite ida nadi, or it can cause much harm. It is the secret technique of yogic psychic healing, of 'laying on of hands', and can also be done for healing oneself by directing the prana directly from ajna chakra, as described in the practice, to the sick or malfunctioning part of the body.

For treating other persons, the prana is directed from ajna to the right hand, which is placed on the ailing portion of the sick person's body. To assist this, the ailing person can also feel the prana flowing from the hand and warming the diseased portion of his own body.

CLASS PRACTICE

Distribution of prana

Stage 1: Preparation

Close your eyes as gently as possible; you are going to practise prana vidya.

In order to avoid distractions, it is very important that the eyes should remain closed.

With regard to the position, you may take any comfortable pose, whether it is lying on the left or right side or lying on the back. You may sit in an easy chair or even recline on your bed, but please remember that your position should not cause any discomfort.

Stage 2: Raising the prana to ajna

As far as the awakening of prana is concerned, I am sure you remember distinctly the spiral movement of prana from mooladhara to ajna from your previous practices.

Start first from the right side and then proceed carefully, keeping pace with your breath.

From mooladhara turn to the right, make a curve and reach swadhisthana.

To manipura move upwards along the left side curve.

From manipura to anahata rise along the right curve.

From anahata to vishuddhi ascend along the left curve.
And from vishuddhi to ajna follow the curve along the right.
Thus takes place the spiral movement from mooladhara to ajna, and thus the awakening of prana.
Continue practising in this way.
In the beginning you have to complete 49 rounds.
But when you become used to the practice, then you no longer need to count because you feel the awakening of prana instinctively.
When the awakening of the pranic force has commenced from mooladhara to ajna and you feel the movements of the pranic force, only then may you commence your next journey.
Please start raising the prana from mooladhara to ajna in the same way as you have been practising during the last few days.
But leave the prana at ajna, do not take it back to mooladhara.
Commence your journey with watchful awareness from mooladhara to ajna. Let your mind and consciousness, with psychic and pranic energies, keep on rising in and through the spinal cord.
Continue diligently with your practice and keep on listening to the vibrationless sound.
The kundalini is to be awakened at mooladhara.
Let it rise gradually to ajna, then pause briefly at ajna in the form of kumbhaka.
Here ends our first round, only to step into the second.
Recommence your journey from mooladhara, stop at ajna with a brief kumbhaka; go on, go on, with absolute concentration, feeling intensely the movement of prana.
Keep on awakening the pranic force along the route mentioned before, but do not forget that the psychic route is from mooladhara to ajna.
When you reach ajna chakra, please remember that you have to remain there in kumbhaka for some time.

Stage 3: Expanding and relaxing the whole body

Now listen carefully.

After performing kumbhaka at ajna you have to exhale and relax your whole body.

You are not exhaling through the spinal cord, but you are exhaling through the body like a balloon releasing air.

With inhalation the body expands, breathing through every pore of the skin.

Relaxation comes with every exhalation, and expansion with every inhalation.

Don't forget this golden rule.

The form of breathing will be ujjayi pranayama. Don't feel it in the spinal cord as you did in your previous practices, but feel it in the body.

Now this ujjayi air becomes all pervading in the body, as if every pore of the body is breathing in ujjayi.

When you inhale, every pore in the body assists you in inhalation and the body expands like a balloon.

When you exhale, your whole body exhales and becomes as light as cotton wool – it is the time of relaxation.

Total body awareness and synchronization of breath consciousness with body consciousness.

Complete awareness of the whole body.

Now inhale, and with the inhalation the whole body is breathing in through the pores, through the skin, through every part of the body. Now your body is expanding with inhalation.

Now exhale. Breathe out, and with exhalation every pore of the body is breathing out.

Now the body relaxes.

Please remember that that the entire process of inhalation and exhalation takes place through ajna chakra behind the centre of the eyebrows. Ajna is the focal point, it is the main distributing agency of the entire respiratory system. It is from ajna chakra that the inhaled air proceeds to the entire body. The air to be exhaled returns to ajna chakra, and from ajna the exhaled air is expelled.

During inhalation there is expansion of the body; during exhalation there is relaxation of the body.
When you inhale from ajna chakra and expand the whole body, feel that it is from ajna chakra, the storehouse of prana, that the prana is being distributed to the entire body.
During exhalation the inhaled air is withdrawn to ajna, but not through the spinal passage.
It reaches ajna directly.
Remember that breathing is to be practised in the form of ujjayi.
Please practise in the following way.
From ajna inhale and distribute the inhaled air throughout the whole body right to the toes.
During exhalation withdraw the prana back to ajna and relax. It is natural to relax when you exhale.
This stage is much easier to follow than the previous one. In the previous exercise you were breathing in through the pores of the body and also breathing out through the same pores, but here the whole breathing process is to be carried out through the agency of ajna chakra.
Ajna chakra may be considered as the storehouse of prana from where, with the help of ujjayi breathing, the prana is distributed to the entire body system, and during exhalation the prana is withdrawn from all directions back to ajna chakra.
But you must be very careful to remember that relaxation follows exhalation.
During relaxation both consciousness as well as prana withdraw themselves from the body to ajna. So you must understand that there is relaxation of the body and not contraction of the body.
You should become so used to ujjayi breathing, that during the process of prana vidya your entire machinery of consciousness, imagination, feeling, thinking and also your physical system should expand with inhalation and relax with exhalation.

You should become so indifferent to the breathing process that not even a fraction of your consciousness remains aware of it.

The prana is causing expansion of the astral body during inhalation.

The prana is also relaxing your astral body during exhalation.

Your total awareness should be focused on the whole process of expansion and relaxation, not on the prana itself.

That is, your centre of gravity should shift from the processes of breathing in and out to the processes of expansion and relaxation.

In short you must transcend the breathing consciousness.

Stage 4: Expanding and contracting the whole body

Now we shall proceed to the next stage, where there is a slight variation.

In this stage there will be expansion of the body with every round of inhalation as in the previous stage, but this time, instead of relaxation accompanying exhalation, there will be contraction of the body during exhalation.

So there is expansion and contraction and not expansion and relaxation.

This point will become very clear to you as we proceed with the practice.

You expand with inhalation, and during the process of inhalation the prana is distributed from ajna chakra to the entire body.

That is, during inhalation prana moves from ajna to various parts of the body and the body expands at the same time.

When you exhale, the prana returns to ajna chakra, causing contraction of the astral body.

Therefore, you can understand the whole exercise if you remember two sets of rules.

The first is that on inhalation there is distribution of prana and expansion of the body.

The other is that on exhalation there is withdrawal of prana and contraction of the body.
Now we will repeat the process for your revision.
First inhale, then distribute the prana from ajna to the whole body, and it will cause expansion of the body.
Now exhale, and it will cause contraction of the body.
The process of expansion and contraction of the body is not physical but mental. You have to stretch your imagination to its limits.
When you direct your prana to any part of the body, for example, the foot, then mentally feel as if your foot is expanding in all directions.
It is not a physical expansion but a physical experience.
Thus, when you inhale you direct your prana in all directions, so that prana, which has started from ajna centre, is extending and covering the entire body.
Your whole body from top to toe is saturated with pranic force.
Feel this intensely.
Simultaneously, you must imagine that your psychic body is expanding extensively in all directions and it has assumed cosmic form.
Similarly, when you exhale, you consciously withdraw your pranas from all parts of the body and direct them to ajna chakra.
As water in the ocean recedes when the tidal flow is reversed, so also prana recedes during exhalation, and contraction takes place.
In contraction, body consciousness is transcended.
But remember, the contraction and expansion is to be effected in the body as a whole, not in parts. The body as one homogeneous unit is to be expanded or contracted as the case may be.
So, to give you a general outline, during inhalation you expand; during exhalation you either release or contract.
When you inhale you distribute the prana from ajna to all parts of the body.

When you exhale you bring the extended the pranic force back to the source via ajna.

Stage 5: Distribution to individual body parts – expansion and relaxation

This time we will do the exercise in parts, starting with the right arm.

Inhale and supply the pranic force from ajna to the right arm.

Expand your right arm, not physically but mentally.

Now exhale, withdraw your prana from the right arm back to ajna and relax your right arm.

When you distribute prana to the right arm, feel the prana there permeating every pore of the limb right down to the fingertips.

Feel the movement of prana.

Come back to ajna, retain your breath. Go to the left arm and supply prana down to the fingertips of the left hand.

Now withdraw the prana back to ajna.

Prana proceeds from ajna to the left arm, it returns to ajna from the left arm.

You are expanding and relaxing your arms alternately with every supply and withdrawal of prana.

Come back to ajna, retain the breath there.

Now inhale, and with inhalation supply the prana to the right leg through the right side of the back.

Mentally feel the expansion of your right leg.

Now exhale, withdraw your prana from the right leg to ajna. With the withdrawal of prana relax your right leg.

Now supply prana to the left leg, right to the tips of your toes. Expansion follows with every round of supply.

Withdraw prana from the left leg and relax.

Now repeat.

Supply...expand; withdraw…relax.

Supply...expand; withdraw...relax.

Bring your prana back to ajna.

From ajna supply prana to your right chest, and withdraw the prana back to ajna during exhalation.

Inhale...supply prana...expand; exhale...withdraw prana... relax.

Now bring your prana back to ajna and retain the breath.

Inhale, supply prana to your left chest and expand your chest mentally.

Exhale, withdraw prana from the left chest, then relax your chest.

Supply...and expand; withdraw...and relax.

Stage 6: Distribution to individual body parts – expansion and contraction

Now return to ajna, retain the breath and listen to the instructions.

This time during the withdrawal of prana, instead of relaxation you will have to contract; with supply you will have to expand as before.

First of all supply prana to the right arm and expand.

Withdraw prana from the right arm to ajna and contract.

Come back to ajna, remain aware of the prana in ajna chakra.

Inhale, supply prana to the left arm and expand your left arm.

Exhale, withdraw the prana and contract.

Both the processes of expansion and contraction are to be done mentally.

Withdraw your prana back to ajna. Retain it in ajna for some time.

Mentally relax your left arm, then go to the right leg.

Supply prana from ajna to the whole right leg, down to the tips of your toes, through the right side of the back, and now expand.

Withdraw prana, exhale, and contract your right leg mentally.

Return to ajna, retain your breath, mentally release your right leg.

Supply prana to the right side of the chest with expansion, withdraw the prana with contraction, come back to ajna, relax the right side of the chest.

Now supply prana to the left side and expand your chest mentally, withdraw prana with contraction, come back to ajna and retain the prana for some time.

Stage 7: Vision of prana shakti

Now you should have a vision of prana shakti.

Supply the prana directly to the whole of your body, then withdraw the prana back to ajna: no contraction, no expansion, no retention.

If they take place on their own, well and good, but don't worry if these processes do not accompany the supply and withdrawal of prana.

The most important thing is to get a vision of light streaks proceeding from ajna to the body during the period of supply.

With withdrawal of prana, shafts of light must withdraw to ajna, just as from a charcoal fire you find little sparks shooting forward with a hissing noise, or you see light streaks shooting forth from fireworks, or sparks during the welding process.

In the same manner, where prana is supplied to the various limbs, visualize the pranic energy in the form of light particles issuing from ajna to the part where prana is directed.

Imagine ajna to be the storehouse of infinite light streaks. It is like a volcanic bed and as soon as eruption takes place, streaks of light particles issue forth with lightning velocity.

These streaks of light permeate the whole body and when the eruption stops, the energy in the form of light sparks withdraws to the source, only to reappear at the next explosion.

Now supply your prana shakti to your right hand thumb. Imagine that your right thumb is melting. You must try to feel this emotion intensely, the feeling of melting.

Feeling your right thumb melting due to the presence of pranic energy there will be very helpful to you in self-healing.

Imagine that you are in a hospital and your right thumb is seriously injured and blood is coming out in a stream. What will be your feeling be?

You have to relive this feeling when you think of melting.

Stage 8: Withdrawal of prana to mooladhara

Now begin to end the practice.

Withdraw your prana back to ajna.

Inhale and retain the breath, concentrating at ajna.

Exhale and let the prana descend from ajna to mooladhara via sushumna passage.

Continue this practice until you are sure all the prana has been returned to mooladhara.

Stage 9: Ending the practice

Then slowly and carefully become aware of your external environment.

Once your awareness is fully externalized slowly move your body and open your eyes.

Hari Om Tat Sat

Note: For more information and further practices refer to *Prana Pranayama Prana Vidya,* published by Bihar School of Yoga.

25

Kundalini Kriyas

The following tantric kriyas provide what is possibly the most efficient method for systematically evolving man's consciousness that has been developed. They were originally written down in the tantric texts by the great masters of the past, and they are said to have been the teaching for transcendental sadhana which Lord Shiva gave to his disciple and wife, Parvati.

These practices are rather advanced and are too powerful for the average aspirant. Before an aspirant takes up their practice, he should have a thorough familiarity and practical experience with all of the preliminary practices included in this book. Additionally, it is advisable that he take up these kriyas only under the guidance of a guru, who can see that the aspirant is fully ready for them and that any obstacles which arise while the aspirant is practising do not cause him harm in the way of disease, mental imbalance or psychic dislocation.

By tradition there are a total of seventy-six kundalini kriyas of kriya yoga. We present the following twenty main practices, which are sufficient for the daily practice of any sincere sadhaka. These practices are divided into three groups:

1. those which induce pratyahara
2. those which induce dharana
3. those which induce dhyana.

It should be noted that three states are actually a continuity of evolution, that is, the consciousness flows from one to the next without any apparent dividing point, so these practices should be done in an unbroken sequence. Of course, from the first day the practice of these kriyas will not necessarily lead to such exalted states of awareness, but if they are practised properly with correct guidance, by an aspirant who is ready for them, then most likely one day they will. It will be at that stage that the constant unbroken progression of awareness will become essential.

For more information on the practices refer to *Kundalini Tantra*, published by Bihar School of Yoga.

PRATYAHARA PRACTICES

1: Vipareeta Karani Mudra (inverted psychic attitude)

Assume vipareeta karani asana.
The chin should not touch the chest.
Practise ujjayi pranayama.
Be sure that your legs are completely vertical.
Close your eyes.
Inhale in ujjayi and simultaneously feel a hot stream of amrit or nectar flowing through the spinal passage from manipura chakra to vishuddhi. The nectar will collect at vishuddhi.
Retain the breath for a few seconds, and be aware of the nectar remaining at vishuddhi and becoming cool.
Then exhale with ujjayi, sensing the nectar travelling from vishuddhi through ajna, bindu and down to sahasrara.
The sensation is that of the nectar being injected with the help of the breath.
After exhalation, immediately return your awareness to manipura and repeat the kriya to bring more nectar down to vishuddhi, and finally sahasrara.
Practise 21 respirations or rounds.

2: Chakranusandhana (the discovery of the chakras)

Assume siddhasana/siddha yoni asana or padmasana.
Close your eyes.
Breathe normally.
There is no connection between the breath and the consciousness in this practice.
Bring your awareness to mooladhara chakra.
Your consciousness will slowly ascend the frontal passage of arohan from mooladhara to the frontal point of swadhisthana at the pubic bone, manipura at the navel, anahata at the sternum, vishuddhi at the throat and across to bindu at the top back of the head.
As you travel upwards mentally repeat 'mooladhara, swadhisthana, manipura, anahata, vishuddhi, bindu' as you pass through these centres.
Then let your awareness slip down the spinal awarohan passage from bindu to mooladhara, saying mentally, 'ajna, vishuddhi, anahata, manipura, swadhisthana, mooladhara', as you pass through these centres.
From mooladhara, immediately start ascending in the frontal passage as before, mentally reciting the chakra names starting with swadhisthana as you ascend.
Continue this rotation of awareness through the chakras in a constant flow of rounds.
Do not make a serious, tense effort to locate the chakras as you pass through them. Merely glance at them as you go by them as you would view the scenery from a fast moving train.
You can visualize your awareness in this kriya as a thin silver serpent travelling in an ellipse within your body.
Practise 9 rounds.

3: Nada Sanchalana (conducting the sound consciousness)

Sit in siddhasana/siddha yoni asana or padmasana.
Exhale completely and open your eyes.
Bend your head forward, so that it drops downward in a relaxed manner.

The chin should not press tightly on the chest.
Bring your awareness to mooladhara chakra.
Repeat mentally, 'mooladhara, mooladhara, mooladhara'.
Then as you inhale with ujjayi, your consciousness should rise up the frontal passage or arohan to bindu.
Have a clear awareness of swadhisthana, manipura, anahata and vishuddhi as you pass by them on your way to bindu, and mentally repeat their names.
As your awareness travels from vishuddhi to bindu during the last segment of your inhalation, your head will slowly rise and tilt back slightly into position, facing about 20 degrees above the horizontal.
With the breath stored inside you and the awareness at bindu repeat mentally, 'bindu, bindu, bindu'.
The power of the awareness will build up as you are repeating the word bindu, and it will explode into the vocal chant of *Om* which will carry you down through the spinal passage or awarohan to mooladhara.
The '*O*' sound on the *Om* will be explosive and sudden.
The '*m*' sound will be long and drawn out, culminating almost in a buzz as you approach mooladhara.
As your awareness descends in the spine, your eyes will gradually close in unmani mudra.
As you descend through the awarohan passage with the *Om* sound, you should also be aware ajna, vishuddhi, anahata, manipura and swadhisthana chakras; no mental repetition.
When you have reached mooladhara, drop your head forward and open your eyes.
Mentally repeat 'mooladhara, mooladhara, mooladhara', with the breath retained outside and start on the ascent as before, with inhalation and repetition of the chakra names as you pass through them.
Practise 13 full rounds or breaths, and end after the last 'mooladhara, mooladhara, mooladhara'.

4: Pawan Sanchalana (conducting the breath consciousness)

Sit in padmasana, siddhasana or siddha yoni asana, and keep your eyes open.

Practise khechari mudra throughout this kriya.

Exhale completely and bend your head forward as in nada sanchalana.

Become aware of mooladhara and repeat mentally, 'mooladhara, mooladhara, mooladhara'.

Then say mentally 'arohan' once and begin your ascent through the frontal passage with a subtle ujjayi inhalation.

As you ascend, be aware of the chakras and as you pass by them, name them mentally.

As your awareness moves from vishuddhi to bindu, slowly raise your head until it leans backward as in nada sanchalana.

At bindu, mentally repeat, 'bindu, bindu, bindu'.

Then say 'awarohan' mentally, and descend through the spinal passage with ujjayi exhalation, mentally reciting the name of each chakra as you pass through it.

As you descend, your eyes will close very gradually to form unmani mudra, the attitude of mindlessness.

At mooladhara, they will be closed.

Repeat mentally, 'mooladhara, mooladhara, mooladhara', and then open your eyes and bend the head forward.

Again begin your ascent with ujjayi inhalation as before.

Practise 49 rounds of complete breaths.

After the last 'mooladhara, mooladhara, mooladhara', open your eyes and end the practice.

5: Shabda Sanchalana (conducting the word consciousness)

Sit in siddhasana, siddha yoni asana or padmasana.

Keep your eyes open and practise khechari mudra throughout the kriya.

Exhale completely.

Bend your head forward and become aware of mooladhara chakra for a few seconds.

Inhale with ujjayi and ascend the frontal passage.

As you ascend, be aware of the breath sound, which takes the form of the mantra *So*.
Simultaneously, be aware of each kshetram, without mental repetition.
As you travel upward from vishuddhi to bindu, the head will move upward as in pawan sanchalana and nada sanchalana.
Then, with the breath retained inside, be aware of bindu for a few seconds.
Then exhale and descend the spinal passage, being simultaneously aware of the natural sound of exhalation and the mantra *Ham*.
Be aware of each chakra without repetition of its name.
After reaching mooladhara, open the eyes and lower your head.
Begin your ujjayi inhalation, rising up the frontal passage with the inhalation mantra of *So*.
Continue in this manner for 59 full rounds or breaths.

6. Maha Mudra (the great psychic attitude)

Sit in siddhasana or siddha yoni asana with the heel of the lower foot pressing firmly in towards mooladhara chakra.
Practise khechari mudra, exhale completely and bend your head forward.
Keep your eyes open.
Repeat mentally, 'mooladhara, mooladhara, mooladhara'.
Ascend through the frontal passage with ujjayi inhalation, being aware of the chakra levels as you pass through them.
Raise your head as you are crossing up from vishuddhi to bindu.
At bindu, repeat mentally, 'bindu, bindu, bindu'.
Practise moola bandha and shambhavi mudra, with the breath still retained inside.
Say to yourself mentally, 'shambhavi, khechari, mool' while at the same time shifting your awareness to the centres of these practices.

Beginners should repeat this shifting of awareness three times.

Advanced aspirants can rotate their awareness up to twelve times.

Then first release shambhavi mudra, then moola bandha.

Bring your awareness back to bindu, and travel down your spinal passage to mooladhara with ujjayi exhalation, being aware of the chakras as you pass them.

On reaching mooladhara, bend your head forward.

Then repeat 'mooladhara, mooladhara, mooladhara', and ascend the frontal passage with ujjayi inhalation as before.

Practise 12 rounds or breaths, and end after the last 'mooladhara, mooladhara, mooladhara'.

Alternative practice: This kriya can also be practised in the asana known as utthanpadasana by stretching one leg forward with the heel of the opposite leg placed against the perineum or inside the edge of the vagina.

Place the hands on the unbent knee.

When practising maha mudra in utthanpadasana, a change must be made in the technique.

After ascending to bindu and repeating 'bindu, bindu, bindu', lean forward and remove your hands from your knee. Hold the big toe of your forward foot with the fingers of both hands.

The stretched knee must not bend.

Now practise shambhavi mudra and moola bandha.

Repeat 'shambhavi, khechari, mool' from 3 to 12 times, while bringing your awareness to the seats of these practices.

Release shambhavi, then moola bandha, then utthanpadasana and place your hands back on your knee.

Bring your consciousness back to bindu, and then descend the spinal passage with the ujjayi exhalation.

Practise 4 rounds with the right leg stretched forward, 4 rounds with the left leg stretched, and 4 rounds with both stretched.

All other details are the same for both methods of practice.

7: Maha Bheda Mudra (the great separating attitude)

Sit in perfect siddhasana/siddha yoni asana.

Practise khechari mudra and keep your eyes open and head down.

Exhale completely and practise jalandhara bandha.

Repeat mentally, 'mooladhara, mooladhara, mooladhara', then release jalandhara bandha.

Inhale in ujjayi while you ascend the frontal passage to bindu.

As you ascend from vishuddhi to bindu, raise your head.

Repeat mentally, 'bindu, bindu, bindu', and then descend the spinal passage to mooladhara with ujjayi exhalation and unmani mudra.

Be sure to notice the chakras as you pass them.

Repeat mentally, 'mooladhara, mooladhara, mooladhara', and then practise jalandhara bandha, with the breath retained outside.

Practise moola bandha, uddiyana bandha and nasikagra drishti.

Repeat mentally, 'nasikagra, uddiyana, mool', while simultaneously placing your awareness at the seats of these practices in turn.

Repeat this cycle of awareness three times if you are a beginner, or up to twelve times if you are experienced.

Then release nasikagra drishti, moola bandha, uddiyana bandha and jalandhara bandha.

Bring your awareness back to mooladhara.

Repeat the mantra 'mooladhara, mooladhara, mooladhara', mentally.

Then rise up the frontal passage with an ujjayi inhalation to bindu for the next round.

Practise 12 full rounds or breaths.

Alternative practice: Sit in utthanpadasana (as described in the previous practice). Place your hands on your unbent knee, exhale completely and bend your head forward, eyes open.

Repeat mentally, 'mooladhara, mooladhara, mooladhara'.

Inhale within ujjayi through the frontal passage from mooladhara to bindu, raising your head while crossing from vishuddhi.
Repeat 'bindu, bindu, bindu', and then exhale in ujjayi through the spinal passage, being aware of the chakras en route.
Repeat mentally, 'mooladhara, mooladhara, mooladhara', and then bend your head downward to form jalandhara bandha.
Bend forward and grasp the big toe of the extended foot and practise moola bandha, uddiyana bandha and nasikagra drishti while still retaining the breath outside.
Repeat mentally the words, 'nasikagra, uddiyana, mool', while simultaneously placing your awareness at the seats of these practices in turn.
Repeat this cycle of awareness three times if you are a beginner, or up to twelve times if you are experienced.
Then release nasikagra drishti, moola bandha, uddiyana bandha and jalandhara bandha.
Bring your hands to your knees and sit up, but keep your head bent.
Bring your awareness back to mooladhara, and then ascend the frontal passage with an ujjayi inhalation.
Practise in this way for four full rounds, or breaths, with your right leg extended, then practise four times with the left leg extended, and finally four times with both legs extended.
After the fourth time in each position, ascend once to bindu with the ujjayi inhalation. Repeat the bindu mantra, descend to mooladhara, repeat its mantra, and relax.

8: Manduki Kriya (the attitude of the frog)

Sit in bhadrasana, the gracious pose.
The eyes should remain open.
The point on your body below mooladhara chakra must touch the ground. If it doesn't, then use a cushion to exert pressure on this point.

Place your hands on your knees and practise nasikagra drishti.
Become aware of your natural breath flowing in and out of your nostrils.
With inhalation the breath flows through both nostrils and merges at the eyebrow centre. As you exhale the two flows diverge from the eyebrow centre and move out through both nostrils.
The breath follows a conical or inverted V-shaped pathway. Feel this.
Simultaneously, be aware of all smells.
The point of this kriya is to smell the aroma of the astral body, which has a scent like that of sandalwood.
If your eyes become tired, close them for some time and then resume nasikagra drishti.
Practise this kriya until it becomes intoxicating.
Do not carry it so far that you become totally absorbed in it and do not wish to end the practice.

9: Tadan Kriya (beating the kundalini)

Sit in padmasana with the eyes open.
Place your palms on the floor at the sides of your body, next to your hips, with the fingers pointing forward.
Bend your head slightly backward and practise shambhavi mudra.
Inhale through your mouth in audible ujjayi pranayama.
As you inhale, feel the breath travelling downward through a tube connecting the mouth to mooladhara chakra.
The breath will collect at mooladhara chakra.
Hold the breath, keep your awareness at mooladhara and practise a very light, subtle moola bandha.
Place your hands next to your hips and lift your body, using your hands to support you.
Then drop your body lightly so that mooladhara is gently beaten.
Repeat this beating a few times.
Do not practise this quickly or harshly.

After the third beating, exhale gently through the nose with ujjayi pranayama.
The breath will seem to diffuse in all directions from its storehouse at mooladhara.
Practise this kriya a total of 7 times.
The number of beatings practised per round can be gradually increased by one a month, until it reaches a maximum of 11.

DHARANA PRACTICES

10: Naumukhi Mudra (closing the nine gates)

Sit in siddhasana, siddha yoni asana or padmasana.
Your eyes should remain closed throughout.
If necessary, use a cushion to ensure that mooladhara is compressed.
Do khechari mudra and bend your head slightly forward (not jalandhara bandha).
Repeat mentally, 'mooladhara, mooladhara, mooladhara'.
Then inhale with ujjayi up the frontal passage to bindu, raising your head as you pass from vishuddhi to bindu.
Practise shanmukhi mudra by closing your ears with the thumbs, the eyes with both forefingers, your nostrils with your middle fingers, the upper lip with the ring fingers and your lower lip with the little fingers.
Practise moola bandha and vajroli mudra.
The nine gates of the body are now closed (eyes, ears, nostrils, mouth, anus and sexual organs).
Become aware of the spinal passage and of bindu.
Now visualize a shining copper trident (trishul), rooted in mooladhara with its stem in the spinal cord and the prongs extending upward from vishuddhi. The prongs are very sharp, and the central one touches bindu.
The trishul will rise up slightly a number of times of its own accord to pierce bindu.
As it pierces bindu, repeat the mantra *bindu bhedan*, which means 'bindu piercing', every time that the trident rises.

After some time, release vajroli mudra and moola bandha.
Open the upper gates and lower the hands to the knees.
Exhale in ujjayi from bindu to mooladhara.
Mentally repeat 'mooladhara' three times.
Then inhale through the frontal passage up to bindu to repeat the kriya.
Practise five full rounds or breaths, and after the fifth round end the practice after exhalation.

Practice note: The back must be straight throughout this kriya or the sensation that follows the piercing of bindu will not be perceived.
It is important that vajroli mudra be correctly performed as it heightens the sensation experienced. The sensation is like an electric current running the full length of vajra nadi to the brain. Try to sensitize your awareness to the point where you actually feel the piercing of bindu like an electric shock.

11: Shakti Chalini (conducting the thought force)

Sit in siddhasana, siddha yoni asana or padmasana.
Your eyes should remain closed throughout.
Practise khechari mudra.
Exhale completely and bring your awareness to mooladhara.
Bend your head forward.
Repeat mentally, 'mooladhara, mooladhara, mooladhara', and then ascend the frontal passage to bindu with ujjayi inhalation, raising your head as you approach bindu.
Retain the breath inside and then practise shanmukhi mudra, closing your ears, eyes, nostrils and lips with the fingers.
Allow your consciousness to rotate in a continuous cycle, descending the spinal passage to mooladhara and rising up the frontal passage to bindu in an unbroken loop, with the breath retained inside.
Visualize a thin green snake moving through the psychic passageways.

The tail of this serpent is at bindu, and the body extends down through mooladhara and up the frontal passage.
The head is also at bindu, with the mouth biting the end of the tail.
If you watch this snake, it will start to move in a circle in the psychic passages, or it may even go off this track and follow a new one of its own.
Just watch this snake, whatever it does.
When your retention of breath is becoming exhausted, release shanmukhi mudra, return your hands to the knees and bring your awareness to bindu.
Then descend to mooladhara through the spinal passage with ujjayi exhalation.
At mooladhara, repeat 'mooladhara' three times, and ascend the frontal passage.
Practise this kriya five times without a break, or for the duration of five breaths.

Practice note: Vajroli mudra and moola bandha can also be performed simultaneously with shanmukhi mudra.

12: Shambhavi (Parvati's lotus)

Sit in siddhasana, siddha yoni asana or padmasana.
Close your eyes and practise khechari mudra.
Visualize a lotus flower with a long thin stem extending downward.
The roots of the lotus are white or transparent green. They spread out from mooladhara chakra,
The thin green lotus stem is in your spainal passage.
The lotus flower is at sahasrara, and it is closed like a bud.
At the bottom of the bud are a few light green immature petals.
The main petals of the flower are pink with fine red veins.
Try to see this lotus clearly.
You visualize it in the space of chidakasha, but you feel it in your body.
Exhale and take your awareness to the root of the lotus at mooladhara.

Inhale with ujjayi pranayama and allow your awareness to rise slowly through the centre of the lotus stem, within the spinal passage.
At the end of inhalation, you will reach the closed bud at the top of the stem.
Your ascent will be like that of a caterpillar, climbing up inside the thin stem.
Hold your awareness at sahasrara with the breath retained inside.
You are inside the lotus, but you can also see it from outside.
It will begin to open very slowly.
As the bud opens out into a beautiful lotus flower, you will see the yellow pollen tipped stamen in its centre.
It will slowly close again, to open again almost immediately.
After the lotus has cease to open and close, and it remains sealed, then slowly descend through the stem to mooladhara, drifting down on the wave of your ujjayi exhalation.
Remain at mooladhara for a few seconds, visualizing the roots spreading out in all directions.
Then once again ascend the stem with ujjayi inhalation.
Ascend and descend 11 times, and then end this kriya.

13: Amrit Pan (the quaffing of nectar)

Sit in siddhasana, siddha yoni asana or padmasana.
Keep the eyes closed throughout and practise khechari mudra.
Bring your awareness to manipura chakra, where there is a storehouse of a warm, sweet liquid.
Exhale fully with ujjayi.
Inhale with ujjayi, drawing a quantity of this liquid up to vishuddhi chakra through the spinal passage with the suction power of your breath.
Remain at vishuddhi for some seconds.
The nectar which you have raised from manipura will become icy cold at vishuddhi.

Then with ujjayi, exhale up to lalana chakra (at the back of the soft palate), through the nectar passage. Blow the cool nectar up to lalana with the breath.
Your breath will immediately disperse by itself once you have reached lalana.
Immediately return your awareness to manipura chakra.
With another ujjayi inhalation, continue the upward transfer of liquid. Practise 9 times in all.

14: Chakra Bhedan (piercing the chakras)

Assume siddhasana, siddha yoni asana or padmasana.
Keep your eyes closed throughout.
Practise khechari mudra and ujjayi pranayama. Breathe without any break between inhalation and exhalation.
Exhale and bring your awareness down to swadhisthana chakra at the base of the spine.
Inhale and direct your consciousness first to mooladhara and then up the frontal passage.
At about the level of vishuddhi kshetram, the breath will run out and you will immediately start exhalation. Exhale from vishuddhi kshetram to bindu and then down the spine from ajna to swadhisthana chakra to complete one round.
The kriya should actually be practised for 59 rounds but if introversion starts to occur before you have completed the rounds, discontinue the practice and go on to the next kriya.

15: Sushumna Darshan (inner visualization of the chakra)

Sit in siddhasana, siddha yoni asana or padmasana.
Close your eyes and practise normal breathing.
There is no relation between the breath and awareness in this kriya.
Bring your awareness to mooladhara.
Imagine a pencil, and with it draw a square at mooladhara.
Draw the largest possible inverted equilateral triangle within that square.

Then make a circle touching all the four corners of that square.
Prepare four petals, one for each side of the square.
Bring your awareness to swadhisthana.
Prepare a circle there of the same radius as the one at mooladhara.
Draw six petals around the edge of the circle, and a crescent moon inside the bottom of the circle.
Now come to manipura.
Draw a circle, and then make the biggest possible inverted triangle to fit this circle.
In the centre draw a ball of fire.
Make ten petals around the circle.
Raise the consciousness to anahata.
Draw two triangles there, one pointing upward and the other inverted. They are interlaced, both crossing each other.
Surround them with a circle having 12 petals.
Then come to vishuddhi.
Draw a circle, and place a smaller circle within the circle, like a drop of nectar.
Make 16 petals around that circle.
Rise to ajna.
Make a circle and inside it write a big Sanskrit *Om*.
Prepare two large petals, one on the right and one on the left side of the circle.
At bindu draw a crescent moon with a very tiny circle above it.
Reach sahasrara.
Prepare a circle there, and make the largest possible upward pointing triangle within that circle.
There are a thousand petals all around the circle.
Try to sec at one glance all the chakras in their proper places.
If it is very difficult to see them all together, then see only two chakras on the first day and add one more chakra to your visualization daily until all appear together.

16: Prana Ahuti (infusing the divine prana)

Sit in siddhasana, siddha yoni asana or padmasana.
Close your eyes and breathe normally.
Feel the soft touch of a divine hand lying on your head.
The hand is infusing divine prana into your body, and the prana is travelling down from sahasrara through the spinal passage.
You may experience it as a wave of cold, heat, energy, electric current, or as a stream of wind or liquid.
Its passage will result in vibrations, shocks, jerks or tickling sensations which course through you.
When the prana has reached mooladhara, then immediately go on to the next kriya without waiting to experience the prana a second time.

17: Utthan (raising the kundalini)

Sit in siddhasana, siddha yoni asana or padmasana.
Keep your eyes closed throughout.
Again the breathing is normal in this kriya.
Bring your awareness to mooladhara chakra.
Try to visualize it clearly and notice all details.
You will see a black shivalingam made of a smoky, gaseous substance.
The top and bottom of the lingam are cut off, and circled around it is a red baby snake.
The red baby snake is trying to uncoil itself so it can move upward through sushumna.
As it struggles to release itself and ascends, it makes an angry hissing sound.
The tail of the snake will remain fixed at the bottom of the shivalingam, but the head and body may move upward and come back down again.
Sometimes both the shivalingam with the snake may shift its position in the body, so you may even visualize them for a time at ajna or at sahasrara.
The head of the snake is very wide, having the same width as your body, but it is not a cobra.

After some time you may feel your body contract.
This will be followed by a sensation of bliss.
When this occurs go on to the next kriya.

18: Swaroopa Darshan (the vision of your Self)

Remain sitting in siddhasana, siddha yoni asana or padmasana and do not open your eyes.
Become aware of your physical body.
Your body is completely motionless, and you maintain total awareness of this fact.
Be sure that you are completely steady, like a rock.
When you are absolutely sure of your bodily steadiness, you should also become aware of your natural breath.
Watch your constant flow of breath, but be sure your body remains steady.
Your body will start to become stiff.
As it becomes stiffer, your awareness will shift completely to your breathing; however, the body will continue to become stiffer and stiffer of its own accord.
When your body has become as rigid as a stone, and it is beyond your control to move it even if you tried, then go on to the next kriya.

19: Linga Sanchalana (astral conduction)

Remain still in your stiffened asana with the eyes closed.
Due to the stiffness of your body your breathing will automatically have become ujjayi breathing, and khechari will have been formed.
Be aware totally of your breathing.
You will notice that with each inhalation your body seems to be expanding.
And with each exhalation your body appears to be contracting.
It is peculiar, though, because your physical body is not moving; it is still as stiff as a statue.
It is your astral body that you experience expanding and contracting.

As you observe this contraction and expansion process, it will gradually become more and more pronounced.
After some time you will begin to lose awareness of the physical body, and you will only be observing the astral body directly.
However, the degree of contraction will become more pronounced.
Eventually you will reach a stage where, on contraction, the astral body reduces to a single point of light.
When this occurs, discontinue the kriya immediately and go on to the next.

DHYANA PRACTICE

20: Dhyana (meditation)

You have realized your astral body as a single point of light.
Now look closer at that point of light and you will see it take the form of a golden egg.
As you watch this golden egg, it will begin to expand.
The golden egg is luminous and glowing intensely; however, it does not give off any rays of light.
As the golden egg becomes larger, it will begin to take on the same shape as that of your astral and physical bodies.
This form, however, is not a material or even a subtle form.
This form is glowing light.
It is your causal self.

Appendices

Phonetic Pronunciation Guide

a *in* mica
ā " far
i " hill
ī " police
u " pull
ū " nude
ṛ " clarity
ṝ " marine
lṛ " rivalry
lṝ " rivalry (*prolonged*)
e " prey
ai " aisle
o " go
au " cow
ṃ " rum
ḥ " bah
k " meek
kh " inkhorn
g " go
gh " yoghurt
ṅ " sing
ch " check
chh" churchhill
j " jab
jh " hedgehog

ñ in canyon
ṭ " true
ṭh " anthill
ḍ " do
ḍh " redhead
ṇ " gong
t " water (*dental*)
th " nuthook
d " bud
dh " adhere (*more dental*)
n " not
p " pay
ph " photo
b " rub
bh " abhor
m " map
y " yoga
r " red
l " bull
v " vice
ś " shield
ṣ " assure
s " sin
h " hit

Appendix B

Mantras from Different Religions

All religions make use of mantras, either knowingly or unknowingly, including the Christian religion and the Catholic faith in particular. We list hereunder for your interest and information a selection of the best mantras. One does not need to be Hindu or Buddhist to make use of a particular mantra; a Christian may also make use of them with great benefit, the only provision being that it should have appeal for him.

The first section of mantras have been selected from vedic and tantric texts, classified according to their deities. Following these are mantras from different religions.

GAYATRI MANTRAS

Gayatri

Oṃ Bhūḥ Bhūvaḥ Svaḥ Tat Saviturvareṇyaṃ
Bhargodevasya Dhīmahi Dhiyo Yo Naḥ Prachodayāt

Ganesha

1. Oṃ Ekadantāya Vidmahe Vakratuṇḍāya Dhīmahi Tanno Dantiḥ Prachodayāt
2. Oṃ Tatkarāṭāya Vidmahe Hastimukhāya Dhīmahi Tanno Dantiḥ Prachodayāt
3. Oṃ Tat Puruṣāya Vidmahe Hastimukhāya Dhīmahi Tanno Dantiḥ Prachodayāt

Brahma

1. Oṃ Vedātmane Cha Vidmahe Hiraṇyagarbhāya Dhīmahi Tanno Brahmā Prachodayāt
2. Oṃ Chaturmukhāya Vidmahe Kamaṇḍaludharāya Dhīmahi Tanno Brahmā Prachodayāt

Vishnu

1. Oṃ Nārāyaṇāya Vidmahe Vāsudevāya Dhīmahi Tanno Viṣṇuḥ Prachodayāt
2. Oṃ Nārāyaṇāya Vidmahe Mahādevāya Dhīmahi Tanno Viṣṇuḥ Prachodayāt

Narasimha

1. Oṃ Vajranakhāya Vidmahe Tīkṣṇadanṣṭrāya Dhīmahi Tanno Nṛasiṅhaḥ Prachodayāt
2. Oṃ Nṛasiṅhāya Vidmahe Vajranakhāya Dhīmahi Tanno Simhaḥ Prachodayāt

Garuda

Oṃ Tat Puruṣāya Vidmahe Suvarṇa Pakṣāya Dhīmahi Tanno Garuḍaḥ Prachodayāt

Rudra/Shiva

1. Oṃ Tat Puruṣāya Vidmahe Mahādevāya Dhīmahi Tanno Rudraḥ Prachodayāt
2. Oṃ Tat Puruṣāya Vidmahe Sahasrākṣasyamahādevasya Dhīmahi Tanno Rudraḥ Prachodayāt

Nandikeshvara

Oṃ Tat Puruṣāya Vidmahe Nandikeśvarāya Dhīmahi Tanno Vṛṣabhaḥ Prachodayāt

Shanmukha

1. Oṃ Ṣaṇmukhāya Vidmahe Mahāsenāya Dhīmahi Tanno Skandaḥ Prachodayāt
2. Oṃ Ṣaṇmukhāya Vidmahe Mahāsenāya Dhīmahi Tanno Ṣaṇamukhaḥ Ṣaṣṭhaḥ Prachodayāt

Surya

1. Oṃ Bhāskarāya Vidmahe Mahādyutikarāya Dhīmahi Tannaḥ Ādityaḥ Prachodayāt
2. Oṃ Ādityāya Vidmahe Sahasra-kiraṇāya Dhīmahi Tannaḥ Bhānuḥ Prachodayāt
3. Oṃ Prabhākarāya Vidmahe Divākarāya Dhīmahi Tannaḥ Sūryaḥ Prachodayāt

Durga

1. Oṃ Kātyāyanyai Vidmahe Kanyākumāryai Dhīmahi Tanno Durgā Prachodayāt
2. Oṃ Mahāśūlinyai Vidmahe Mahādurgāyai Dhīmahi Tanno Bhagavati Prachodayāt

Saraswati

Oṃ Aiṅ Vāgdevyai Cha Vidmahe Kāmarājāya Dhīmahi Tanno Devī Prachodayāt

Rama

Oṃ Dāśarathāya Vidmahe Sitā-vallabhāya Dhīmahi Tanno Rāmaḥ Prachodayāt

Hanuman

Oṃ Āñjaneyāya Vidmahe Vāyu Putrāya Dhīmahi Tanno Hanumān Prachodayāt

Krishna

Oṃ Devakīnandanāya Vidmahe Vāsudevāya Dhīmahi Tanno Kṛṣṇaḥ Prachodayāt

Gopal

Oṃ Gopālāya Vidmahe Gopijana-vallabhāya Dhīmahi Tanno Gopālaḥ Prachodayāt

Parashuram

Oṃ Jāmadajñāya Vidmahe Mahāvīrāya Dhīmahi Tanno Paraśurāmaḥ Prachodayāt

Tantrika (Brahma)

Oṃ Parameśvarāya Vidmahe Parama Tattvāya Dhīmahi
Tanno Brahmā Prachodayāt

Lakshmi

Oṃ Mahādevī Cha Vidmahe Viśṇu-patnī Cha Dhīmahi
Tanno Lakṣmīḥ Prachodayāt

Shakti

Oṃ Sarva-sammohinyai Vidmahe Viśva-Jananyai Dhīmahi
Tannaḥ Śaktiḥ Prachodayāt

Annapurna

Oṃ Bhagavatyai Cha Vidmahe Māheśvaryai Cha Dhīmahi
Tanno Annapūrṇā Prachodayāt

Kali

1. Oṃ Kālikāyai Vidmahe Śmaśānavāsinyai Dhīmahi Tanno Aghorā Prachodayāt
2. Oṃ Ādyāyai Vidmahe Parameśvaryai Dhīmahi Tanno Kālīḥ Prachodayāt

Dakshinamurti

Oṃ Dākṣiṇāmūrtaye Vidmahe Dhyānasthāya Dhīmahi
Tanno Dhīśaḥ Prachodayāt

Guru

Oṃ Gurudevāya Vidmahe Parabrahmaṇe Dhīmahi Tanno
Guruḥ Prachodayāt

Hamsa

1. Oṃ Hamsāya Vidmahe Paramahamsāya Dhīmahi Tanno Hamsaḥ Prachodayāt
2. Oṃ Paramahamsāya Vidmahe Mahattattvāya Dhīmahi Tanno Hamsaḥ Prachodayāt

Hayagriva

Oṃ Vāgīśvarāya Vidmahe Hayagrīvāya Dhīmahi Tanno Hamsaḥ Prachodayāt

Sivananda

Oṃ Tat Puruṣāya Vidmahe Śivānandāya Dhīmahi Tanno Brahma Prachodayāt

Ajapa

Oṃ Hamsa Hamsāya Vidmahe Sohaṃ Hamsāya Dhīmahi Tanno Hamsaḥ Prachodayāt

MANTRAS FROM UPANISHADS

1. Oṃ
2. Hariḥ Oṃ
3. Hariḥ Oṃ Tat Sat
4. Ahaṃ Brahmāsmi
5. Tattvamasi
6. Ayamātmā Brahmā
7. Prajñānam Brahmā
8. Śivoham
9. Sachchidakam Brahmā

SEED MANTRAS

Mantra	Devata or deity
1. Oṃ	Sound of cosmic being
2. Hrauṃ	Śiva
3. Duṃ	Durgā
4. Krīṃ	Kālikā
5. Hrīṃ	Mahāmāyā
6. Aiṃ	Mahāsarasvati
7. Śrīṃ	Mahālakṣmī
8. Klīṃ	Kṛṣṇa or Kāmadeva
9. Huṃ	Bhairava
10. Gaṃ	Ganeśa
11. Kṣrauṃ	Nāṛasimha

GANESHA MANTRAS

For Gayatri see section on Gayatri.

1. Oṃ Śrī Gaṇeśāya namaḥ
2. Oṃ Śrī Mahāgaṇapataye namaḥ
3. Oṃ Śrīṃ hrīṃ krīṃ glauṃ gaṃ gaṇapataye vara varada sarvajanaṃ me vaśamānaya svāhā
4. Hriṃ gaṃ hriṃ gaṇapataye svāhā
5. Oṃ gaṃ Oṃ
6. Oṃ Gaṃ Gaṇapataye namaḥ
7. Oṃ Namo Bhagavate Gajānanāya
8. Vakratuṇḍāya huṃ

SHIVA MANTRAS

For Gayatri see section on Gayatri.

1. Oṃ namaḥ Śivāya
2. Oṃ Haraye namaḥ
3. Oṃ Tryambakaṃ yajāmahe sugandhiṃ puṣṭivardhanaṃ Urvārukamiva bandhanāt mṛtyormukṣīya māmṛtāt
4. Oṃ Namaḥ Nīlkanṭhāya
5. Hrauṃ
6. Hrauṃ hrīṃ ṭhaḥ
7. Raṃ kṣaṃ maṃ yaṃ auṃ ūṃ

VAISHNAVA MANTRAS

For Gayatri see section on Gayatri.

1. Oṃ Nārāyaṇāya namaḥ
2. Oṃ Viṣṇasve namaḥ
3. Oṃ Viṣṇave parājyotye namaḥ
4. Oṃ Paramātmane namaḥ
5. Oṃ Anantāya namaḥ
6. Oṃ Achyutāya namaḥ
7. Oṃ Govindāya namaḥ
8. Oṃ Achyutānanta Govindāya namaḥ
9. Oṃ Klīṃ Hriṣikeśāya namaḥ

10. Oṃ Śrī Śridharāya namaḥ
11. Oṃ Śrī Madhusūdanāya namaḥ
12. Oṃ Dāmodarāya namaḥ
13. Oṃ Namo Narayaṇāya
14. Oṃ Śrīman Nārāyaṇa-charaṇau-śaraṇaṃ prapadye

SRI RAMA MANTRAS

For Gayatri see section on Gayatri.

1. Oṃ Śrī Rāma jaya Rāma jaya jaya Rāma
2. Oṃ Śrī Rāmāya namaḥ
3. Oṃ Śrī Sitārāmachandrābhyāṃ namaḥ
4. Rāmāya Rāmabhadrāya Rāmachandrāya vedhase Raghunāthāya nāthāya Sitāyāḥ pataye namaḥ
5. Oṃ Śrī Rāmaḥ śaranaṃ mama
6. Oṃ Śrī Śrī Sitārāmaḥ śaranaṃ
7. Oṃ Śrī Rāmachandra-charaṇau-śaraṇaṃ prapadye
8. Raṃ Rāmāya namaḥ
9. Haṃ so Rāmāya namaḥ sohaṃ
10. Hrīṃ Rāmāya namaḥ hrīṃ
11. Hrauṃ Rāmāya namaḥ hrauṃ
12. Aiṃ Rāmāya namaḥ
13. Klīṃ Rāmāya namaḥ

KRISHNA MANTRAS

For Gayatri see section on Gayatri.

1. Oṃ namo bhagavate Vāsudevāya
2. Oṃ Śrī Kṛṣṇāya Govindāya Gopījana-vallabhāya namaḥ
3. Oṃ Śrī Kṛṣṇāya namaḥ
4. Oṃ Śrī Kṛṣṇaḥ śaraṇam mama
5. Klīṃ
6. Kṛṣṇaḥ
7. Klīṃ Kṛṣṇāya
8. Klīṃ Kṛṣṇāya Govindāya klīṃ

SHAKTI MANTRAS

Kali

1. Hrīṃ śrīṃ krīṃ Parameśvaryai svāhā
2. Hrīṃ śrīṃ krīṃ Parameśvari Kālike hrīṃ śrīṃ krīṃ svāhā
3. Oṃ śrī Kālikāyai namaḥ
4. Oṃ hrīṃ me svāhā (Kāli Hridaya)
5. Krīṃ krīṃ krīṃ huṃ huṃ hrīṃ hrīṃ dakṣiṇe Kālike krīṃ krīṃ krīṃ huṃ huṃ hrīṃ hrīṃ svāhā
6. Krīṃ hrīṃ śrīṃ

Durga

1. Oṃ śrī Durgāyai namaḥ
2. Oṃ hrīṃ duṃ Durgāyai namaḥ

Saraswati

1. Oṃ śrī Sarasvatyai namaḥ
2. Oṃ hrīṃ aiṃ hrīṃ Oṃ Sarasvatyai namaḥ

Mahalakshmi

1. Hrīṃ śrīṃ krīṃ Mahālakṣmyai namaḥ
2. Oṃ śrīṃ hrīṃ kamale kamale kamalālaye prasīda prasīda śrīṃ hrīṃ śrīṃ Mahālakṣmyai namaḥ

Radha

1. Śrī Rādhāyai svāhā
2. Oṃ hrīṃ Rādhikāyai namaḥ

Annapurna

Hrīṃ namo bhagavatī māheśvarī Annapūrṇe svāhā

Indrakshi

Oṃ śrīṃ hrīṃ aiṃ Indrākṣyai namaḥ

Chamunda

Oṃ aiṃ hrīṃ krīṃ chāmundāyai vichche

SIDDHA MANTRAS OF HANUMAN

The following siddha mantras are used for power and siddhis.
For Gayatri see section on Gayatri.

1. Oṃ Hanumate namaḥ
2. Oṃ namo bhagavate āñjaneyāya mahābalāya svāhā
3. Oṃ Hanumate rudrātmakāya huṃ phaṭ
4. Oṃ pavana nandanāya svāhā
5. Oṃ namo bhagavate āñjaneyāya amukasya śrinkhalā troṭaya troṭaya bandha mokṣam kuru kuru svāhā
6. Pūrvakapimukhāya pañchamukha hanumate ṭaṃ ṭaṃ ṭaṃ ṭaṃ ṭaṃ sakala śatru saṅharaṇāya svāhā
7. Oṃ paśchimamukhāya garuḍānanaya pañchamukha hanumate maṃ maṃ maṃ maṃ maṃ sakala viṣahara svāhā

MATRIKA MANTRAS & BIJA MANTRAS
IN THE SHAT CHAKRAS

Chakra	Matrika mantra	Bija mantra	Tattwa
Mooladhara	Vaṃ śaṃ ṣaṃ saṃ	Laṃ	Earth
Swadhisthana	Baṃ bhaṃ maṃ yaṃ raṃ laṃ	Vaṃ	Water
Manipura	Ḍaṃ ḍhaṃ ṇaṃ taṃ thaṃ daṃ dhaṃ naṃ paṃ phaṃ	Ram	Fire
Anahata	Kaṃ khaṃ gaṃ ghaṃ ṅaṃ chaṃ chhaṃ jaṃ jhaṃ ñaṃ ṭaṃ ṭhaṃ	Yam	Air
Vishuddhi	Aṃ āṃ iṃ īṃ uṃ ūṃ ṛṃ ṝṃ lṛṃ lṝṃ eṃ aiṃ oṃ auṃ aṃ aḥ	Ham	Ether
Ajna	Haṃ kṣaṃ	Oṃ	Mind

MISCELLANEOUS MANTRAS

These mantras are used for fulfilment of desires, curing diseases, achieving sound health, removing difficulties, etc., in day to day life.

To keep safe from snakes

1. Oṃ Narmadāyai vichāraṇā
2. Anantaṃ vāsukiṃ śeṣaṃ padmanābhaṃ cha kāmbalaṃ Śankhapālaṃ dhṛtarāṣtraṃ takṣakaṃ kālīyaṃ tathā munirājaṃ āstikaṃ namaḥ
3. Oṃ plaḥ sarpakulāya svāhā aśehakula sarva kulāya svāhā

For removing the venom of snakes

1. Nāma prabhāu jāna Śiva niko Kālakuṭa phalu dīnha amiko
2. Garuḍadhvajānusmaraṇāt viṣavīryam vyapohati

For removing the poison of scorpions

Chhapa svāhā

For removing any disease

1. Oṃ hrīm hamsaḥ
2. Oṃ śrīm hrīm klīm aīm Indrākṣyai namaḥ
3. Oṃ sam sām sum sim sum sū sem saim sam saha vam vām vim vīm vum vūm vem vaim vom vauṃ vam vām saha amṛta varech svāhā

Curing fever

1. Oṃ namo bhagavate ruḍrāya namaḥ krodheśvarāya namaḥ jyoti pataṇgāya namo namaḥ sīddhi rudra ajāpayati svāhā
2. Oṃ vindhya vānana hum phaṭ svāhā
3. Oṃ namo bhagavate chhandi chhandi amukasya jvarasya śara prajjvalita paraśupāṇaye paraśāya phaṭ
4. Oṃ namo mahā uchchhiṣṭa yogini prakirṇa danṣṭrā khādati tharvati naśyati bhakṣyati Oṃ ṭhaḥ ṭhaḥ ṭhaḥ ṭhaḥ

For sound health

1. Mām bhayāt sarvato rakṣa śrīyam vardhaya sarvadā
   Sharīrārogyam me dehi deva deva namostute
2. Oṃ aim hrīm śrīm namaḥ sarvadharāya bhagavate asya mama sarva roga vināśāya jvala jvala enam dīrghāyuṣam kuru kuru svāhā
3. Achyutam chāmṛtam chaiva japedauṣadhikarmāṇi
4. Oṃ namo paramatmane para brahma mama śarīre pāhi pāhi kuru kuru svāhā

For wealth

1. Oṃ Lakṣmī vam śrī kamalādhāram svāhā
2. Jimi saritā sāgar mahu jāhī
   Jadyapi tāhi kāmanā nāhī
3. Viśva bharana poṣana kara joī
   Tākara nāma bharata aṣa hoi
4. Oṃ śrīm hrīm śrīm kamale kamalālaye mahyam prasida prasida prasida svāhā
5. Oṃ śrīm hrīm mahālakṣmyai namaḥ

For removing obstructions and difficulties

1. Sakal vighna vyāpahin nahin tehī
   Rāma sukripā bilokahin jehīn
2. Sarvābādhāpraśamanaṃ trailokyasyākhileśvarī
   Evameva tvayākāryamasmad vairi vināśanam
3. Oṃ rām rām rām rām rām ro ro rām kaṣṭam svāhā
4. Oṃ namaḥ śānte praśānte gum hrīm hrīm sarva krodha praśamani svāhā
5. Rāma Rākṣā stotra (the whole chapter)

Removal of the evil eye

Śyāma Gaura sundara dou jorī
Nirakhahin chhabi jananī trina torī

For sound sleep

Oṃ agasti...śāyinaḥ

For peace and detachment

1. Daihika daivika bhautika tāpā
   Rāma rāja nahin kāhū byāpā
2. Bharata charita kari prabhu tulasī ne sādar sunahin
   Siyā Rāma pada prema vasi hoi bhava rasa birati

For removing doubt

Rāma kathā sundar karatārī
Sanśaya bihaga uḍāvana hārī

For purification of thought

Tāke juga pada kamala manāvauṇ
Jāsu kripā niramala mati pāvauṇ

For children's diseases

Avyādajoaṅgdhri maṇimānstava jānvathoru,
yajṇoachyutaḥ kaṭi taṭam jaṭharam kā hayāsya

For piles

Oṃ chhaī chhuī chhalaka chhalāī āhum
Ahum klam klām klīm hūm

For pox

Oṃ śrīm śrīm śrūm śrām śraum śraḥ Oṃ kharasthā
digambarā vikaṭa nayanām toyāsthitām bhajāmi svāhā
Svāṅgasthāṃ prachandarupāṃ namāmyātmabhibū taye

For stimulating digestive fire

Agastyaṃ kumbhakaraṇaṃ cha śamincha vāḍavānalaṃ
Bhojanam pachanārthāya smaredabhyāṃ cha pañchakaṃ

To have a son

1. Sarvābādhāvinirmukto dhanadhānyasutānvitaḥ
   Manuṣyo matprasāden bhaviṣyati na samśayaḥ
2. Oṃ hrīm lajjā jalyam ṭhaḥ ṭhaḥ laḥ Oṃ hrīm svāhā

For marriage

1. Taba Janaka pāi Vaśiṣtha āyasu byāha sāja savāri kai
   Mandavī śruta kirati Urmilā kuwari lāi hankāri kai
2. Kātyāyani mahāmāye mahāyoginyadhīśvarī
   Nandagopasutam devi patim me kurute namaḥ

For safety of the child in the womb

Oṃ ṭham ṭhām ṭhim ṭhīm ṭhum ṭhūm ṭhem ṭhaim ṭhom
ṭhaum ṭhaḥ ṭhaḥ Oṃ

For long life

1. Hraum Oṃ jom sā Oṃ bhūrbhuvah svāhā Oṃ
2. Tryambakam yajāmahe sugandhim puṣṭivardhanam
   Urvārukamiva bandhanāt mṛtyormukṣīyamāmṛtāt

To keep safe from theft

1. Oṃ kaphall-kaphall-kaphall
2. Oṃ karālinī svāhā Oṃ kapālinī svāhā hraum hrīm hrīm
   hrīm choram bandhaya ṭhaḥ ṭhaḥ ṭhaḥ

For winning court cases

Pavana tanaya bala pavana samānā
Buddhi viveka bigyāna nidhānā

For vision of Sitaji

Janakasutā jagajanani jānakī
Atisaya priya karunānidhāna kī

To please Hanuman

Sumiri pavana suta pāvana nāmū
Apane vaśa kari rākhe Rāmū

For devotion to God

Bhagata kalpataru pranatahita kripāsindhu sukhadhāma
Soi nija bhagati mohi prabhu dehu dayā kari Rāma

For acquiring knowledge

Chhiti jala pāvaka gagana samirā
Pañcha rachita yaha adhama śarīrā

For God's forgiveness

Anuchita bahuta kaheun agyatā
Kṣamahun kṣamā mandira dou bhrātā

Note: For peace, glory and power see the important suktas and mantras from the text *Siddha Prarthana*.

TEXTS

The following tantric texts containing mantras, hymns and prayers are extremely powerful in bestowing siddhis. Even Adi Shankaracharya when affected by black magic was cured by praying to Shakti. These prayers became the sixty-five tantras and are known as *Saundarya Lahari*. The following are also used as upachara (healing) mantras:

- *Durga Saptashati*
- *Ananda Lahari*
- *Devi Sukta*
- *Atharva Shirsha*
- *Kshama Yachana*
- *Thirty-two names of Durga*
- *The mantras of the ten Mahavidyas*

This completes the section on vedic and tantric mantras. The following are taken from different religions.

BUDDHIST MANTRAS

1. Buddhaṃ Śaraṇaṃ Gachchhāmi
2. Dhammaṃ Śaraṇaṃ Gachchhāmi
3. Sanghaṃ Śaraṇaṃ Gachchhami
4. Oṃ Svabhāvaśuddhāḥ Sarvadharmāḥ
   Svabhāvaśuddhohaṃ

5. Oṃ Sarvatathāgatātmakohaṃ
6. Oṃ Maṇipadme Huṃ
7. Oṃ Ah Huṃ Vajra Guru Padmasiddhi Huṃ
8. Ah Dharmadhātu Ah
9. Hri Ma Ma Ḍakinijua Mandarā Sarva-Siddhi Huṃ
10. Oṃ Padmo Yogini Jayā Varā-hai Huṃ
11. Oṃ Muni-Muni Mahāmuni ye Saha
12. Oṃ Ah Ṛa Pa Cha Na Dhe Saha
13. Oṃ Amrita Prabhe Amrita Huṃ
14. Oṃ Amrita Vajra Pani Huṃ Phaṭ
15. Oṃ Amrita Vajra Mahā Kala Khrin Tapi Gha Ṇa Bināyak Huṃ
16. Nāṃ Myoho Reṇgai Kyo (Nicharin Shoshu)

JAIN MANTRAS

1. Om
2. Siddha
3. Arhint
4. A-si-ā-u-sā
5. Arhint siddha
6. Ṇamo arihantāṇam ṇam ṇamo siddhāṇam ṇamo āiriyāṇam
7. Ṇamo uvajjhāyāṇām ṇamo loe sabvasāhūṇam

ISLAMIC MANTRAS

1. Bismillā-Hirrahaman-Nir-Rahim
2. Lā Ilāha Illallāh Muhammadur Rasulullāh
3. Allāh hū Allāh hū (audible japa)
4. Allāho Hāziri, Allāho Nāziri
   Allāho Shahidi, Allāho Māi (whispering japa)
5. Kuliadauaallāh Aviadauaarrhmān
   Ayyamamā Tadaufhal hual Asmāualahusnāa
6. ...Allāh Huval Hakku

SIKKH MANTRAS

1. Sat nāma
2. Vāhe guru
3. Sat śri akāla
4. Ek sat nāma omkāra karatā purakhu nirabhau niravairu
   akālamūrati ajūni saibham guru prasādi
   Adi sāchu jagādisāchu
   Hāi bhāi sāchu nanaka hosī bhāi sāchu

ZOROASTRIAN MANTRAS

1. Aṣaṃ Vohu (secret root mantras of Avesta)
2. Yathā Ahū Vairyo
3. Yathā Ahū Vairyo Athā Ratuṣ Aṣāt Chit Hachā
   Vaṅgahaush Dajdā Maṅgho Śyothananāṃm Aṅghaush
   Mazdāi Kshathremachā Ahurāi A Yiṃ Driguvyo Dadat
   Vāstārṃ
4. Fravārāne Mazda Yasno Jarthushtrish
   Vidaevo Ahura-Takaeṣo Hāvanae
   Aṣaone Aṣahe Raṭhave Yasnāich Vahmāich
   Kshanaothrāich Phrasastayaech

HEBREW MANTRAS

1. *Shema Yisroel*
   Adonoi Elohenu
   Adonoi Echod

   Hear O Israel
   The Lord our God
   The Lord is one.

2. *Boruchu es Adonoi Hamvorah*
   Boruch es Ataw Adonoi Liyolam Voed
   Boruch Ataw Adonoi
   Elohenu Melech Haolam

Boruch Ataw Adonoi
Vinatan Lanues Toraso
Boruch Ataw Adonoi
Hametz U'Tairah

Blessed art thou O Lord our God
Blessed art thou, who created the universe
Blessed art thou, who is our lord
You are the king of the universe.
Blessed art thou our lord
Who has created the law.
Blessed art thou our lord
Who has given us the law.

CHRISTIAN MANTRAS

Kyrie Eleison

Kyrie Eleison *(3 times)*
Christe Eleison *(3 times)*
Kyrie Eleison *(3 times)*

Hail Mary

Hail Mary full of grace
The Lord be with thee.
Blessed art thou among women
And blessed is the fruit of thy womb Jesus.
Holy Mary Mother of God
Pray for us sinners
Now, and at the hour of our death.
Amen.

The Sign of the Cross

In nomine Patris, et Filii et Spiritus Sancti
Amen.

In the name of the Father, the Son and the Holy Ghost
Amen.

Agnus Dei

Agnus Dei
Qui tollis peccata mundi
Miserere nobis.
Agnus Dei
Qui tollis peccata mundi
Miserere nobis.
Agnus Dei
Qui tollis peccata mundi
Dona nobis pacem.

Lamb of God
Who takest away the sins of the world
Have mercy upon us.
Lamb of God
Who takest away the sins of the world
Have mercy upon us.
Lamb of God
Who takest away the sins of the world
Grant us thy peace.

Paster Noster

Our Father
Which art in heaven
Hallowed be thy name.
Thy kingdom come
Thy will be done
On earth as it is in heaven.
Give us this day our daily bread
And forgive us our trespasses
As we forgive those who trespass against us.
Lead us not into temptation
But deliver us from evil
For Thine is the kingdom
And the power and the glory
For ever
Amen.

God be in my heart

God be in my head
And in my understanding.
God be in my heart
And in my thinking.

Sanctus

Sanctus Sanctus Sanctus
Hosanna in excelsis.
Gloria in excelsis Deo.

Holy Holy Holy
Hosanna in the highest.
All glory in the highest to God.

Glossary

Adrenal glands – located above kidneys; respond to stress by secreting adrenaline.
Adrenaline – hormone secreted during times of stress, danger or fear; responsible for 'fight or flight' reaction.
Ahimsa – non-violence in thought and deed.
Ajapa japa – spontaneous repetition of a mantra.
Ajna – the chakra or psychic centre that is the seat of intuition, also known as the 'third eye'.
Ajna's tube – psychic passageway running from the eyebrow centre through ajna chakra to the back of the head.
Akasha – ether; the ether of inner space as in chidakasha; the ether of outer space as in mahakasha.
Alpha waves – brain wave pattern emitted during milder states of meditation.
Amrit – psychic nectar that drops from lalana chakra to vishuddhi chakra, causing a feeling of blissful intoxication.
Anahada – sound without boundaries; non-tone.
Anahata – unstruck sound.
Anahata chakra – heart chakra; root of all emotions; associated with the psychic sounds experienced in meditation.
Anandamaya kosha – the third dimension of consciousness; the 'bliss body'.
Antar kumbhaka – retention of breath inside the body.
Anushthana – the performance, observance or accomplishment of an act; the resolve to act with absolute discipline.

Apana vayu – vital energy in the lower part of the body, below the navel.
Aparigraha – non-possessiveness; the attitude of non-attachment to material possessions.
Archana – worship in its ritualistic form.
Archetypes – symbols of the information contained in the collective unconscious.
Ardhanarishwara – Hindu god; the form of Lord Shiva and Parvati combined in one body; presides over vishuddhi chakra.
Arohan – psychic passageway in the subtle body.
Asana – a comfortable and steady position of the body.
Asteya – the ideal of complete honesty and non-theft.
Astral body – the subtle psychic body; finer than the physical body.
Autonomic nervous system – involuntary nervous system; governs respiration, circulation and internal organs. It is composed of the sympathetic and parasympathetic systems.
Avatara – divine incarnation, e.g. Krishna, Buddha, Christ, Ram, Mohammed.
Awarohan – psychic passageway in the subtle body.
Bahiranga kumbhaka – retention of breath outside the body.
Baikhari – sound produced by striking two objects.
Baikhari japa – audible repetition of a mantra.
Bandhas – locks designed to hold prana, or psychic energy, within certain areas of the body so that its pressurized force can be directed and utilized.
Basti – methods of cleaning the intestines.
Beta waves – brainwave patterns predominantly emitted during daily waking life.
Bhakta – one who practises bhakti yoga.
Bhakti yoga – the yoga of devotion.
Bhastrika – bellows; type of pranayama.
Bhrumadhya – the eyebrow centre; the trigger point for ajna chakra.
Bija – literally 'seed'

Bindu – the chakra, or psychic centre, associated with the moon and psychic sounds. Very important in the practices of kundalini yoga.
Biofeedback instruments – concerned with monitoring and measuring electric waves emitted from the brain.
Brahma – Hindu god; creator of the universe; presides over mooladhara chakra.
Brahmacharya – sexual control; the redirection of sexual energy towards spiritual or meditational practices; one who lives in higher consciousness.
Brahma granthi – type of knot separating beads on a mala; knot of creation.
Brahmamuhurta – the most appropriate time for meditation, from 4.00 a.m. to 6.00 a.m.
Bhramari – a bee; type of pranayama.
Carotid sinuses – structures at the rear of the throat that detect blood pressure.
Cervix – mouth of womb where it joins the vagina.
Chakra – major centre in the psychic or subtle body.
Chidakasha – the psychic space behind the forehead where all psychic events are viewed.
Chitta shuddhi – mental purification.
Conical passages – psychic passageways beginning behind the eyebrow centre and extending to a point just outside each nostril.
Daharaksha – the space at mooladhara chakra.
Dakini – Hindu goddess who controls the skin element in the body; presides over mooladhara chakra.
Delta waves – brainwave patterns closely linked with deep dreamless sleep.
Dharana – state of concentration.
Dharma – one's duty.
Dhauti – methods of cleansing the alimentary canal.
Dhyana – state of meditation.
DNA – responsible for the transmission of genetic information from generation to generation; found in every cell of the body.

Drashta bhava – the attitude of a witness.

Ego – the centre of individual physical, emotional and mental functioning.

Electroencephalograph (EEG) – amplifier system that detects electrical activity in the brain.

Frontal passage – psychic passageway visualized as extending up the front of the body from the navel to the throat.

Glottis – the opening between the pharynx and windpipe.

Guru – guide; dispeller of darkness; spiritually awakened one who opens his disciples' eyes to the infinite truth.

Hakini – Hindu goddess who controls the subtle mind; presides over ajna chakra.

Hatha yoga – the yoga path primarily concerned with bodily purification practices which tranquilize the mind and discipline the body.

Hridayakasha – the psychic heart space visualized in the centre of the chest.

Ida nadi – important psychic passageway in the subtle body.

Isha – Hindu god; the Lord in his all pervading form; presides over anahata chakra.

Ishta – one's personal form of God.

Ishwara pranidhana – self-surrender; the surrender of all of one's actions to God.

Japa – to rotate; repetition of a mantra; type of meditation practice.

Jnana yoga – yoga of higher intuitional knowledge.

Jugular vein – blood vessel connecting heart to brain.

Kakini – Hindu goddess; ruler of the fat element in the body; presides over anahata chakra.

Kapalbhati – a type of pranayama; method of purifying the frontal portion of the brain.

Karma yoga – the yoga path of selfless action.

Kleshas – Sanskrit name for the causes of human suffering.

Kriyas – the practices of kundalini yoga; literally an action.

Kumbhaka – breath retention.

Kundalini shakti – manifested power of consciousness in the individual.

Lactate – substance produced mainly in muscles during intense activity; the build-up of lactate leads to fatigue.
Lakini – Hindu goddess; controls the flesh element of the body; presides over manipura chakra.
Lalana – one of the minor chakras, or psychic centres; responsible for the secretion of amrit.
Larynx – central region of the throat.
Laser – device for concentrating light waves.
Likhit japa – written repetition of a mantra.
Madhyama – 'in between' sound; whispering sound with almost no audible effect.
Mala – bead rosary for counting.
Manipura – the chakra or psychic centre associated with vitality and energy.
Mantras – mystical combinations of sound that were realized by sages and rishis during stages of deepest meditation.
Mantra shastra – the science of mantra.
Metabolism – the processes of breaking down and building up in the body.
Mooladhara – the chakra, or psychic centre, which is the seat of the sexual and spiritual energy in man.
Mouna – silence.
Mudras – physical and mental attitudes which play an important role in yoga in bringing about controlled psychic states and occurrences.
Nada yoga – the yoga of subtle sound.
Nadi – passageway for the flow of energy in the psychic body.
Nama sankirtan – continuous repetition of the names of God in song form.
Nauli – the practice of control of the abdominal muscles.
Nectar passage – psychic passageway between vishuddhi chakra and lalana chakra.
Neti – methods of nasal cleansing.
Nirvana – enlightenment; samadhi; harmony between the individual consciousness and the universal consciousness.
Niyamas – the five observances, or rules of personal

discipline, laid down by Patanjali to help render the mind tranquil in preparation for meditation.

Paramshiva – the Hindu god symbolizing formless consciousness; presides over ajna chakra.

Para nada – transcendental sound.

Parasympathetic nervous system – that part of the involuntary nervous system responsible for the reduction of tension; governs inner organs.

Parathyroid glands – small glands at the throat.

Pashyanti – mental sound.

Patanjali – ancient yogi who codified the techniques for attaining states of meditation; his system is known as 'raja yoga'.

Pathology – science of diseases.

Perineum – the area between the genitals and the anus.

Phobia – deep-rooted irrational fear.

Pingala nadi – psychic passageway travelling from mooladhara chakra to ajna chakra.

Pooraka – inhalation during pranayama.

Prana – vital energy in the body; bioenergy.

Prana vayu – vital energy in the region of the body between the larynx and heart.

Prana vidya – technique of energy control and healing.

Pranayama – the control of vital and psychic energy in the body.

Pranic body – the energy body that is finer than the physical body.

Pratyahara – withdrawal of the senses; elimination of sense impressions communicated to the brain.

Psychosomatic diseases – diseases of the mind which manifest in the body.

Psychosynthesis – system of psychology originated by Roberto Assagioli, aiming at self-realization; uses many of the techniques of yoga.

Raga – musical notes; classical music of India.

Raja yoga – a systematic method of attaining states of meditation as codified by the ancient yogi Patanjali.

Rakini – Hindu goddess; controller of the element of blood in the body; presides over swadhisthana chakra.
Rechaka – exhalation in pranayama.
Reticular activating system – that part of the brain which controls the information that reaches conscious perception; the physiological seat of the ego.
Rudra – Hindu god; the destroyer of the universe; presides over manipura chakra.
Rudraksha mala – rosary of rudraksha beads used for japa.
Sadhaka – spiritual seeker.
Sadhana – spiritual practice that aims at eventually experiencing self-realization of divine knowledge.
Sahasrara – the highest chakra, or psychic centre, which symbolizes the threshold between the psychic and spiritual realms.
Sakini – Hindu goddess who controls the bones of the body; presides over vishuddhi chakra.
Samadhi – the climax of meditation; state of unity with the object of meditation and the universal consciousness.
Samkhya – philosophy associated with yoga; based on the division of existence into purusha and prakriti.
Samskaras – past mental impressions.
Sankalpa – resolve; short sentence of moral significance.
Sanskrit – ancient language of India, in which most of the yogic texts are written.
Santosha – contentment; attitude of acceptance of events that leads to inner contentment.
Satya – truth; the ideal of absolute truthfulness.
Satori – flash of intuition, revelation, perhaps even samadhi.
Self-actualization – psychological term for the full flowering of individual potential.
Septum – that region of the brain which releases tension and creates relaxation in body and mind.
Shakti – primal energy; manifested consciousness.
Shaucha – purity of mind and body.
Shivalingam – symbol of consciousness.
Shoonya – the void.

Shravan – Hindu month of July-August.
Sinuses – cavities in the skull.
Smarana – continuous remembrance of God by performing japa; the mental repetition of the name of God.
Sphincter muscle – muscle at the opening of the anus.
Sravana – one of the methods of bhakti yoga, reading or hearing of different scriptures.
Sumeru – terminal bead in a mala.
Sumirani japa – repetition of a mantra for 24 hours a day.
Sushumna nadi – the most important psychic passageway in the subtle body.
Swadhisthana – the second chakra, or psychic centre, associated with the unconscious mind.
Swadhyaya – self-study; awareness of one's actions and reactions to further self-knowledge.
Sympathetic nervous system – part of involuntary nervous system; maintains physical activity; responsible for the build-up of tension in the body.
Tapas – austerity; the practice of small austerities to strengthen willpower.
Theta waves – brainwave patterns emitted during sleep.
Third eye – the psychic centre of intuition; another name for ajna chakra.
Thyroid gland – master gland situated at the throat.
Trataka – method of developing the powers of concentration.
Trikuti – meeting point of the two nasal passages and ida and pingala nadis.
Tulsi mala – type of mala used for japa.
Unknown point – physical trigger point for one of the psychic centres; located in the centre of the head between the ears.
Upanishads – yogic texts; commentaries on the oldest known religious texts, the Vedas.
Upanshu japa – whispered repetition of a mantra.
Vairagya – non-attachment; state where one is calm and tranquil in the midst of the tumultuous events of the outside world.

Vandana – prayers to God.

Vasanas – the desires that are the driving force behind every thought and action in life.

Vedas – the oldest known religious texts; written about 5000 BC.

Vishnu – Hindu god; preserver of the universe; presides over swadhisthana chakra.

Vishuddhi – the throat chakra; the psychic centre of purification.

Yamas – the five self-restraints, or rules of conduct, designed to remove emotional disorders in preparation for higher yoga practices.

Yoga nidra – psychic sleep; type of meditation practice.

Yoga Sutras – texts written by Patanjali setting down the system of raja yoga.

Further Reading

Aurobindo, Sri, *On the Tantras,* Sri Aurobindo Ashram, Pondicherry, 1970.

Bose, D.N. & Halder, H., *Tantras: Their Philosophy and Occult Secrets,* 3rd edn, Oriental Pub Co, Calcutta, 1981.

Gupta, S.B., *An Introduction to Tantric Buddhism,* Calcutta University, Calcutta, 1974.

Leadbeater, C.W., *The Chakras,* Theosophical Pub. House, Madras, 1971.

Madhusudan, Kaul, *Sri Malini Vijayottara Tantram,* Butala & Co., Delhi, 1984.

Mookherjee, Ajit, *Tantric Art,* 1st edn, Ravi Kumar, Delhi, 1971.

Ostrander, S. & Schroeder, L. *PSI – Psychic Discoveries Behind the Iron Curtain,* Abacus, UK, 1973.

Pandit, M.P., *Studies in the Tantras and the Vedas,* 1st edn, New Delhi, Sterling publ. 1977.

Pandit, M.P., *Lights on the Tantras,* 5th edn, New Delhi, Sterling publ, 1977.

Pandit, M.P., *Gems from the Tantras,* 1st edn, Madras, Ganesh & Co., 1975.

Saraswati, Swami Niranjanananda, *Dharana Ḍarshan,* 2nd edn, Bihar Yoga Bharati, Munger, Bihar, 1999.

Saraswati, Swami Niranjanananda, *Prana Pranayama Prana Vidya,* Bihar School of Yoga, Munger, Bihar, 1998.

Saraswati, Swami Satyananda, *Amaroli,* Bihar School of Yoga, Munger, Bihar, 1978.

Saraswati, Swami Satyananda, *Asana Pranayama Mudra Bandha*, Bihar Yoga Bharati, Munger, Bihar, 1996.

Saraswati, Swami Satyananda, *Four Chapters on Freedom*, Bihar School of Yoga, Munger, Bihar, 1983.

Saraswati, Swami Satyananda, *Hatha Yoga Pradipika*, Bihar School of Yoga, Munger, Bihar, 1985.

Saraswati, Swami Satyananda, *Kundalini Tantra,* Bihar School of Yoga, Munger, Bihar, 1984.

Saraswati, Swami Satyananda, *Moola Bandha*, Bihar School of Yoga, Munger, Bihar, 1978.

Saraswati, Swami Satyananda, *Sure Ways to Self-Realization,* Bihar School of Yoga, Munger, Bihar, 1983.

Saraswati, Swami Satyananda, *Taming the Kundalini*, Bihar School of Yoga, Munger, Bihar, 1982.

Saraswati, Swami Satyananda, *Yoga Nidra*, 6th edn, Bihar School of Yoga, Munger, Bihar, 1998.

Saraswati, Swami Satyananda, *Yoga from Shore to Shore,* Bihar School of Yoga, Munger, Bihar, 1980.

Snellgrove, D., *The Hevajra Tantra,* Oxford University Press, London, 1980.

Woodroffe, John, *Garland of Letters*, Ganesh & Co., Madras, 1963.

Woodroffe, John, *Principles of Tantra,* Ganesh & Co., Madras, 1986.

Woodroffe, John, (trans. and comm.), *The Great Liberation (Mahanirvana Tantra)*, Ganesh & Co., Madras, 1963.

Woodroffe, John, *The Serpent Power,* Ganesh & Co., Madras, 1958.

Woodroffe, John, *Tantra Raja Tantra,* Ganesh & Co., Madras, 1954.

Woodroffe, John, *Shakti and Shakta,* Ganesh & Co., Madras, 1959.

Woodroffe, John, *Kama Kala Vilas*, Ganesh & Co., Madras, 1961.

Woodroffe, John, *The World as Power,* Ganesh & Co., Madras, 1966.

Index of Practices

A Abstract Meditations
- Categories 280
- Commune with Nature 278
- Divine Symphony 280
- Fullness 281
- Perfect Oneness 278
- The Essence of Existence 278
- The Life Stream 277
- The Pulsating Throb of Life 279
- The Sea of Bliss 279
- Who Am I? 280

Agochari Mudra 127
Ajapa Japa 165
Akashi Mudra 127
Amrit Pan 321
Antar Mouna 211
Antar Trataka 261
Anuloma Viloma 162
Ardha Padmasana 111
Ashwini Mudra 130
Ashwini-Vajroli/Sahajoli-Moola Alternation 132

B Baikhari 154
Bhadrasana 116
Bhastrika Pranayama 144
Bhramari Pranayama 148

C Chakra Bhedan 322
Chakra Shuddhi 164
Chakranusandhana 310
Chidakasha Dharana 242
Seated in a meditation posture 243
Lying in shavasana 248
Chin Mudra 121

D Dhyana 326

I Inner visualization techniques
Association of ideas 232
Contraction and expansion of scenery 233
Contraction and expansion of viewpoint 234
Object visualization at will 234
Recall by visualization 233

J Jalandhara Bandha 132
Jnana Mudra 121

K Kapalbhati Pranayama 146
Khechari Mudra 124

L Likhit Japa 155
Linga Sanchalana 325

M Maha Bandha 136
Maha Bheda Mudra 315
Maha Mudra 313
Manasik Japa 155
Manduki Kriya 316
Manipura Shuddhi 160
Moola Bandha 130

N Nada Anusandhana Asana 119
Nada Sanchalana 310
Nada Yoga 272

Nadi Shodhana Pranayama 139
Nasagra Mudra 122
Nasikagra Drishti 127
Naumukhi Mudra 318

P Padmasana 112
Pawan Sanchalana 312
Pingala Shuddhi and Ida Shuddhi 162
Prana Ahuti 324
Prana Shuddhi 163
Prana Vidya 297
Psychic screen 292

S Shabda Sanchalana 312
Shakti Chalini 319
Shambhavi 320
Shambhavi Mudra 126
Shanmukhi Mudra 123
Shavasana 118
Siddha Yoni Asana 114
Siddhasana 113
Sukhasana 110
Sumirani Japa 157
Sushumna Darshan 322
Swaroopa Darshan 325
Swastikasana 115

T Tadan Kriya 317
Trataka on a candle flame 256
Trikuti Sandhanam 163

U Uddiyana Bandha 135
Ujjayi Pranayama 143
Unmani Kriya 285
Upanshu Japa 155
Utthan Kriya 324

V Vajrasana 116
Vajroli/Sahajoli Mudra 128
Vak Shuddhi 163
Vipareeta Karani Asana 117
Vipareeta Karani Mudra 309
Vishuddhi Shuddhi 161
Visualization test 235

Y Yoga Nidra
Short practice 183
Long practice 185
Complete practice 194

General Index

Abstract meditation 277
Active meditation 12
Ahimsa 70
Ajapa japa 165
Ajna chakra 44
Ajna's tube 47
Anahata chakra 43
Antar kumbhaka 139
Antar mouna 211
Antar trataka 254
Aparigraha 71
Arohan psychic passage 46
Asanas 75
Association of ideas 232
Asteya 70
Austerity 73
Autosuggestion 52
Awarohan psychic passage 46

Bahiranga kumbhaka 139
Baikhari 269
Baikhari japa 154
Bhakti yoga 84
Bhrumadhya 45
Bindu chakra 44
Biofeedback 23
Brahmacharya 71
Breath control 138
Breath retention 139

Cell consciousness 28
Chakras 41
Chidakasha 45
Chidakasha dharana 242
Concentration 79
Concentration – object of 106
Conical psychic passage 47
Contentment 72

Detachment 54
Dharana 79
Dhyana 58, 80
DNA molecule 28

Ego 29

Fight or flight mechanism 35
Frontal psychic passage 46

Hatha yoga 91
Honesty 70
Hridayakasha 45

Ida nadi 46

Inner visualization 225
Intellectual knowledge 15
Intuitive knowledge 15
Ishwara pranidhana 73

Japa anusthana 156
Japa – rules for practice 157
Japa yoga 153

Karma yoga 88
Kleshas 64
Kundalini kriyas 308
Lalana chakra 45
Likhit japa 155

Madhyama 269
Mala – use of 153
Manasik japa 155
Manipura chakra 42
Mantra 153
Mantra siddhi yoga 160
Meditation 9
Meditation poses 108
Miscellaneous meditations 282
Mood control 22
Mooladhara chakra 41

Nada yoga 269
Nadi 45
Nectar passage 47
Niyamas 71
Non-possessiveness 71
Non-violence 70

Object of concentration 106
Object visualization 234
Observances 71
Obstacles to meditation 68, 101, 104

Para nada 269
Pashyanti 269
Passive meditation 12
Patanjali's yoga 67
Physiological effects of meditation 33
Pingala nadi 46
Pooraka 139
Postures 75
  for meditation 108
  therapeutic 75
Prana vidya 297
Pranayama 76, 138
Pratyahara 77
Preparations for meditation 101
Psychic body 41
Psychic centres 41
Psychic pathways 45
Psychic screen 292
Psychology and yoga 18
Psychosomatic disease 36
Purity 72

Raja yoga 67
Recall by visualization 233
Rechaka 139
Reticular activating system 29

Sahasrara chakra 44
Samadhi 81
Santosha 72
Satya 70
Science and yoga 17
Self 10
Self-actualization 19
Self-realization 11
Self-restraints 69
Self-study 73
Self-surrender 73

Sense withdrawal 77
Sexual control 71
Shaucha 72
Subconscious mind 9
Suffering – causes of 64
Sumirani japa 157
Sushumna nadi 45
Swadhisthana chakra 42
Swadḥyaya 73
Sympathetic nervous system
arousal 35

Tantric kundalini yoga 90
Tantric yoga 96
Tapas 73
Therapeutic postures 75
Third eye 44
Trataka 254
Truthfulness 70

Unconscious meditation 287
Unconscious mind 9
Unknown point 45
Unmani kriya 285
Upanshu japa 155

Vairagya 54
Vishuddhi chakra 43
Visualization 227

Windpipe psychic passage 46

Yamas 69
Yoga nidra 181

INTERNATIONAL YOGA FELLOWSHIP MOVEMENT (IYFM)

The IYFM is a charitable and philosophical movement founded by Swami Satyananda at Rajnandgaon in 1956 to disseminate the yogic tradition throughout the world. It forms the medium to convey the teachings of Swami Satyananda through its affiliated centres around the world. Swami Niranjanananda is the first Paramacharya of the International Yoga Fellowship Movement.

The IYFM provides guidance, systematized yoga training programs and sets teaching standards for all the affiliated yoga teachers, centres and ashrams. A Yoga Charter to consolidate and unify the humanitarian efforts of all sannyasin disciples, yoga teachers, spiritual seekers and well-wishers was introduced during the World Yoga Convention in 1993. Affiliation to this Yoga Charter enables the person to become a messenger of goodwill and peace in the world, through active involvement in various far-reaching yoga-related projects.

BIHAR SCHOOL OF YOGA (BSY)

The Bihar School of Yoga is a charitable and educational institution founded by Swami Satyananda at Munger in 1963, with the aim of imparting yogic training to all nationalities and to provide a focal point for a mass return to the ancient science of yoga. The Chief Patron of Bihar School of Yoga is Swami Niranjanananda. The original school, Sivanandashram, is the centre for the Munger locality. Ganga Darshan, the new school established in 1981, is situated on a historic hill with panoramic views of the river Ganges.

Yoga Health Management, Teacher Training, Sadhana, Kriya Yoga and other specialized courses are held throughout the year. BSY is also renowned for its sannyasa training and the initiation of female and foreign sannyasins.

BSY provides trained sannyasins and teachers for conducting yoga conventions, seminars and lectures tours around the world. It also contains a comprehensive research library and scientific research centre.

SIVANANDA MATH (SM)

Sivananda Math is a social and charitable institution founded by Swami Satyananda at Munger in 1984, in memory of his guru, Swami Sivananda Saraswati of Rishikesh. The Head Office is now situated at Rikhia in Deoghar district, Jharkhand. Swami Niranjanananda is the Chief Patron.

Sivananda Math aims to facilitate the growth of the weaker and underprivileged sections of society, especially rural communities. Its activities include: distribution of free scholarships, clothing, farm animals and food, the digging of tube-wells and construction of houses for the needy, assistance to farmers in ploughing and watering their fields. The Rikhia complex also houses a satellite dish system for providing global information to the villagers.

A medical clinic has been established for the provision of medical treatment, advice and education. Veterinary services are also provided. All services are provided free and universally to everyone, regardless of caste and creed.

YOGA RESEARCH FOUNDATION (YRF)

The Yoga Research Foundation is a scientific, research-oriented institution founded by Swami Satyananda at Munger in 1984. Swami Niranjanananda is the Chief Patron of the foundation.

YRF aims to provide an accurate assessment of the practices of different branches of yoga within a scientific framework, and to establish yoga as an essential science for the development of mankind. At present the foundation is working on projects in the areas of fundamental research and clinical research. It is also studying the effects of yoga on proficiency improvement in various social projects, e.g. army, prisoners, children. These projects are being carried out in affiliated centres worldwide.

YRF's future plans include literary, scriptural, medical and scientific investigations into other little-known aspects of yoga for physical health, mental well-being and spiritual upliftment.

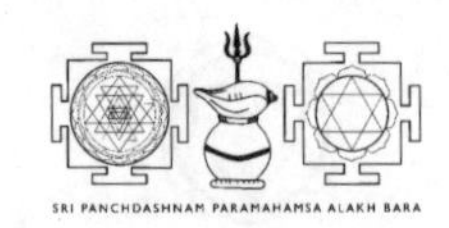

SRI PANCHDASHNAM PARAMAHAMSA ALAKH BARA (PPAB)

Sri Panchdashnam Paramahamsa Alakh Bara was established in 1990 by Swami Satyananda at Rikhia, Deoghar, Jharkhand. It is a charitable, educational and non-profit making institution aiming to uphold and propagate the highest tradition of sannyasa, namely vairagya (dispassion), tyaga (renunciation) and tapasya (austerity). It propounds the tapovan style of living adopted by the rishis and munis of the vedic era and is intended only for sannyasins, renunciates, ascetics, tapasvis and paramahamsas. The Alakh Bara does not conduct any activities such as yoga teaching or preaching of any religion or religious concepts. The guidelines set down for the Alakh Bara are based on the classical vedic tradition of sadhana, tapasya and swadhyaya, or atma chintan.

Swami Satyananda, who resides permanently at the Alakh Bara, has performed the Panchagni Vidya and other vedic sadhanas, thus paving the way for future paramahamsas to uphold their tradition.

BIHAR YOGA BHARATI (BYB)

Bihar Yoga Bharati was founded by Swami Niranjanananda in 1994 as an educational and charitable institution for advanced studies in yogic sciences. It is the culmination of the vision of Swami Sivananda and Swami Satyananda. BYB is the world's first accredited institution wholly devoted to teaching yoga. A comprehensive yogic education is imparted with provision to grant certificates and diplomas in yogic studies. It offers a complete scientific and yogic education according to the needs of today, through the areas of Yoga Philosophy, Yoga Psychology, Applied Yogic Science and Yogic Ecology.

Residential courses of four months to one year are conducted in a gurukul environment, so that along with yoga education, the spirit of seva (selfless service), samarpan (dedication) and karuna (compassion) for humankind is also imbibed by the students.

YOGA PUBLICATIONS TRUST (YPT)

Yoga Publications Trust (YPT) was established by Swami Niranjan-ananda in 2000. It is an organization devoted to the dissemination and promotion of yogic and allied knowledge - psychology (ancient and modern), ecology, medicine, vedic, upanishadic, tantric darshanas, philosophies (Eastern and Western), mysticism and spirituality - nationally and internationally through the distribution of books, magazines, audio and video cassettes and multimedia.

YPT is primarily concerned with publishing textbooks in the areas of yoga philosophy, psychology and applied yogic science, research materials, practice texts and the inspiring talks of eminent spiritual personalities and authors aimed at the upliftment of humanity by means of the eternal yogic knowledge, lifestyle and practice.